Applied Research Methods in Public and Nonprofit Organizations

The Instructor's Guide to accompany *Applied Research Methods in Public and Nonprofit Organizations* is available for free at www.wiley.com/college/brownhale.

Applied Research Methods in Public and Nonprofit Organizations

Mitchell Brown
and
Kathleen Hale

A Wiley Brand

Published by Jossey-Bass
A Wiley Brand
One Montgomery Street, Suite 1200, San Francisco, CA 94104-4594—www.josseybass.com

Jossey-Bass books and products are available through most bookstores. To contact Jossey-Bass directly call our Customer Care Department within the U.S. at 800-956-7739, outside the U.S. at 317-572-3986, or fax 317-572-4002.

Wiley publishes in a variety of print and electronic formats and by print-on-demand. Some material included with standard print versions of this book may not be included in e-books or in print-on-demand. If this book refers to media such as a CD or DVD that is not included in the version you purchased, you may download this material at http://booksupport.wiley.com. For more information about Wiley products, visit www.wiley.com.

Library of Congress Cataloging-in-Publication Data has been applied for and is on file with the Library of Congress.

ISBN 978-1-118-73736-1 (pbk.); ISBN 978-1-118-90443-5 (ebk); ISBN 978-1-118-90450-3 (ebk)

Printed in the United States of America

FIRST EDITION
PB Printing   10 9 8 7 6 5 4 3 2 1

CONTENTS

List of Figures and Tables   xiii

Acknowledgments   xvii

The Authors   xix

INTRODUCTION   **1**

Integrating Case Studies into Learning About Applied
   Research Methods   2

The Cases   3

  Community Garden Initiative: Exploring Community
    Interest in Local Food Projects   4

  Statewide Needs Assessment: Understanding the Status
    of Aging Women   6

  Election Administration and Technology: Understanding
    the Implementation and Implications of Election Policy Decisions   8

  National Program Evaluation: Domestic Violence Prevention
    and Faith-Based and Community Organizations   11

  Criminal Justice Policy Reform: Exploring Innovation Across Sectors   13

Structure of the Book and Message to Instructors   15

PART ONE: Research Basics: What Do We Want
to Know and Why?   19

CHAPTER ONE Overview and Context of
the Research Process   21

The Research Process   21
   The Applied Research Context   25
   Public Administration, Nonprofit Studies, and Other Subfields   27
   Information Literacy   28
   Information Quality and Types of Sources   29
   Finding High-Quality Information   37
Values, Beliefs, and Certainty in Applied Disciplines   38
   Grand Theory and Theories of the Middle Range   40
   Case Comparisons   41
Ethics and Institutional Review Boards   43
   Specific Concerns for Public Administration and Nonprofit Studies   45
Decision Trees   47
   Applied Research Project Planning   47
   Typical IRB Review Considerations   48
Conclusion   49
Overview of the Book   50
Chapter Support Materials   51

CHAPTER TWO Applied Research Questions,
Literature, and Theory   55

Asking Good Research Questions   56
   Case Illustrations of Research Questions   57
   Research Questions and Sponsored Research   60
   Case Illustrations of Research Questions in Sponsored Research   60
Using Literature and Building Theory   62
   The Literature Review   62
   Literature Sources   63
   Literature Searches   65
   A Note About Citations   69
   Theory Building   71
   Developing Research Expectations and Hypotheses   75
Theories of Change and Logic Models   79
   Theories of Change   79
   Logic Models   82
   Steps for Development of Theories of Change   86

Decision Tree 90
   Decisions About Applied Research and Using a Theory of Change 90
Conclusion 91
Chapter Support Materials 92

CHAPTER THREE Applied Research Designs 99

General Parameters of Design 99
Major Design Types 100
   Experimental Design 100
   Quasi-Experimental Design 105
   Nonexperimental Design 108
   Case Illustrations of Research Design Approaches 113
Sampling 117
   Random or Probability Sampling 118
   Nonrandom or Nonprobability Sampling 121
   Sample Size 123
   Case Illustrations of Sampling Approaches 123
Decision Trees 127
   Selecting a Research Design Type 127
   Choosing a Sampling Strategy 129
Conclusion 130
Chapter Support Materials 131

PART TWO: Data Collection: Where and How
Can We Gather Information? 135

CHAPTER FOUR Qualitative Data Collection in the Field 137

Validity, Reliability, and Error in Qualitative Research 138
The Process of Conducting Field Research 142
Interviews 146
   Writing Interview Questions 148
   Putting Respondents at Ease 149
Focus Groups 151
Direct Observation 152
Content Analysis 154

Case Studies 159

Case Illustrations of Data Collection 161

    Statewide Needs Assessment 161

    Election Administration and Technology 162

    National Program Evaluation 163

Decision Tree 163

    Data Collection Strategy 164

Conclusion 165

Chapter Support Materials 165

CHAPTER FIVE Survey Research 171

The Survey Research Process 172

Survey Design 175

    Crafting Quality Questions 176

    Response Categories 181

    Demographic Questions 188

Problems and Controversies in Survey Research 189

Case Illustrations of Survey Use 191

    Statewide Needs Assessment 191

    Criminal Justice Policy Reform 192

    National Program Evaluation 192

Decision Tree 193

    Decisions About Methods of Survey Distribution 193

Conclusion 194

Chapter Support Materials 195

PART THREE: Analyzing Data and Communicating About
Them: What Do They Mean? How Can They Be Used? 199

CHAPTER SIX Data Analysis 201

Context and Descriptive Analysis 202

Qualitative Analysis 203

Quantitative Analysis 207

    Coding 208

Levels of Measurement   209

Descriptive Statistics   210

Statistical Significance   216

Bivariate Statistics   219

Multivariate Statistics   225

Codebooks   232

Case Applications of Qualitative and Quantitative Analysis   233

Decision Tree   240

Conclusion   242

Chapter Support Materials   242

CHAPTER SEVEN Writing and Presentations   **249**

General Tips for Writing   250

A Productive Writing Process   250

Feedback and (Constructive) Criticism   251

Readability and Appeal   252

A Note About Style   254

Types of Writing   256

Needs Assessments and Asset Mapping   256

Grant Applications   258

Funder Reports   264

Stakeholder Documents   266

Journal Articles   268

Applied Dissertations   270

Presentations   271

Presenting Material to Stakeholders   274

Academic Presentations   275

Case Illustrations of Writing and Presentation   277

Decision Tree   277

Decisions About Making Presentations   277

Conclusion   280

Chapter Support Materials   282

Glossary   287

Bibliography and Works Cited   303

Index   309

LIST OF FIGURES AND TABLES

FIGURES

1.1	The Research Process	22
1.2	Inside the Steps of the Research Process	23
1.3	Top Ten Information Sources from Google Search for "Homeless Women"	37
1.4	Typical Research Roles Covered by IRB Requirements	44
1.5	Decision Tree for Planning a Research Process	48
1.6	Decision Tree for Typical IRB Review Process	49
1.7	Research Process Outline Worksheet	54
2.1	List of Selected Scholarly Journals for Applied Research in Public Service	66
2.2	Examples of Scholarly Sources Used in Case Studies	67
2.3	Journal Article Worksheet	68
2.4	Deductive and Inductive Approaches to Theory	72
2.5	Theory-Fact Relationships in Deduction and Induction	72
2.6	Time Horizons and Outcomes in the Theory of Change Model for the Community Garden Case	85
2.7	Logic Model/Theory of Change to Increase Democratic Functioning Through Voting	85
2.8	Program Evaluation Logic Model for Study of Community Organizations	89
2.9	Decision Tree for Using a Theory of Change Model	91
2.10	Annotated Bibliography Entry Worksheet	97
2.11	Logic Model Worksheet	98

3.1	Common Sources of Secondary Data	112
3.2	Decision Tree for Selecting Research Design Type	128
3.3	Decision Tree for Choosing a Sampling Strategy	129
4.1	The Field Data Collection Process	143
4.2	Decision Tree for Data Collection Strategy	164
5.1	Approaches to Question Wording	178
5.2	The Influence of Word Order and Response Set Choices	183
5.3	Illustration of Ordered Scales	184
5.4	Illustration of Likert Scale	185
5.5	Decision Tree for Choosing Paper or Web-Based Survey Approach	194
6.1	Qualitative Data Display Illustration: Discussion of Partners in Statewide Needs Assessment	206
6.2	Illustration of Coding for Quantitative Analysis	209
6.3	Graphic Display of Descriptive Statistics	212
6.4	Codebook Example for Election Administration and Technology Project	234
6.5	Proposed Theory of Change Model Developed from Statewide Needs Assessment Case	239
6.6	Decision Tree for Approaching Qualitative and Quantitative Analyses	241
7.1	SWOT Analysis Display for the Community Garden Case	257
7.2	Gantt Chart Example for Statewide Needs Assessment	260
7.3	Planning Process Example for National Replication of the Statewide Assessment	261
7.4	Budget Summary and Budget Narrative	263
7.5	Poster for Community Presentation on Statewide Needs Assessment (online only at www.wiley.com/college/brownhale)	
7.6	Community Presentation on Community Garden (online only at www.wiley.com/college/brownhale)	
7.7	Decision Tree for Approaching a Presentation	279

TABLES

| 1.1 | Association of College and Research Libraries Information Literacy Standards and Benchmarks | 30 |

1.2	Top News Sources by Media Type	34
1.3	Case Comparison of Research Question, Theory, Reasoning, and Tools	42
2.1	Case Comparison of Approaches to Theory, Literature, and Hypotheses or Research Expectations	74
2.2	Case Comparison of Concepts and Operationalization	76
3.1	Measurement and Intervention Sequence for Major Forms of Experimental Design	102
3.2	Major Forms of Quasi-Experimental Design	107
3.3	Approaches to Nonexperimental Data Collection	109
3.4	Case Comparison of Research Designs	114
3.5	Case Comparison of Sampling Strategies	124
4.1	Case Comparison of Case Selection Methods	142
4.2	Illustration of Content Analysis Strategy for Examining Innovations in Voter Guides	156
5.1	Index of Engaged Healthy Living Activities	187
6.1	Frequency Distribution Example: State Requirements for Certification of Election Equipment	211
6.2	Illustration of Calculation Matrix	216
6.3	Measures of Central Tendency and Dispersion by Level of Measurement	217
6.4	Bivariate Tests by Level of Measurement	219
6.5	Illustration of Bivariate Crosstab Table for Soft Skills Class	222
6.6	Multivariate Tests Based on Dependent Variable Measurement	226
6.7	Relationship Between Soft Skills Course Participant Background and Course Attendance to Posttest Performance	229
6.8	Case Comparison of Use of Qualitative Analysis	236
6.9	Case Comparison of Use of Quantitative Analysis	237
6.10	Codebook for Soft Skills Class	246
7.1	Illustration of Table Format and Style	255
7.2	Case Comparison of Types of Writing and Presentations	278

For James

You helped make possible
this and so much more.
Thank you.
March 12, 2014

ACKNOWLEDGMENTS

First and foremost, we thank our students in various undergraduate and graduate research methods courses over the past several years. Their feedback on exercises, instructions, and general understanding of the text was essential in shaping this book. Graduate research assistant Andrew Sullivan and undergraduate research assistant Shelbie Keel assisted with the glossary. Graduate research assistant Tameka Davis helped us with a careful reading and final edit of the text. Most important, John Powell Hall piloted earlier versions of book chapters in several undergraduate research methods courses and solicited and collated feedback from students. We thank him for his thoughtful commentary throughout the process. We also owe a special thanks to Gerry Gryski, who during his tenure as department chair provided critical administrative support in the form of summer resources that allowed us to pilot and coteach a new field research seminar to graduate students and a few very hardy upper-division undergraduates.

We are indebted especially to our own teachers over the years who taught us how to be engaged and quality researchers. We count faculty who taught us in formal classroom settings and faculty and practitioners who taught us by example. The critical feedback and collegial support they provided helped positively shape our understanding and practice. Along the way, we also learned the power and limitations of applied research and hope to pass our understanding along through this book.

The book would not be possible without the unflagging energy and support of our editor, Alison Hankey, and her belief in our concept. We also extend our sincere appreciation to Rob Brandt, Nina Kreiden, Michele Jones, Diane Turso, and the entire team at Jossey-Bass/Wiley. Anonymous reviewers provided critical commentary and guidance that shaped the final manuscript, and we thank them for their thorough and thoughtful feedback and suggestions.

We also thank our colleagues with whom we have dissected various strategies for teaching students how to become engaged in the communities around them through research and analysis. We hope that this book makes a contribution to that conversation.

Not least, we thank our families for their forbearance during the project; they know how much we love this work, which they make all the more enjoyable through their patience and support.

THE AUTHORS

Mitchell Brown, PhD, is an associate professor in the Department of Political Science at Auburn University, and teaches in Auburn's MPA program and PhD program in public administration and public policy. Brown's broader research agenda focuses on the empowerment efforts of marginalized communities, which she pursues particularly through applied research. With Dr. Kathleen Hale, she is codirector of the Community Governance Research Project, an initiative designed to investigate the politics and policies surrounding critical contemporary governance issues using a lens that looks at the intersection of the government, nonprofit, and private sectors. She is the author of numerous articles in the fields of political science, public policy, public administration, and pedagogy. She is the recipient of the 2013 SGA Outstanding Faculty Award for the College of Liberal Arts at Auburn University, the 2009 Distinguished Diversity Researcher Award through the Research Initiative for the Study of Diversity and the Office of the Vice President for Research at Auburn University, and an Outstanding Service Award in 1998 from the Center for Mental Health Services, among others. She currently serves on the boards of the Alabama Department of Child Abuse and Neglect Prevention, Auburn University Women's Resource Center, and the *Journal of Political Science Education*, among others.

Kathleen Hale, JD, PhD, is an associate professor and MPA program director at Auburn University, where she teaches graduate and undergraduate courses in public administration, nonprofit studies, and public policy. Her work focuses on applied research about the capacity and outcomes of intergovernmental and nonprofit organizational arrangements. She is the author of *How Information Matters: Networks and Public Policy Innovation* (Georgetown University Press, 2011), winner of the Best Book Award from the Academy of Management Public and Nonprofit Section, and honored by the National Media Award from the National Association of Drug Court Professionals. She is the coauthor and coeditor of *Scholarship in Action: Communities, Citizens, and Change* (Common Ground/World University Press, 2013), and the recipient of the 2012 Award for Community and Civic Engagement from Auburn University and the 2012 Award for Excellence in Teaching from the American Political Science Association. Her research has appeared in numerous public administration, public policy, and nonprofit journals. She is currently a member of the board of directors of the Alabama Association of Nonprofit Organizations and of the Election Center, a national professional association devoted to the improvement of the public administration of elections. Together with Dr. Mitchell Brown, she directs the Community Governance Research Project, devoted to applied research questions.

Applied Research Methods
in Public and Nonprofit
Organizations

INTRODUCTION

A*pplied Research Methods in Public and Nonprofit Organizations* is designed as a guide to understanding and implementing applied research in practical settings common to public agencies and nonprofit organizations. All public service scholars and practitioners in public administration, nonprofit organizations, or public policy engage in applied research at some point in their careers. Similarly, every person who works in a nonprofit organization or public agency is involved in applied research in one way or another.

For a few scholars and practitioners, research is a significant portion of their work and involves sophisticated methodological designs, strategies, and tools. For most, however, the applied research experience is less obvious and takes different forms. For many practitioners, these less obvious "research" experiences include such projects as charting a new course for an organization or program, making a case for funding, determining what stakeholders find meaningful, or figuring out "what works" in a particular program or service arena. Contemporary public sector administrators working in government agencies and nonprofit organizations lead these and other similar efforts every day. In doing so, they are also asking their staffs and collaborative partners to engage in applied research strategies that include data collection and analysis using quantitative and qualitative methods, as well as tools to communicate research findings. Some of these research experiences are episodic, such as conducting a needs assessment for a new initiative. Some occur simultaneously but independently, such as a needs assessment for strategic planning purposes and production of an annual report about community programs. Others are integrated into a longer-range strategy for the organization or agency, such as regular benchmarking of program accomplishments or designing strategies to change policy.

We distinguish applied research from basic social science research, although both follow a rigorous process. The key distinction is that applied research projects are primarily concerned with solving a contemporary problem. Applied research follows the tenets of sound basic research. Namely, we conduct literature reviews and develop hypotheses or research expectations, and we follow the protocols for ethical data collection and the precepts of qualitative and quantitative analysis. In addition, in applied research we take specific steps to identify public problems, interventions to address those problems, and how the interventions ought to work. Following this approach permits us as researchers to think through how to create a research design that captures the logic of a program as well as any anticipated or unanticipated consequences we can measure.

In the chapters that follow, we present a systematic and integrated guide to the research tools and skills commonly used in nonprofit organizations and public agencies to gather and analyze information, and link those tools and skills to the specific context of applied research. We connect the research process and the decisions that are required to cases studies and to reports and presentations that are commonly used to communicate about applied research findings. Our goal is to enable students and public service practitioners to understand and use the research and literature relevant to their work, and to conduct applied research about questions that concern them. By *public service* we mean the work of defining and resolving public problems. This work typically draws on the social science disciplines, comprising public administration, nonprofit studies, public policy, and political science. It involves the activities of government agencies and nonprofit organizations, but can involve communities and other formal and informal groups as well.

INTEGRATING CASE STUDIES INTO LEARNING ABOUT APPLIED RESEARCH METHODS

The concepts discussed in this book are reflected in five case studies drawn from our own research on public service questions in the U.S. intergovernmental system. Fundamentally, the intergovernmental system is a network of public agencies and nonprofit organizations that exist at the national level and in states and localities. As a whole, the cases reflect the range of institutions and actors common to public service and familiar to public administrators and nonprofit program staff. The studies engage questions in common substantive areas of public service, consisting of sustainable community-based initiatives, services for aging populations, election administration, domestic violence prevention, and criminal justice reform.

These case studies are important for several reasons. One is that they illustrate a wide range of approaches to the research process. Some of the cases arose out of questions that were posed by communities or practitioners in particular areas of public service. Some involve research conducted at the request of specific funders. Some arose because they addressed issues of intrinsic interest to the researchers. Across the cases, you will find different versions of the elements of the applied research process, including the origin of applied research questions, links between theory and data, methods of data collection and analysis, and dissemination of results. Each of these cases also demonstrates the rich and direct connection between applied research and the practice of public service. The cases connect to typical research-based activities that occur in public and nonprofit organizations and around the programs that they design and deliver, such as needs assessments, policy and program implementation, and program evaluation. In every case, we engaged directly with public agencies, nonprofit organizations, formal and informal community leaders, and various configurations of nonprofit organizations and government agencies in different types of organizational arrangements.

The section that follows contains a summary description of each case, beginning with a relatively simple example and moving to more complex illustrations of the applied research process. In each chapter that follows, we explore the interior of the cases in greater detail to illustrate particular concepts, issues, and concerns that flow throughout the research process. Through these case illustrations, we also demonstrate that applied research is essentially about making choices. In every case, and at every stage of the research process, we had to select among many potentially good and viable options in order to proceed. We share our choices about design, data, and analysis because the choices are common to most applied research projects. The consequences of choices made in the research process are also common—the choices we made inevitably shaped the study findings in ways however small, and, in turn, our findings and our thoughts about our choices also served as starting points for new research.

THE CASES

In the following sections, we describe each of five case studies.

Community Garden Initiative: Exploring Community Interest in Local Food Projects

Access to healthy food is a topic that has captured public attention amid growing public concern and political attention to the links between food and public health. At one end of the spectrum, policymakers have looked for ways to penalize the sale of certain food content. For example, taxes on sugary beverages and sodas are on the agenda in major cities such as San Francisco and New York City; at least one major city (New York) has enacted limits on fat in restaurant foods. At the other end, various "share-the-harvest" collectives have become popular vehicles to encourage broad public participation and to serve needs beyond alleviating hunger. Community gardens and community-supported agriculture are two variations on this theme. Community gardens involve common land gardened collectively by a group. The goals include direct community labor, neighborhood improvement, and civic engagement. Community gardens take many forms, but are public bodies in the sense that they are typically owned in trust by local nonprofits either alone or in partnership with local governments. Community-supported agriculture (CSA) exists on a slightly larger scale as a model for growing and distributing food that relies on a network or association of individuals who agree to support local farms and share both risks and benefits. In a typical CSA, members buy shares or otherwise pledge to cover the cost of the farm operation and share in the harvest (and lack of same) through weekly produce baskets. Growers benefit through steady financial support from shareholders and reduced costs for marketing. At the local level, communities have focused increasingly on community gardens as a tool that can promote individual well-being along with other civic ends such as sustainability and civic participation.

In this case, a study was initiated by students in one of our graduate courses at the request of a community leader in a nearby city. The community leader was interested in finding out whether and how the city and the surrounding area could begin a civic initiative around the broad concepts of CSA and sustainability. The research project was designed and executed by graduate students around the concept of a needs assessment. The study was designed to be exploratory, and the overarching research question was typical of the "What should be done/ What is our role?" questions that organizations and communities pose when considering broad initiatives that have multiple goals, when examining problems with multiple causes, and when confronting change. The research began by defining two communities: one community consisted of the city and one consisted of the broader university environment that the students encountered on a daily basis. The study next focused on finding and understanding the literature about practical applications of sustainability, including CSAs and community gardens. Building on this base, the study proceeded to identify existing and potential resources and needs in both communities and focused on the viability of a community garden. The research process encompassed every aspect of the garden, including where it should be located, whether and how the university could play a role in supporting the garden, the purposes it should serve, how it should be governed, and how it should be sustained in terms of resources.

Data were collected in a variety of ways, including personal interviews, surveys, focus groups, visits to prospective garden sites and the surrounding areas, community meetings, and reviews of public documents and funder reports. Personal interviews were conducted with stakeholders in the city and within the university, and a decision was made to focus on locating the community garden in the city community. Surveys were conducted of city residents. City leaders and stakeholders met in focus groups, and the project culminated with a written report and presentation to the community at large.

The analysis involved identifying the strengths, weaknesses, opportunities, and threats of various sites and their purposes, governance options, and resource streams. At the end of the course, the final report recommended selection of an empty elementary school in the city as the grounds for the community garden; the school had a working kitchen and ample space for food preparation and instruction, and the site was also a designated recipient of revitalization funds from national and local foundations and government sources. The final report included recommendations to pursue specific funding options to maximize community involvement and the potential for program growth. The report also included recommendations for a governance structure for the community garden and its related programs, and a plan for future development.

The consequences of the study were not what the research team expected; however, the results were common for these types of projects. The community was unable to identify sufficient leadership or participation to construct a governing board or otherwise sustain interest to proceed with a community garden at the elementary school site that was recommended. A research team of students continued in subsequent semesters to pursue funding options for various configurations of a community garden and/or CSA with civic components.

Interest did emerge, however, among some members of the community around a second site that was identified in the study but not recommended as the top choice. A new and different coalition of community members emerged to consider planning for a community garden at this second site, which included public housing projects and involved residents in gardening and similar activities.

This study illustrates the fluid nature of applied research in community settings. It also illustrates the coproduction of new ideas that can occur when communities and universities engage in research together. Here, the research findings and recommendations of the project team were not adopted by the community but clearly led the community to generate new solutions to the conditions that they were experiencing.

For additional reading, see:

Baker, Barbara, Kathleen Hale, and Giovanna Summerfield, eds. 2013. *Scholarship in Action: Communities, Leaders, and Citizens*. Chicago: Common Ground.

Statewide Needs Assessment: Understanding the Status of Aging Women

The physical, financial, social, and emotional well-being of an aging population poses growing challenges for policymakers across America. The population over age sixty-five will double from 2000 to 2030 to reach approximately 20 percent of the total; the vast majority of the oldest old (age eighty-five and older) are expected to be female. Government agencies and nonprofit service providers and advocates have a significant stake in identifying and meeting these emerging needs.

Frequently, government agencies and nonprofits seek academic expertise to conduct studies that generate information about the needs of specific groups, changing conditions, or the value of particular services. The request for proposals (RFP) issued by the Alabama Women's Commission (ALWC) is an example of one such request for assistance. The ALWC was established by the Alabama legislature in 1971 as a vehicle for determining policy options and legislation in areas that affect Alabama's women. In 2010, the ALWC issued its RFP to commission a study on the status of older women in the state age sixty-five and older. The purpose of the study was to understand issues facing this age group and best practices for meeting the needs of these women.

In response to the RFP, we proposed a study to identify services available to Alabama women age sixty-five and older, to identify participant perceptions of these services, and to identify best practices for serving the needs of this group. Our research questions were broadly framed around three areas. We were interested in identifying the capacity of existing organizations in Alabama to deliver services to this group of Alabama women and to meet future needs, and whether there were important differences between the services being provided by government agencies in comparison to nonprofit organizations. We also were interested in the perceptions of the women who were receiving public services about the support that they obtained and what their additional needs might be, if any. Our third category of inquiry involved identifying best practices through examination of service providers.

Our corresponding research design included a survey of all potential organizations serving women age sixty-five and older in the state (including nonprofits, government agencies, and for-profit service providers); individual interviews with a sample of Alabama women sixty-five and older; and site visits to locations in conjunction with the interviews. The organizational survey gathered information about programs, resources, and current services; it also gathered information about future needs and pressures on these organizations. Through personal interviews with women age sixty-five and older, we collected information about their needs and their perceptions of the public services that they were currently receiving. These interviews were conducted with women across Alabama and coincided with site visits at a variety of organizations ranging from government-operated adult day centers to nonprofit community-based wellness centers.

What we found was expected in some ways. In its mix of government agencies, nonprofits, and for-profit companies, the service environment was tilted heavily toward nonprofit organizations. Nonprofits made up half the service providers; the other half were divided relatively equally between government agencies and for-profit companies. Most organizations serving this population were well established, served one or a few counties, and operated with relatively limited resources. Local providers tended to serve a single county or several-county area. A small proportion (10 percent) had budgets in excess of $10 million along with hundreds of staff and volunteers; however, approximately half of the organizations operated on $500,000 a year or less and with a handful of staff and volunteers. In terms of individuals, personal needs varied widely based on income; private retirement benefits were rare outside major cities. Quality of life for individual women was influenced directly by resources and indirectly influenced by race, education, and previous employment status.

Not surprisingly, the greatest challenge facing public service providers in both government and the nonprofit sector was the lack of resources available for serving this population. These resource deficiencies include funding, staff, volunteers, and services in general with a particular emphasis on affordable home-based services. Best-practice facilities were observed typically in areas where significant public and/or private philanthropic resources were also deployed to address the older population in general (wellness, socialization, and planned activities), whether or not special needs were addressed.

What is encouraging about our findings is that best practices were also observed in areas with minimal resources. In these cases, best-practice facilities exhibited several important characteristics that were also common to facilities in high-resource areas. Best-practice facilities in both environments were able to connect to existing resources and leverage them toward services for this population. Facilities in resource-rich environments leveraged local fundraising expertise and relationships with businesses to support development. They were able to rely on a strong tax base (which they supported through their operations) and could also utilize fee-for-service funding for programs and services. In resource-scarce environments, best-practice facilities leveraged resources as well. These programs typically evolved around another existing service area in which resources were more readily available, such as transportation. They were also able to attract in-kind resources from the surrounding area. Best-practice facilities in challenging resource environments were also characterized by their skilled and impassioned leaders. These findings suggest the value of collaboration and that interdependencies can be identified and used to create new initiatives even in tight times.

For additional reading, see:

Brown, Mitchell, and Kathleen Hale. 2011. *State-Wide Assessment of Alabama Women 65+: Organizations, Practices, and Participant Perspectives. Final Report to the Alabama Women's Commission*. Auburn, AL: Auburn University.

Election Administration and Technology: Understanding the Implementation and Implications of Election Policy Decisions

Election 2012 marked ten years since the adoption of the Help America Vote Act (2002) and its package of federal reforms intended to improve U.S. elections. A centerpiece of the Help America Vote Act (HAVA) was a comprehensive mandate to replace America's voting equipment supported by an infusion of federal grants dedicated to that purpose. Wholesale replacement of voting systems would be possible only with federal funding support; although elections are conducted primarily through local county governments, funding for these efforts is varied, sporadic, and limited. All across the country, local election offices replaced their punch-card machines and lever machines with electronic voting systems. Some jurisdictions already had electronic systems in place; these systems were modernized as well. In total, more than 75 percent of the $3.1 billion in HAVA funds went to buying new equipment.

Federal support also included an optional program that would certify the operation of new electronic voting systems and verify that the hardware and software met particular operating standards for accuracy and reliability. This voluntary certification program would provide states with assurance about the equipment that they used and was seen as a critical element in assuring the public of the integrity of voting systems—that votes were not lost, flipped, or hacked, and that vote totals and election equipment were free from either internal or external manipulation. The federal standards, known as Voluntary Voting System Guidelines (VVSG), were developed through an extensive consultation between technology experts and federal, state, and local election officials.

The transfer to electronic voting equipment might seem to be a relatively straightforward event in the evolution—some would call it modernization—of public service. Since 2000, the public at large has embraced and fueled a massive shift toward individual use of personalized and portable technology. On the surface, it would seem that electronic voting systems were just another aspect of the technology revolution sweeping virtually every aspect of American life. Yet there might be reasons for concern. We observed in our own lives that individuals were "refreshing" their personal technology every few years as new products became available; however, government offices such as those that conduct elections did not have that option—at least, it seemed clear that no new federal funds were in the pipeline to support that option, nor are many states and localities forthcoming with the financial resources that it would require to purchase new hardware and software so frequently. The election equipment market is also characterized by a very wide array of options, including multiple vendors and many variations in equipment design. The most common types of equipment generally are those that use a touch screen (also known as direct-read electronic, or DRE) and those that scan a paper ballot (also known as optical scan); another major variation is whether the equipment provides the election official with a paper verification of the vote (known generally as a paper audit trail). Various types of equipment are thought to be more acceptable to different groups of voters, including voters with disabilities and their advocates, elderly voters, younger voters, and so on. This varied context suggested that a set of federal standards would offer a level of certainty to states that their equipment would result in a consistent and accurate voting experience. At the same time, we heard election officials express concerns about aging equipment, lack of software and maintenance ability, and the limited number of ways to address problems in elections in the near term.

Against this backdrop, we set out to learn more about the choices that election officials had made regarding the voluntary federal certification program for election equipment and to learn more about the status of electronic voting systems in practice, given the significant investment in this intergovernmental initiative and its overall importance for democratic functioning in general. We were concerned with understanding the implications for intergovernmental theory and practice, given that federal grant programs and federal standards are a cornerstone of today's public service environment.

We used a mixed-methods approach combining quantitative analysis of existing data about election equipment in use in the states with qualitative analysis of interview data and our own observations. We constructed and fielded a series of semistructured interview questions with a variety of election officials. We also attended various conferences and workshops on election administration and gathered observational data about this issue.

We found that federal certification was not widespread across the states, and that most states had adapted modified methods for addressing system integrity or had opted out altogether. The choice to follow federal practices does not seem to be linked to partisanship, unlike other election administration reforms spurred by HAVA, such as the adoption of new voter ID requirements. States that chose to participate in VVSG had greater technological sophistication and higher levels of election administration professionalism, and were more likely to adopt touch-screen voting machines. Even so, all states are uncertain about their capacity to conduct elections with aging equipment, limited maintenance options, and no real viable new equipment or innovations on the horizon. A significant roadblock to the development of new systems was in fact the federal certification program. Our findings have implications for understanding the limits of voluntary federal programs and the importance of technological capacity and professional human resources in U.S. election administration.

For additional reading, see:

Hale, Kathleen, and Mitchell Brown. 2013. "Adopting, Adapting, and Opting Out: State Response to Federal Voting System Guidelines." *Publius: The Journal of Federalism* 43:428–451.

Hale, Kathleen, and Ramona McNeal. 2010. "Election Administration Reform and State Choice: Voter Identification Requirements and HAVA." *Policy Studies Journal* 38:281–302.

National Program Evaluation: Domestic Violence Prevention and Faith-Based and Community Organizations

Rural victims of domestic violence exemplify what it means to be marginalized. Oppression is a significant part of this type of victimization. Circumstances are compounded further by the typical struggles attendant to victims in rural areas today, which include low resources, chronic joblessness, lack of transportation, social stigma, sexism, racism, lower educational attainment, and minimal outlets for support. Domestic violence victims, usually women, exist truly on the margins of society. The organizations that exist to serve this population are typically charitable nonprofit or grassroots organizations that operate on small budgets and rely on volunteers and their in-kind contributions to get by.

The Bush administration developed a pilot program implemented through the Office of Violence Against Women (OVW) at the U.S. Department of Justice titled the Rural Domestic Violence and Child Victimization Grant Program Special Initiative: Faith-Based and Community Organization Pilot Program (called the Rural Pilot Program, or RPP) to see if the faith community could help fill this gap in the provision of social services to domestic violence victims in rural areas.

The RPP was designed to enable small grassroots organizations in rural areas to "create new avenues of partnership and collaboration between small faith-based and community organizations and law enforcement officers, prosecutors, victims' advocacy groups, and other related parties," and to reach faith-based and community organizations (FBCOs) not already providing domestic violence services in order to expand the availability of services (Office of Violence Against Women 2005). Funds were allocated to the RPP, which were then distributed by intermediary organizations in small grants ranging from $10,000 to

$100,000 to FBCOs in rural areas to provide domestic violence services over a one-year period.

The RPP was designed by the OVW as an intermediary model, as was typical for most of the Bush administration faith-based programs. An intermediary model is one in which a federal agency selects one or more organizations to fund, and these organizations in turn issue their own RFPs, receive and review funding applications, oversee their sub-awardees' work, collect reports, and receive and respond to reimbursement requests. The intermediary model was selected because the OVW expected that the types of organizations targeted by the RFP would not respond to a request from a federal government grant program. In addition, the OVW expected that most of the organizations recruited would have limited organizational capacity and would need the assistance of the intermediary in order to respond to the requests for information associated with reporting to the federal government.

Ultimately, the OVW funded three intermediary organizations. Each intermediary served a different geographical catchment area, and each provided different types of technical assistance to the small organizations. Among these three intermediaries, 54 FBCOs were funded out of more than 150 organizational applicants from around the country. Two-thirds of those funded were community-based organizations, and one-third were faith-based organizations. Although the activities of these organizations varied, most provided direct victim assistance through advocacy, shelter, and counseling.

An applied research study to evaluate the RPP was funded by the National Institute of Justice (NIJ). One dimension of the evaluation was a capacity study, which we use across the chapters to illustrate various concepts and dilemmas in applied research. The capacity study focused on organizational baseline capacity levels and change over the life of the RPP and afterwards.[*]

In the capacity study, we collected several types of data that allowed us to compare the organizations that would receive federal funding and intermediary

---

*Other components of the evaluation included a process evaluation, an outcome evaluation, and a study of the value of the faith dimension. The overall evaluation was undertaken by a group of evaluators from several different organizations, including Andrew Klein, PhD, Advocates for Human Potential, co-principal investigator; Mitchell Brown, PhD, Auburn University and the Institute for Community Peace, co-principal investigator; Mark Small, JD, PhD, Clemson University, co-principal investigator; Rob Fischer, PhD, Case Western Reserve; and Debby Tucker, MA, National Center on Domestic and Sexual Violence. The capacity study was directed by Mitchell Brown.

assistance against similar organizations that would not. First, we developed and fielded a capacity survey for all organizations in the geographical areas served by the intermediary organizations and administered the survey before the funding decisions were announced. We also administered the survey at the end of the funding year and six months after funding ended. Second, we held focus groups with leaders and representatives of organizations that received funding. Third, we conducted case studies with eight of the grantee organizations; these studies included document reviews, site visits, and monthly interviews. Fourth, we conducted monthly interviews with representatives from the intermediary organizations.

What we found, in short, was that the capacity of the successful organizations was higher than expected in many areas. We also found that funded organizations realized positive, sustained changes that were not experienced by the unfunded organizations. These funded organizations improved their ability to raise money, expanded the array of areas from which they recruited volunteers, increased grassroots and media attention, and experienced positive changes in staffing levels and technological capacity.

For additional reading, see:

Brown, Mitchell. 2008. "Improving Organizational Capacity Among Faith- and Community-Based Domestic Violence Service Providers." In *Innovations in Effective Compassion*, edited by Pamela Joshi, Stephanie Hawkins, and Jeffrey Novey, 39–60. Washington, DC: Department of Health and Human Services.

Brown, Mitchell. 2012. "Enhancing and Sustaining Organizational Capacity." *Public Administration Review* 72:506–515.

Klein, Andrew, Mitchell Brown, Mark Small, Rob Fischer, and Debby Tucker. 2009. "Evaluation of the Rural Domestic Violence and Child Victimization Grant Program Special Initiative: Faith-Based and Community Organization Pilot Program." NCJ 225722. Washington, DC: National Institute of Justice, U.S. Department of Justice. http://www.ncjrs.gov/pdffiles1/nij/grants/228192.pdf.

Criminal Justice Policy Reform: Exploring Innovation Across Sectors

For more than forty years following the 1960s Rockefeller drug laws in New York State, American communities embraced tough-on-crime policies. From the 1970s forward, counties and cities have experienced a meteoric rise in prison and jail populations as a result of three-strikes laws, mandatory minimum sentences, and harsh sentences for drug crimes. One consequence of these policies is that many offenders are caught in a revolving door of drug use and criminal behavior to support drug use, with little chance to break the cycle.

Small-scale innovations were attempted in local courts around the idea that a combination of treatment and intensive interaction with the court itself could be a successful model for treating addiction and reducing criminal recidivism for some drug offenders. One such innovation was the idea of a drug court for low-level, nonviolent drug offenders, which began in Miami, Florida, in 1989. Today, more than three thousand drug courts operate across the country, with at least one such court in every state.

This study explored the evolution of this policy innovation, with a focus on the policy environment that created room for the innovation to take hold and the relationships between local public administrators and nonprofit leaders that made this happen. More broadly, this study focused on how successful programs began and continued—how policy innovation occurred and became sustainable. There are several studies about the rise of drug courts. What made this study unique was its focus on the interior of the policy, inside the offices of public administrators and nonprofit executives, and its examination of different forms of information that these administrators used and how that information influenced their choices. Those choices led, ultimately, to the sustainability of drug court policy as a viable policy idea. Sustainability mattered because drug court programs are not mandated, and although federal grant support existed as seed money for planning and implementation, the cost of operations was ultimately paid at the local level in county and city court systems.

The study was completed over a period of three years and included a variety of qualitative and quantitative data and methods of analysis. Interviews with nonprofit leaders around the country created a basis for operationalizing key concepts. A national survey of state program administrators in every state provided data about information relationships and types of information utilized by successful courts. Archival research examined state laws, regulations, and judicial codes in every state. Extensive field work in six states culminated in case study comparisons. Government studies and data collected and maintained by federal agencies provided material for quantitative analysis over time about the state-level factors that influenced the diffusion of this innovation across the country.

Findings established a national nonprofit information network that generated and circulated particular kinds of information to nonprofits and government offices working in this policy area. Links forged around the network led to sustainability. Study findings also demonstrated that particular forms of information generated by nonprofit organizations served to promote program design, implementation, and successful operation.

The study findings were published as a book that garnered the attention of practitioners. One key national nonprofit organization, the National Association of Drug Court Professionals, recommended the book for its four thousand members and awarded the publication its National Media Award. The book has been the subject of numerous talks and presentations to academic audiences and to the National Association of Drug Court Professionals membership.

For additional reading, see:

Hale, Kathleen. 2011. *How Information Matters: Networks and Public Policy Innovation*. Washington, DC: Georgetown University Press.

STRUCTURE OF THE BOOK AND MESSAGE TO INSTRUCTORS

In the chapters that follow, we discuss the research process in its entirety and then break down and explicate each of the components. In Chapter One, we provide an overview of the entire process, introduce major concepts, and discuss information literacy and ethics in research. In Chapter Two, we write about developing useful questions, empirical theories, and testable hypotheses. In Chapter Three, we discuss approaches to research design, validity, reliability and error, and sampling strategies. In Chapter Four, we take up the nuts and bolts of collecting data in the field. In Chapter Five, we extend our discussion of data collection to survey research. In Chapter Six, we lay out the logic and steps behind analyzing our data, including both quantitative and qualitative analysis. Finally, in Chapter Seven, we discuss different approaches to writing up and presenting our findings to a variety of audiences.

This book was designed with multiple purposes in mind. In sum, we wanted to provide a comprehensive, readable, and practical guide to conducting applied research through the use of guided cases. In addition, we imagined a variety of users—advanced undergraduate students studying public administration, non-profit management, public policy, or political science; master's students in public administration programs; or practitioners who need a refresher on engaging in the research process. We also structured the chapters and assignments such that instructors could pick and choose among the topics. For example, Chapter Two could be used as a whole or parsed into two parts, with the first speaking more to an academic audience and the second to a practitioner audience.

To optimally engage with the materials in the text, students should be assigned to read this Introduction to become familiar with the cases. Applied research is always a series of trade-offs. We suggest that the cases be used to enhance discussion of these trade-offs, comprising (1) questions that arise during the practical aspects of conducting applied research; (2) sources of error and bias; (3) what we can claim to know, and why we can claim knowledge with a level of confidence; and (4) how much more (or less) could we know if we had designed and implemented the research differently. In each chapter, we include examples of the case studies to illustrate key concepts and decisions. In addition, each chapter includes one or more summary tables that compare and contrast the case studies to highlight the ways that the skills and tools from that chapter were used. We also include decision trees, or outlines of decision paths that we encounter, on many common questions in the design and execution of applied research and in communicating about the results.

In each chapter, we augment our discussion of research methods in several ways to make the book more useful to the reader. Across the chapters, we discuss our approaches to the relevant elements of the research process in the five different case studies. Each of the chapters contains specific components designed to engage a variety of teaching and learning styles, and tools to help users connect in a practical way with the material. These consist of:

- Key terms. To help reinforce important terminology, key terms in the narrative are identified in boldface type and defined in the Glossary at the back of the book.

- Suggestions for exemplary articles. We list several journal articles that exemplify the best of the concepts we cover. These can be assigned as additional reading if one of the purposes of the course is to teach students how to read academic articles or if instructors want to focus on deeper conceptual understanding.

- Discussion questions. We provide discussion questions designed to elicit a deeper understanding of the major concepts in the chapter. These questions can be used for class discussion, as homework assignments, or as essay test questions. We have used these questions with success in all three of these ways.

- Exercises. Following the discussion questions, we provide exercises that are meant to be brief (taking about thirty to sixty minutes each) to practice the skills presented in the chapter. These short exercises are designed to be used as the basis for in-class practice sessions or for homework. We have used these questions in both ways. If the questions are used as in-class exercises, they work well when assigned to small groups of three to five students. We do not provide answers for the exercises, as they are open ended, and appropriate answers will vary depending on the emphasis of the course and the focus of the instructor.

- Linked assignments. These assignments are essentially components of a single project, and can be used to develop an entire research project from start to finish with the guidance of an experienced researcher or instructor. We have used this approach in guiding students through the entire research process over the course of a semester. Students can work on these assignments as individuals or in small groups. We have taken both approaches, and find that small groups work best, particularly for undergraduate students, unless the research project is designed by the instructor in advance and is very specific and easy to conduct.

- Online materials. We provide links to more intensive Web-based assignments based on readings, data, and related exercises that are more extensive. In these, students read published material for critique or manipulate actual data for replication. Although we do not provide an answer key for these assignments and exercises, proper application of the materials included in each chapter, particularly with the guidance of an instructor or the feedback of peers, will provide positive and useful skill-building results.

We suggest pacing for a fourteen-week semester-length course that moves through the book and related materials at two weeks per chapter. However, the seven-chapter format can be adjusted to allow additional focus on particular topics. The format also lends well to customizing course syllabi to emphasize particular data collection methods or methods of analysis, and to highlight program requirements for (or student interest in) gaining applied experience through field research or practicums.

For example, if instructors want to build in class time to practice the various approaches to field research and qualitative approaches to data collection discussed in Chapter Four, this may take three weeks instead of two; a reasonable trade-off would be to spend only one week on Chapter One. Instructors planning to teach data analysis skills in conjunction with Chapter Six may want to devote additional time to preparing class lectures (a quality open-source resource for instructional materials, ideas, and discussion is www.http://opossem.org) or teaching students how to use data analysis software.

It goes without saying that the research process is time intensive and that students will need ample time in class and outside class to practice the skills and tools included in each chapter. All of the assignments require considerable and regular feedback from faculty. We have found that it is particularly important to set aside time during the semester to allow students to revise their work.

In sum, our purpose in writing this book is to help students gain a greater appreciation for the research process by enhancing normal text with applied examples, as well as through crafting myriad assignments that can be tailored to an array of levels and the interests of students. We hope that this book will help you (whether student, instructor, or researcher) structure and execute research about public problems and the actors and organizations involved in them.

PART ONE

Research Basics: What Do We Want to Know and Why?

chapter ONE

Overview and Context of the Research Process

To establish a common point of departure for understanding the research process, we begin with an overview of that process and a review of the particular vocabulary associated with it. Learning to be comfortable with this vocabulary is a necessary part of becoming capable consumers and producers of applied research.

THE RESEARCH PROCESS

The research process is the result of a combination of good ideas and questions about theory and practice, systematic and appropriate data collection and analysis, and communication about results. In short, the research process encompasses the steps shown in Figure 1.1. These steps consist of

1. Forming ideas and research questions

2. Developing theories and hypotheses

3. Constructing a research design as a plan for data collection and analysis

4. Implementing the research design through the collection of data

5. Analyzing those data

6. Drawing conclusions and communicating about research

As Figure 1.2 illustrates, each of these steps encompasses a collection of concepts and approaches and can proceed in different ways.

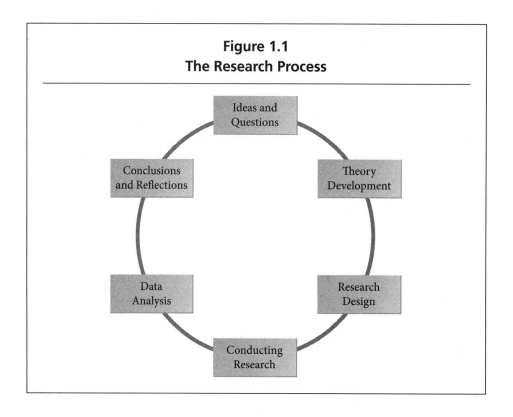

Figure 1.1
The Research Process

Ideas and Questions

Theory Development

Research Design

Conducting Research

Data Analysis

Conclusions and Reflections

Although each of these stages appears to be distinct, the research process is actually an **iterative** one, meaning that we continually review and refine our work while we are involved in each step and across the steps. In some approaches, particularly qualitative research, we are also expected to review prior steps of our work and refine them based on our analysis and findings. Through iteration, we are continually reviewing and refining to make improvements to our work. A significant dimension of the research process involves examining the various components of each stage and making decisions about how to proceed; this examination also results in considerable revision along the way.

The concept of an iterative process may run counter to what some of us think about the research process. We may think of the research process as linear and may believe that these midcourse corrections distort its scientific integrity. However, although there is a logical progression of steps that we follow, in practice the process often folds back on itself, and we continually make revisions as our own learning as researchers expands.

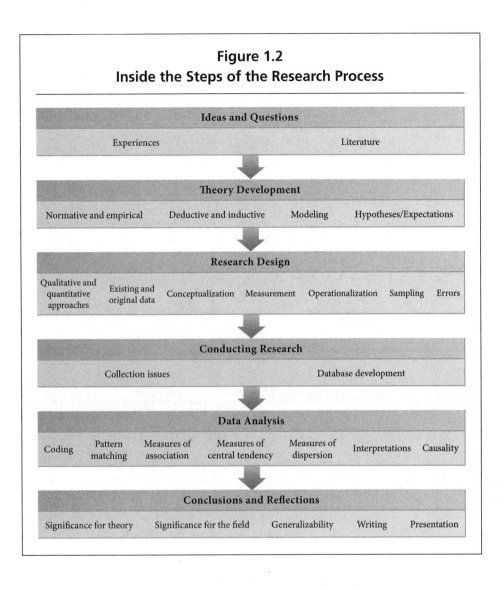

**Figure 1.2
Inside the Steps of the Research Process**

Ideas and Questions

Experiences   Literature

Theory Development

Normative and empirical   Deductive and inductive   Modeling   Hypotheses/Expectations

Research Design

Qualitative and quantitative approaches   Existing and original data   Conceptualization   Measurement   Operationalization   Sampling   Errors

Conducting Research

Collection issues   Database development

Data Analysis

Coding   Pattern matching   Measures of association   Measures of central tendency   Measures of dispersion   Interpretations   Causality

Conclusions and Reflections

Significance for theory   Significance for the field   Generalizability   Writing   Presentation

Our research ideas and questions come from our own experiences and are also informed by the published work of others. We use the previous work of others on similar questions to help us understand what has been accomplished and what is already understood about the area in which we are interested. In applied research, we focus on the practical world and its problems and conditions. It is common for researchers to draw on and seek out the ideas and experiences of practitioners in order to design this type of research, provide data, and implement solutions. We refer to this published work as the **literature** on a given question or subject.

In terms of the research process, we read and observe and think about the world around us in order to develop a **research question**. Good research questions typically have relevance to real-life problems, issues, or concerns. For example, a nonprofit organization dedicated to promoting rehabilitation for drug addicts as an alternative to prison might ask, "Is a rehabilitation program more effective than prison in preventing return to drug use?" or "Is one form of rehabilitation better than another?" A public commission interested in developing new public service programs for older citizens might ask, "Do the current services provided in our city meet the needs of our older citizens?"

The literature that has been developed by others helps shape an **empirical theory** that will serve as the foundation of our research process. An empirical theory essentially reformulates the research question based on current knowledge from research, observation, and logic about the phenomena under investigation. Our empirical theories are almost always based in the literature. After developing an empirical theory, we develop **hypotheses**. Hypotheses are simply the statements that propose an explanation of how the concepts that we are investigating work together. For some research questions, hypotheses are related to our ideas or understandings about cause—one or more factors are thought to cause a particular result. Hypotheses should flow naturally from the empirical theory.

In some instances, new phenomena emerge, and there is no literature that addresses them. In these instances, we engage in **exploratory research**, which investigates these new phenomena and contributes to the development of new theories based on our observations. A theory that emerges from exploratory research is commonly referred to as **grounded theory**, which means generally that it is grounded in interpretations of observations.

The next step in the research process is to plan for data collection, which involves a number of practical concerns, such as where and how we can obtain the data necessary to answer our questions. A key component of this stage is **operationalization**. This simply means that we need to define each of the elements of the research question and the hypotheses. More specifically, we need to describe each element, identify how it will be measured, and specify the data that we will use to measure it. In our example of a public commission interested in providing new services to its older constituents, we could be interested in the concept of "need." We could operationalize "need" as the opinion of the affected group about the desire for particular services such as meals, transportation, or companionship, and measure that need by collecting data from a survey of older constituents.

There are, of course, myriad ways to operationalize, measure, and collect data. Often the most exciting part of the research process is collecting the relevant data. When we collect our own data, we call these data **primary data**. When we use data that someone else has collected, those data are referred to as **secondary data**. Continuing with our illustration, if we collect data through a survey of older constituents, those are primary data. In contrast, if we gather data about the opinions of older adults from surveys that were conducted by others—the U.S. Census, for example—then we are using secondary data. After data have been collected, we analyze them and compare our results to the hypotheses that we proposed earlier in the process. We relate our results either to the theory that we are testing or to the theory that we are building. The techniques we use to analyze data depend on the types of data we have collected. The final steps in the process involve interpreting the results of our analysis and communicating about them in order to better understand our world, improve policies and programs, and refine our theories.

The Applied Research Context

There are multiple ways to approach the universe of social science research. A key distinction that we make in this book is to focus on applied research as opposed to basic research. The purpose of **applied research** is to understand and help solve practical problems. This typically includes problems associated with whether and how to undertake new programs or modify existing programs, and includes questions about design, resources, planning, development, implementation, and improvement—all of which are aspects of the work conducted by public agencies and nonprofit organizations. It is important to note that applied research focuses on problems as opposed to fields of academic study per se. Applied research may combine literature and/or theory from multiple academic disciplines in order to understand an issue or to identify particular solutions. Applied research also typically involves interaction between researchers and stakeholders, perhaps even entire communities. We will cover that interaction throughout the chapters as we discuss the various aspects of the research process, including design, data collection, analysis, and reporting.

In contrast, the purpose of **basic research** is to advance knowledge and look for relationships between theoretical constructs and their related variables. For example, if we were interested in studying the relationship between weather and voter turnout, a basic research question might ask, "Is turnout higher on election days in which the weather is sunny?" In comparison, an applied research question would go further, investigating why turnout would be lower in bad weather and attempting to determine what programs could best ameliorate the potentially dampening effect of weather on turnout.

Applied research operates within the common framework of the research process, which is predicated on some basic assumptions. First, applied research is concerned with **empirical analysis**. Empirical analysis refers to analysis of evidence of how things actually are, or evidence of reality. Empirical analysis is distinctly different from **normative analysis**, which is based on how things "ought to be." Second, knowledge is not an absolute, but rather is contingent and subject to disproof. This aspect of science is sometimes referred to as **falsifiability**. Third, support for our educated guesses, or hypotheses, must come from **systematic observation** and data collection, not from anecdotes, suppositions, or beliefs about how things ought to be. Fourth, we have to be able to clearly articulate and communicate all parts of the research process to others so that they can fully examine our findings and conduct further tests of any evidence we find and conclusions we attempt to draw; in other words, quality research is **communicable**. Fifth, although each research study is limited to particular events, groups, or phenomena, we are often interested in extending what we find in one study or analysis of a specific case or cases to other similar instances. Thus we are concerned about **generalizability**. The exception to this is exploratory research about a new phenomenon or event; in exploratory research, our interest is in exploring and describing what is new. Sixth, we prefer explanations that are as simple and straightforward as possible. Such explanations leave the least room for chance or error. Thus we are concerned with **parsimony**.

The universe of empirical research is divided, broadly, into three groups of approaches. **Qualitative research** focuses primarily on observing complex political and social phenomena and then describing and analyzing those phenomena based on the observations we made. Qualitative research is typically conducted through case studies, elite interviews, focus groups, ethnographies, and analysis of text. **Quantitative research** is focused on reducing political and social phenomena to numbers by giving them numerical codes and then analyzing them with statistical techniques. Increasingly, researchers are choosing to use both quantitative and qualitative approaches in their work. Quantitative research provides information about general relationships and trends, and qualitative research helps shed light on *why* those relationships and trends exist. This third group of approaches, known as **mixed-methods** research, has evolved to blend techniques from these two general groups. In this book, we will explore all three of these approaches.

Public Administration, Nonprofit Studies, and Other Subfields

The applied research focus of this book is substantively directed to applied questions in the field of public administration broadly, which includes the work of public agencies and nonprofit organizations directed toward public service. This substantive field of study encompasses how government institutions are arranged in intergovernmental relationships; the activities of institutions outside government proper, including nonprofit organizations; how rules are made and implemented by government; and how goods and services are provided by government and nonprofit organizations. Public administration is concerned with the design and delivery of public policy decisions in the public sphere. Broadly, this subfield includes administration and policy at the local, state, national, or transnational levels. Some applied questions arise concerning bureaucratic and self-governing organizational arrangements and operations; questions range across such topics as the deployment of human and financial resources, ethics, civic participation and representation, and political legitimacy.

Throughout this book, we define public service to encompass the work of public agencies and nonprofit organizations, because of the virtually inseparable nature of these two sectors (government and nonprofit) in designing and delivering services to meet public need. It is important to also call attention to the distinct subfield of nonprofit studies, which focuses on the practices and effectiveness of nonprofit organizations and the nonprofit sector. This subfield includes the study of organization governance and administration as well as unique legal, ethical, and policy questions that arise from advocacy activities and extensive reliance on volunteers. With increasing frequency, applied research questions involve some aspect of this subfield.

The questions that arise around questions of policy design, implementation, and evaluation also engage the subfields of public policy and policy analysis. Public policy is concerned with the political and economic factors that shape policy formulation, public decision making, and analysis of the stages of public policymaking. Related, the subfield of policy analysis focuses on the systematic analysis of resource allocation and the evaluation of outputs and outcomes. Both subfields place considerable emphasis on applied problem solving and analysis.

Public administration is considered one of several areas of study within the general academic discipline of political science—the discipline that studies the political world. The following section briefly describes the terminology used to identify the other subfields within political science. Together, these subfields give us guidance about the literature that may be most relevant in identifying relationships between concepts in order to build or test theory.

The American politics subfield is typically divided into behavioral research (how people behave in the political world through voting and other means of expression; factors that influence behaviors, such as age, race, gender, public opinion, ideology, and religious beliefs) and institutional research (how the institutions of government in the executive, legislative, and judicial branches are structured and function). A third dimension of this subfield is the study of American political development, which, as the name indicates, explores the development of American politics through an approach that is largely historical.

The comparative politics subfield is engaged in drawing comparisons at the country and regional levels that are developed through in-depth case studies. Emerging research in this subfield includes quantitative analyses that compare virtually every country. Related, the subfield of international relations studies the relationship between international actors such as nation-states, international organizations, multinational corporations, or nongovernmental organizations within the context of the international system, laws, and struggles for power. Increasingly this subfield includes research on national security and terrorism.

The subfield of political theory includes the concept of normative theory, in which researchers ask such questions as "How should people be governed?" "Who should govern?" and "What is the purpose of government?" The study of political theory also includes formal theory or rational choice deductive theory, where approaches such as game theory and spatial modeling are applied to the kinds of substantive issues found in the other subfields. In this latter variation, formal theory is actually more of a method of analysis than it is a subfield of political science, though among academics it is frequently discussed as a separate subfield.

Information Literacy

In this book, we are also concerned with the general notion of **information literacy** and its relationship to applied research. In short, information literacy encompasses understanding what kinds of information people need to have in order to answer questions and solve problems. Under that large umbrella, information literacy includes being able to find information, knowing how to determine whether information is of high quality, being able to read and understand the information, having the skills to use the information, and understanding the context in which the information arises. Not least, information literacy also includes being able to apply the information in an ethical way without violating any laws—in other words, application without plagiarizing information or violating copyright protections.

Information literacy is a critical aspect of our capacity to understand the contemporary world around us. Technological changes have made information prolific and nearly immediately accessible to almost all people. This explosion of information and access to it ought to be a good thing; however, it has significant drawbacks. Central to these drawbacks is the fact that not all people have the training or knowledge to be able to discern the veracity of available information, and thus must rely on others' authority to analyze and interpret information for them. This limitation applies to almost all of us, particularly in regard to information about complex or technical subjects. However, not all of the available information is accurate, appropriately analyzed, balanced, unbiased, or truthful. Moreover, in the face of unlimited information, it is more important than ever that communication about research be grounded in our ability to locate, sift, and organize information. We must also be able to integrate information that is generated in different ways and presented in various forms.

As a consequence, the Association of College and Research Libraries has issued a set of guidelines (*Information Literacy Competency Standards for Higher Education*) for colleges and universities to follow in order to enhance students' information literacy. These guidelines, summarized in Table 1.1, range across five standards that comprise abilities to (1) understand the nature and quantity of information needed for different tasks; (2) effectively and efficiently access information; (3) evaluate information and incorporate it to expand knowledge of particular tasks; (4) use information to accomplish particular tasks; and (5) use information ethically and with comprehensive understanding of the implications of the information gathered. The guidelines also include indicators of these abilities and possible outcomes that align with activities in the research process.

Information Quality and Types of Sources

There are a variety of sources of information to which almost all people have access. One of the first hurdles in developing information literacy is

Table 1.1

Association of College and Research Libraries Information Literacy Standards and Benchmarks

Standard	Indicators	Possible Outcomes
Standard One: The ability to understand what kind and how much information is needed for different activities and tasks	1. Understands when information is needed	1. Communicates need and identifies concepts/terms
	2. Understands the type(s) of information needed	2. Understands and can access appropriate sources
	3. Understands the costs and benefits of attaining this information	3. Weighs what is needed versus what is available
	4. Reevaluates what information is needed	4. Reformulates or clarifies information needs
Standard Two: The ability to effectively and efficiently access information	1. Understands the different ways to collect information	1. Identifies and selects the best way to obtain information
	2. Develops an appropriate data collection plan	2. Develops the best terms and search strategy to retrieve information
	3. Retrieves online or in-person information	3. Implements plan to obtain most appropriate information
	4. Refines search strategy as necessary	4. Assesses quality of information and repeats modified search as necessary
	5. Reviews, summarizes, records, and manages information	5. Reviews and uses information for purpose

Standard Three:

The ability to evaluate the information collected and incorporate it in a way to expand knowledge base to accomplish activity or task

1. Summarizes main points of material
2. Evaluates quality of material
3. Synthesizes information and uses it for knowledge production
4. Compares new and old knowledge
5. Understands utility of new information
6. Processes information by sharing with others
7. Applies information to initial task to reevaluate the purpose of the project

1. Reads and restates relevant information
2. Analyzes quality and recognizes context, error, and bias
3. Recognizes and extends concepts
4. Identifies quality of information and compares across sources to draw conclusions and develop theories
5. Weighs and draws conclusions
6. Uses information in class and assignments
7. Reviews purpose in light of new information and makes necessary refinements

Standard Four:

The ability to use information to accomplish activity or task

1. Applies collected information appropriately
2. Revises the project as necessary
3. Effectively communicates final project

1. Organizes, articulates, and integrates information
2. Systematically reflects on process
3. Selects best approach to communicate information clearly

Standard Five:

The ability to ethically use material and to comprehensively understand the implications (economic, legal, and social) of the information gathered

1. Understands ethical issues involved in information use
2. Follows laws, regulations, and policies concerning information use
3. Acknowledges sources

1. Applies concepts of privacy, security, fair use, and copyright
2. Complies with processes and standards for information use
3. Appropriately documents source materials used in products

Source: Adapted from Association of Colleges and Research Libraries, "Information Literacy Competency Standards for Higher Education," approved 2000, http://www.ala.org/acrl/standards/informationliteracycompetency.

understanding how to identify what we refer to in this book as quality information. By **quality information**, we mean information that is factually accurate, derived from a credible source through a public and transparent process, and produced using rigorous and standard techniques that adhere to appropriate ethical standards. Related, information consumers need to be able to discern among sources of information and to identify quality sources of information that can be used with confidence, sources that require caution when using, and sources that should be discarded altogether.

One approach to thinking about the quality of various sources of information is to divide them into two groups: scholarly and popular. The *APA Manual of Style*, among other resources, gives us a useful comparison between these two broad groups.

The highest-quality information in **academia**, or university-based work, is found in **double-blind peer-reviewed journals**. **Peer review** means that the work is evaluated by anonymous experts prior to acceptance for publication. The criteria for acceptance generally include subject matter expertise, accuracy, and adding value to our understanding of the topic.

The process for publishing in these sources is very specific. Authors send a manuscript of their work to a journal editor with all identifying information about the authors stripped from the manuscript. The editor in turn identifies several experts who also study and write about the topic of the manuscript, and sends that manuscript to the experts. The experts read the manuscript and make comments and suggestions for ways to improve it. They also provide the journal editor with a frank assessment of whether the quality of the research is sufficiently high to be published. The editor collects this information from the experts and makes a decision about whether to publish the manuscript. Most often the editorial decision is not to publish the piece; many peer-reviewed journals report rejection rates well in excess of 80 percent. However, sometimes the editor will ask the authors to make revisions to the piece and then resubmit it for a second round of consideration by the same experts or additional reviewers. In either case, the editor sends the authors the feedback provided by the experts to help the authors understand how to improve the submission. This feedback is stripped of all identifying information about the experts. The authors do not know who has read their work and made the comments, and the experts do not know who wrote the manuscripts that they review—thus the term double-blind peer review.

Frequently, **university press books** go through a blind review process, and are therefore also considered to contain information that is of high quality. Many for-profit presses also subject manuscripts to a peer-review process before publication. In general terms, the use of blind review by experts in the subject area is expected to enhance the quality of the information that emerges from the publication process. However, reviews conducted by for-profit presses may not be blind, and thus there is some concern that manuscripts will be less critically reviewed. Self-published and fee-for-publication books (put out by what some call "vanity presses") are generally viewed to be of lower quality than peer-reviewed publications.

Newspapers and news magazines are also often used as sources of information. Although most journalists adhere to high-quality journalistic standards, there is also a sense of a quality hierarchy among the newspapers and news magazines. This is true for audio and visual media as well. One way to consider quality is through the level of trust ascribed to particular news outlets. Table 1.2 offers a snapshot of highly trusted news sources for mainstream and independent newspapers and other news media, both national and international.

Government publications and information produced by nonprofit organizations, interest groups, and think tanks are more difficult to assess in terms of quality. These sources are commonly used by those working in public service, whether in administration or policy, and whether working inside government or in a nonprofit organization. One way to distinguish among sources is to consider the reason or motivation that guided the creation of the information. This motivation can be gleaned from an examination of the intended audience, the method of dissemination, and the opportunity for challenge or critique of the information by those who may disagree with it in such a way as to shape future information (Hale 2011). No information is ever entirely neutral, so it is important to be able to identify motives and make these types of assessments as we evaluate information.

Many government publications are high-quality sources and can be treated as having the same quality as peer-reviewed journal articles and books. In fact, many government publications go through rigorous internal scrutiny and review prior to publication and are quite transparent in disclosing the processes by which data were gathered and analyzed. In addition, some government publications are peer reviewed. Simultaneously, though, it is also the case that these publications can be highly partisan; information presented as fact may actually

Table 1.2

Top News Sources by Media Type

Blogs	Magazines	Newspapers	Online	Radio	TV	Wire Service
Daily Kos	Mother Jones	Christian Science Monitor	AlterNet	All Things Considered	Aljazeera	Associated Press
Global Voices	National Geographic	Los Angeles Times	FactCheck	NPR	Daily Show	Bloomberg
Informed Comment	New Yorker	New York Times	PolitiFact		Democracy Now	Inter Press Service
Robert Reich's Blog	Rolling Stone	The Guardian	ProPublica		NewsHour	McClatchy
Think Progress	The Nation	Washington Post	Salon			

Source: Adapted from NewsTrust, "Trusted Sources," 2012, www.newstrust.net.

be an interpretation of facts put forth with a particular goal in mind. The task for information consumers is to determine which is which.

Reports issued by the Government Accountability Office (GAO; formerly the General Accounting Office) are seen as highly credible. These reports frequently include a detailed description of the methods used to collect and analyze data, and also include commentary from representatives of the organizations or processes that are studied; this type of commentary offers insight into the findings of each study by providing additional information about points on which interested organizations disagree, and why that is the case. Reports from elected officials and their administrations (for example, White House reports or reports from governors' offices) have less credibility as objective sources of information because the objectives of these offices are aligned with a particular motivation, typically associated with partisan political views or to advance a particular policy agenda. Documents from such sources may, however, be excellent evidence of the views of an office, agency, or official. Here, it is important for the researcher to distinguish the purpose for which the information is intended. Information produced by outside researchers, but funded by government agencies, is most often neutral and of high quality.

In examining questions about public service, it is also important to note that government documents are actually the authoritative source for laws and regulations. The *U.S. Code* contains the laws of the United States; related, the *Code of Federal Regulations* contains all the federal administrative rules and regulations adopted by federal executive branch agencies and departments. Similarly, state codes of law and regulation are the authoritative sources for laws and administrative rules and regulations that have been adopted at the state level.

Information produced by think tanks, interest groups, and other nonprofit organizations is more difficult to gauge. Most of these types of organizations are established to promote a particular perspective that they desire to persuade others is correct, and this motivation should automatically give readers pause (Radin 2006). The use of a particular perspective does not automatically render information inaccurate, but consumers of information from these sources have a responsibility to consider the motivations at play and to seek competing perspectives in order to gain a representative view. Many of these organizations employ well-trained scholars who can and do generate credible and accurate information. In these cases, readers must have access to background information about the sources of evidence provided and types of analyses performed in order to make an informed judgment about information quality. Much information from these sources is not peer reviewed in the academic sense. However, many of these organizations (typically, national nonprofit groups) interact regularly with one another within an issue area and regularly monitor the information and communication of peer organizations in what are known as information networks; this interaction promotes accuracy and diligent attention to detail in many cases (Hale 2011). As a general rule, readers should further investigate the think tanks, nonprofits, and interest groups in order to learn about their missions, their goals, how they operate, and the sources of their funding. From this information, readers will gain a better understanding of the quality of information generated by these organizations.

A critical issue in determining whether information is of high versus low quality is today's common use of the Internet in obtaining information. It is not usually possible to determine the credibility of the source from the position of the link when it appears on the list of responses that is generated by a typical Internet random word search. An example is an ordinary Google search for the term "homeless women." The top ten results of this search (conducted November 12, 2013) are listed in Figure 1.3.

The first link is to images of homeless women. Interestingly, each image is linked to a nonprofit organization's website; however, there is no immediate information that identifies the subjects or the photographers. The second link is to a Wikipedia page about homeless women in the United States. Three links are to news items; two of these items have to do with homeless women veterans, perhaps because this particular search was conducted the day after Veterans Day. Four of the links direct readers to studies and reports from government agencies or nonprofit organizations; one of these is specific to Alabama, perhaps because we are located in that state. The remaining links direct readers to resources including homeless shelters (in Alabama) and a directory for homeless women veterans. In order to assess the credibility of each of these sources, readers have to investigate further.

Our interpretation of the multiple sources of information about "homeless women" is complicated further by the practice of paying for placement of information in search engines and the ability to manipulate data placement in the list of sources. Our example list also suggests that search results will vary according to the location of the searcher and the time of year (here, Alabama and Veterans Day). In addition, the fact that an information source appears on a list of search

Figure 1.3
Top Ten Information Sources from Google Search for "Homeless Women"

1. Images of homeless women
2. Homeless women in the United States—Wikipedia entry
3. News about homeless women (three entries)

   "In remembrance of the ex-servicemen and women who ended up homeless" (*The Guardian*)

   "Helping homeless veterans win battle" (*New York Daily News*)

   "Shelter offers hope for pregnant homeless women" (Fox News)
4. Up With Women—facts about homelessness (www.upwithwomen.com)
5. Domestic Violence and Homelessness—National Coalition for the Homeless (www.nationalhomeless.org)
6. ACOG—Health Care for Homeless Women (www.acog.org)
7. State Brief—The Institute for Children, Poverty, & Homelessness (www.ICPHusa.org)
8. Shelters, Homeless Housing, Halfway Houses (www.shelterlistings.org)
9. Homeless Women Veterans—National Resource Directory (www.nrd.gov)
10. Homeless Women (www2.webster.edu)

results does not attest to the credibility of the information. All of the information sources listed in Figure 1.3 place materials on the Internet, but less credible ones do as well. As a rule, any source linked through university libraries is likely to be of high quality. In contrast, although blogs may be quite interesting, they are typically not a good source unless they are used for content analysis or to demonstrate the beliefs of the bloggers (see Chapter Four for more discussion). This is not to suggest that there are no blogs with high-quality data and analysis. Online media and blogs are increasingly mentioned in reports about trusted media sources, as shown in Table 1.2; however, blogs in particular rarely go through a review process, and, in general, it is better to err on the side of caution.

Finding High-Quality Information

Today, a search for high-quality information will most likely begin with the Internet and a list of curated databases that contain scholarly articles. This section briefly discusses a variety of such sources that can guide researchers to high-quality information. In Chapter Two, we explore different types of information in greater detail.

Google Scholar is a free, comprehensive search engine that covers scholarly materials in a wide variety of disciplines, such as those discussed earlier, and others. The tool facilitates full-text search of scholarly books, scholarly articles published in many leading peer-reviewed journals, and some other materials. Other similar services are available through subscription. Many institutions subscribe to JSTOR, or Journal Storage, which offers full-text search of thousands of current-issue and back-issue journals. The Social Science Citation Index is available through the ISI Web of Science subscription service. The Social Science Research Network provides access to academic articles in the social sciences and humanities; articles are posted by authors and can be downloaded for a fee through institutional subscribers. Searches for laws and regulations are likely to focus on a legal database. LexisNexis and Westlaw are two such subscription services. These and other services provide access to federal and state case law, law review articles, treatises, and other legal scholarship, as well as news articles. Encyclopedias published by academic or other similar presses can also provide useful summaries of the general state of the field on a given topic (for example, program evaluation or voter identification). The *Encyclopedia of Public Administration and Public Policy* (Berman 2007) is one example of a general purpose, peer-reviewed encyclopedia that provides article-length introductions on a wide range of themes and subfields.

It is important to note that no single source of information will meet all of our research needs for theoretical development, methodological approaches, or data. We have to gather multiple sources of information and synthesize theory, methods, data sources, and findings. What matters is that we gather and use accurate information that collectively reflects a complete picture of relevant issues and data, and that we acknowledge the various biases and perspectives contained therein.

VALUES, BELIEFS, AND CERTAINTY IN APPLIED DISCIPLINES

As we have noted previously, applied research focuses on problems that exist in the real world. It may seem unusual, but the concept of "reality" and, by extension, the nature of the "real world" are actually subjects of considerable controversy and study. For the study of public problems, public services, and all of the various "public" questions that surround applied research, a key dimension of the real world has to do with values and beliefs. Because people are always a part of the world that we study through applied research, values and beliefs are always incorporated into our analysis in some way.

The fields of public administration, nonprofit studies, public policy, and policy analysis in particular are concerned with values and beliefs from two distinct perspectives that are linked to American institutions. One perspective is reflected in the decision processes and results of the political process. American politics is characterized by majority rule and winner-take-all election practices. As a consequence, most policy debates are reflected by two broad sets of competing values; these values are also typically reflected in the positions of the two major political parties (although that is not always the case). The political majority is continuously reconfigured through a constant process of elections; today's majority view may be the political minority view in the future. Another perspective comes through in the institutional arrangements of the public sector, including nonprofit organizations and networks of public and nonprofit organizations and individuals. These institutional arrangements comprise various stakeholders—some close to the action on a particular issue and some more distant. Some are currently engaged in looking at issues and problems, and some will be engaged in the future. These champions, challengers, bystanders, and supporters reflect different values and beliefs about how public problems are defined and about the ways to address particular conditions; the interaction of these values and beliefs is a critical aspect of public policy innovation (Hale 2011). Stakeholder views are an essential element of the analysis of a public environment; stakeholders are constantly reconfiguring in new arrangements, and they present researchers and communities with an ever-evolving set of values and beliefs that must be taken into consideration.

Riccucci (2010) argues that the values and beliefs inherent in the study of matters of public concern are evidence of an environment that is inherently different from the physical world. This means that the nature of what we study is always infused with our values, including our particular views about what is important, about who is deserving, about who should benefit from government, and about who should be assisted by charity or nonprofit organizations. For the purposes of applied research, this means that the field of study is always changing and always includes the values (and the values debates) that pertain to the problem or situation under study, the ways that these values take shape in public policy decisions (in legislation and administration), and the values of the researcher. This also means that the tools that are used to conduct applied research must be able to explicitly access and accommodate values at various levels of understanding.

Another dimension of the conversation has to do with certainty about the external world. Certainty is linked to the existence of **paradigms**, or particular ways of thinking about problems and the tools used to investigate them that accumulate over time and become the commonly accepted way of thinking; these paradigms are the underpinning of what has come to be known as normal science (Kuhn 1970), which is based on our very specific assumptions that are commonly understood to be true. Paradigm shifts occur when the tools of an existing paradigm are exhausted; Kuhn argues that this process is quiet and occurs only after sufficient research is published that acknowledges the new paradigm.

In contrast, the positivist school of thought holds that the world in which we exist comprises realities and truths, and though we may never arrive at complete understanding and knowledge because our ability to collect full data is necessarily incomplete, our job as researchers is to pursue the accumulation of evidence in such a way as to best model reality. For example, King, Keohane, and Verba (1994, 6) write "that it is possible to have some knowledge of the external world but that such knowledge is always uncertain." Scholars in this tradition tend to favor quantitative approaches to data collection and analysis, and when they do utilize qualitative data collection approaches, tend to do so using structured protocols (see Chapter Four for detailed discussion). Contrast this to interpretivists, who hold that knowledge is socially constructed and situated and that thus truth is impossible to obtain. Scholars who hold this conception tend to engage in data collection techniques that are largely qualitative, using more fluid and less structured protocols.

Grand Theory and Theories of the Middle Range

Regardless of the approach we take to the idea of certainty and values, we are also guided by long-standing traditions about how to classify our research questions. **Grand theory** includes the big ideas that guide the types of research questions we ask. Within American politics generally, scholars tend to work in one of two "schools," traditions, or grand theories, referred to as behavioralism and institutionalism. Behavioralists ask questions about political behavior within the American context—for example, "Does voting matter?" Institutionalists ask questions about how the major institutions of American politics operate and ask such questions as "What role do committees play in congressional lawmaking?" The study of public service involves both schools of thought, and applied research about public service looks at both behavior and institutional arrangements. In public service, one central tension lies between the normative desire to separate public administrative practice from values of any kind, including political influence, and the constitutional imperative to reconcile administrative (bureaucratic) discretion with changeable public values. Related, scholars of nonprofit organizations are concerned with theories of charity, community, and civic space.

But, as social scientists, we tend to spend most of our time developing **middle-range theories**. Middle-range theories are concerned with developing explanations for specific phenomena. Across the public space in general, scholars and practitioners are concerned with cooperation, collaboration, and reciprocal relationships as well as performance and accountability. We develop theories that explain these and other concepts in order to produce useful, testable hypotheses, or our best guesses about how and why the phenomena we investigate operate. These hypotheses then help us develop the best possible research designs in order to gather data to test our research questions.

Case Comparisons

The cases that we discuss in this book take a variety of approaches to research questions, theory, reasoning, and tools used to accomplish the projects. A summary of these are illustrated in Table 1.3. This summary table is an introduction to the framework of these particular cases and presents the range of questions and approaches to applied research and the basic concepts that we have discussed in this chapter thus far. Each element is also explored in more detail in the chapters that follow.

Each case is a typical example of applied research. Three of the studies were directed at resolving particular applied questions, and the two studies that began as basic research studies produced findings useful to, and used by, practitioners. Although the subject matter varies widely across the cases, the cases lean strongly on mixed methods and a combination of inductive and deductive thought processes. We think that this combined approach is ideally suited for applied research questions.

Table 1.3
Case Comparison of Research Question, Theory, Reasoning, and Tools

	Community Garden	Statewide Aging Assessment	Election Administration and Technology	National Program Evaluation	Criminal Justice Policy Reform
Type of Research	Applied	Applied	Basic/Applied	Applied	Basic/Applied
Gist of the Research Question	How can a local government best develop a Community Supported Agriculture and sustainability initiative?	What are the current resources and needs in the state for this population?	What factors influence state compliance with suggested federal guidelines about voting equipment?	What is the organizational capacity of faith-based and community groups providing violence prevention services?	How do organizational networks influence public policy innovation?
Middle-Range Theory	Public participation in hunger and health	Role of government and nonprofits in delivering human services as a result of changing demographics	Intergovernmental arrangements and state responses to federal pressures	Capacity of nongovernmental organizations in an era of increasing devolution	Unique role of information generated by nonprofit networks
Reasoning	Inductive	Deductive and inductive	Inductive	Inductive	Deductive and inductive
Tools	Qualitative	Qualitative and quantitative	Qualitative and quantitative	Qualitative and quantitative	Qualitative and quantitative

ETHICS AND INSTITUTIONAL REVIEW BOARDS

Often when we are conducting research, we involve human subjects in one way or another. When dealing with human subjects, there are two concerns researchers need to think about simultaneously. The first is whether what we are planning is ethical at a basic level. The second involves institutional rules governed by our **Institutional Review Board (IRB)** about whether and how to get permission to conduct our research.

In short, our focus on ethics in research is a response to horrific research conducted by scientists at various points in recent history, most notably Nazi experimentation during World War II and projects like the Tuskegee syphilis experiment in America. A consequence of reflecting on these instances is the understanding, at least in Western countries, that research subjects must be able to provide what is referred to as informed consent. **Informed consent** includes participant knowledge about the purpose and expectations of research projects in which they have been asked to participate, and free and willing participation with the opportunity to stop participating at any point for any reason.

The U.S. government has clear guidelines that govern human subject research, based on three principles:

1. **Beneficence**—maximizing positive outcomes for humanity while minimizing harm

2. **Respect for subjects**—including protection of their autonomy and, in some cases, anonymity

3. **Justice**—ensuring that research does not exploit others

IRBs are composed of scholars who review research proposals to determine that all of these principles are upheld. In their most basic form, these principles mean that the subjects of our research need to provide voluntary consent to the intervention of our research into their lives only after having full information, to the extent possible, about the research. This means that subjects are aware of any risks, as well as any benefits, of the research; that they can withdraw from a study at any point; that they are not deceived; and that their privacy and **confidentiality** are maintained, up to and including remaining **anonymous**. The IRB process also considers and provides procedures for risk mitigation for subjects under circumstances where researchers feel that they cannot fully explain their research to subjects—that they ought to deceive subjects.

Practically, this means that once a project has been designed, researchers need (usually) to obtain IRB approval, develop consent procedures and maintain records of consent, and develop and maintain procedures for ensuring anonymity or confidentiality of data. IRB procedures vary from institution to institution, and reflect the nature of the research that is typically conducted there and that is supported by significant federal funding. For example, an institution with a medical school or pharmacy program might impose a more rigorous set of requirements than a small liberal arts college. Note also that the IRB requirements typically cover any person who has a significant role in the study, including graduate students. IRB procedures apply typically to individuals based on the role(s) that they serve in the project. Figure 1.4 illustrates several key roles that are common to applied research projects. Each of these individuals, whether faculty members or student assistants (and others as designated by the institution), must complete online training for certification. The training is widely available through the Comprehensive Institutional Training Initiative (CITI; University of Miami) for member institutions.

Each institution also interprets its obligations regarding federal requirements in different ways and may cover additional activities; the time to obtain approval varies from a few weeks to many months. The main point here for researchers is to become very familiar with the IRB requirements that will apply to their specific projects.

After approval to begin research is received, scholars must then develop secure processes and places to maintain consent documents and data files. Usually this involves private computers, password-protected files, locked offices,

---

Figure 1.4
Typical Research Roles Covered by IRB Requirements

Principal investigator

Coprincipal investigators

Individual(s) receiving grant awards or contracts

Individual(s) listed as contacts on consent forms

Individual(s) listed as contacts on documents used to recruit study participants

Individual(s) who plan to obtain informed consent from participants in a study

and locked filing cabinets. IRBs retain the privilege of reviewing these files and all documentation of informed consent at any point in order to ensure that researchers have complied with the aforementioned standards. IRBs also require that regular reporting be made throughout the process of data collection and at the end of the research project.

Specific Concerns for Public Administration and Nonprofit Studies

Two of the case studies presented particular ethical considerations that are common to applied research.

Statewide Needs Assessment   One aspect of the statewide needs assessment involved conducting interviews with women age sixty-five and older. This population is a classic example of a vulnerable population by virtue of age. These women were also vulnerable because of the setting in which we chose to identify them and speak to them. Some women were receiving public services in the day care setting (most typically a meal and companionship); in this setting, meals and activities are provided according to a specific schedule. We made efforts to schedule our interviews at times that did not conflict with scheduled events; however, it is important to note the possibility that our presence might be interpreted as somehow threatening or disruptive to their scheduled daily events. This was less of a concern for the interviews conducted in assisted living facilities because the women typically had more latitude in arranging their time.

We took a number of steps to mitigate any concerns that the women might have had. Most obviously, we provided each woman with a consent form that included information explaining the project and her rights, including her ability to withdraw at any time without penalty. We asked each woman to read and sign the form before we could begin the interview; the interview did not begin unless the consent form was signed.

This approach exposed several interesting dimensions of the consent process that should be considered when working with any group, and with vulnerable groups in particular. One dimension involves general literacy. Not all prospective interview subjects could read, and it was clear that some could not read well enough to understand the language of the consent form. One option for addressing this situation is to read the form to an interview subject. Even so, it is also necessary to be well prepared to paraphrase some language or to confirm understanding after each paragraph or complex phrase. Some women we interviewed were unable to write their names, but indicated consent with their mark instead (for example, an X). The written consent form itself may have caused some women to choose not to participate.

Another issue involves human understanding on a broader level. In a few instances, women volunteered to be interviewed and signed the consent form, but were clearly unable to understand the questions once the interviews began. In these instances, we politely terminated the interviews as quickly as possible; we recorded these experiences as interviews that were initiated but not concluded, and we did not use any data from these experiences.

Finally, the physical surroundings should be considered in terms of confidentiality. In every facility, we first asked to conduct interviews in the office of the facility administrator, which was typically a private office with a door that closed. In some cases, however, that space was not available to us. In some instances, we conducted interviews at a table in the common area of the facility. The interviews conducted in the common area were held at a distance away from the other center participants so as to ensure that the conversations were not heard by the others. Even so, the interviews conducted in the common areas attracted considerable attention. Our interviews were interrupted by other center attendees who asked to be interviewed. Interviews were also interrupted by curious men who wondered why our interviews were limited to women, and by "nosy" neighbors who simply wanted to listen in on the interviews. We consistently redirected these onlookers; interestingly, the interview subjects were also typically quite strident in directing these onlookers to leave the area. In other cases, we conducted interviews in private rooms within the facility; in those instances, we did not experience any interruptions.

Many of these circumstances also pertain to matters that we should consider when we design interview procedures. We discuss them in this chapter to highlight the significance of the ethical considerations, which arise in rather routine ways.

National Program Evaluation   Because the purpose of the national program evaluation was to assess organizational capacity as opposed to the experiences and outcomes of victims of interpersonal violence, the ethical concerns were minimal. We wanted to ensure that the organizations would be protected if negative information came out about their organizational structure, resources, and capacity, so in public reporting we agreed to describe general characteristics of the organizations and give them alternative names.

Unconnected to the capacity study, another portion of the evaluation identified a potentially unethical practice on the part of one of the grantees during the course of data collection, and the evaluation team agreed to immediately turn this information over to the Department of Justice, which then took the appropriate steps to rectify the situation. Here we encountered an ethical question: If harm could come to a study participant from an organizational practice, what was the correct step for us as outside observers conducting presumably neutral and value-free research? Do we adhere to our promise of confidentiality for organizations in the study, or do we report findings to the funder, identifying the organization? If we report the findings to the funder, do we do so immediately or after the study period? Our decision was that the safety of study participants was more important than our "integrity" as researchers, and thus we immediately informed the funder of our findings.

DECISION TREES

Planning an applied research project involves multiple considerations, as we have begun to discuss in this chapter. Decisions abound at every turn within the design, implementation, and analysis of even the simplest of projects. As researchers, we have essentially complete control over how the research is designed, executed, and analyzed. This infinite variety can be overwhelming, yet the choices we make are at the heart of discovery. We have found that posing a few straightforward questions can help organize our thoughts and efforts throughout the research enterprise; we present these questions in the form of decision trees throughout the book.

Applied Research Project Planning

To guide the initial planning of a project, we propose a series of decisions formed around the set of questions shown in Figure 1.5.

The answers posed in the decision tree help sketch an early framework for applied research design. We should expect that our first responses to these questions will be revised, because our responses to each of these questions often generate further questions, alternatives, and choices. Often, our initial conceptualization has to be refined in one area or another based on the answers to these initial questions. These questions give us a place to begin, although our initial answers may not be reflected in the final project plan.

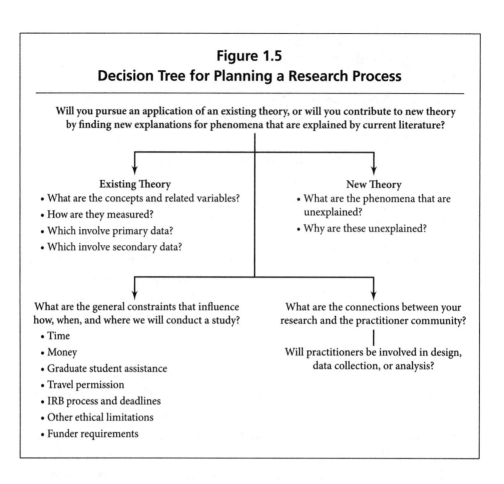

Figure 1.5
Decision Tree for Planning a Research Process

Will you pursue an application of an existing theory, or will you contribute to new theory by finding new explanations for phenomena that are explained by current literature?

Existing Theory
- What are the concepts and related variables?
- How are they measured?
- Which involve primary data?
- Which involve secondary data?

New Theory
- What are the phenomena that are unexplained?
- Why are these unexplained?

What are the general constraints that influence how, when, and where we will conduct a study?
- Time
- Money
- Graduate student assistance
- Travel permission
- IRB process and deadlines
- Other ethical limitations
- Funder requirements

What are the connections between your research and the practitioner community?

Will practitioners be involved in design, data collection, or analysis?

Throughout the chapters that follow, we use decision trees to illustrate some of the common decisions that we have faced in our work. These choices reveal in some measure why projects followed particular paths and also illustrate some of the paths not taken.

Typical IRB Review Considerations

The IRB process focuses on ethical decisions about data collection and protection of the rights of human subjects. The decision tree in Figure 1.6 illustrates the typical questions that have to be resolved in determining whether IRB review is required.

Of course, each institution has internal requirements and timelines for review and also a process for considering research that may be exempt from review, and we do not address those here. Instead, we focus on the major decisions that guide

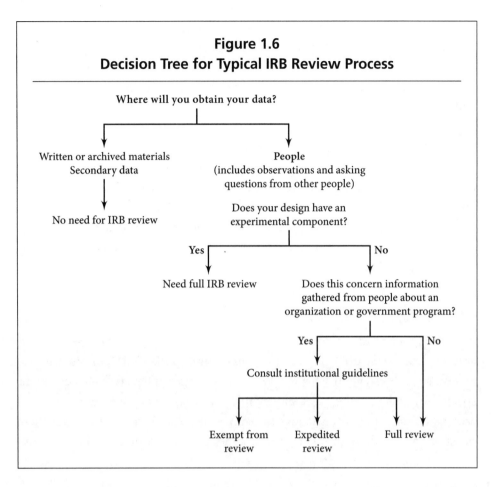

Figure 1.6
Decision Tree for Typical IRB Review Process

Where will you obtain your data?

Written or archived materials
Secondary data

People
(includes observations and asking
questions from other people)

No need for IRB review

Does your design have an
experimental component?

Yes — Need full IRB review

No — Does this concern information
gathered from people about an
organization or government program?

Yes — Consult institutional guidelines

No

Exempt from
review

Expedited
review

Full review

whether IRB review is required and whether that review will most likely be a full board review or some form of expedited review. For example, experimental designs typically require a full IRB review. In contrast, when data are collected from written or archived materials, an IRB review is typically not required. An intermediate form of review, known as expedited review, is available if the institution's IRB rules permit. Expedited review may be an option if the data pertain to organizational activities and government programs.

CONCLUSION

In this chapter, we provided an overview of the research process and several key concepts that underlie all research efforts. These include the general concept of quality research; the stages of the research process; and the iterative, reflexive nature of the process, which always involves feedback and revision. We also considered the ethical concerns present in research that involves human beings, and the Institutional Review Boards designed to protect us in those efforts. Also, we introduced the concepts of information literacy and quality information, both of which are crucial to conducting research and to disseminating and understanding results.

We also introduced the basic context of applied research as a problem-based inquiry that bridges many disciplines and fields of study that focus either directly or indirectly on public service problems. Related, we emphasized the importance of values, beliefs, and perceptions in studying the human condition and developing public service prescriptions to address social issues. These values exist within the larger realm of the philosophy of science, which guides scientific inquiry across all fields of study.

OVERVIEW OF THE BOOK

The remainder of this book explores each of the elements of the research process in detail. The book is organized into three parts. Part One focuses on planning and design. In Chapter Two, we take up applied research questions specifically and describe steps and techniques for asking applied questions that are answerable, and discuss how to use literature and theory to refine these questions and build high-quality research designs. In Chapter Three, we lay out these research designs and provide discussion and tools to help readers determine which designs and data collection methods are best for different applied research questions and given various resource constraints. We also describe approaches to sampling, sampling techniques, and the strengths and weaknesses of different sampling strategies.

In Part Two of the book, we shift from planning and design to actual data collection. In Chapter Four, we discuss and provide tips and techniques for field research, with a focus on site visits, interviews, direct observation, and focus groups. In Chapter Five, we take up survey research and describe survey basics as well as modifications for specific audiences.

In Part Three, we discuss what we do with data once we have them. In Chapter Six, we detail various qualitative and quantitative techniques for analyzing different types of data. In Chapter Seven, we outline the different forms of writing that evolve from applied research, including needs assessments, stakeholder documents, funder reports, grant applications, academic journal articles, and doctoral dissertations. We also discuss presenting information to various stakeholders and using information for program planning and development.

CHAPTER SUPPORT MATERIALS

Chapter One Relevant Articles

Boser, Susan. 2007. "Power, Ethics, and the IRB: Dissonance over Human Participant Review of Participatory Research." *Qualitative Inquiry* 13:1060–1074.

Brians, Craig. 2010. "Review of the 'Information Literacy Instruction Handbook.'" *Journal of Political Science Education* 6:87–88.

Lee, Carole J. 2012. "A Kuhnian Critique of Psychometric Research on Peer Review." *Philosophy of Science* 27:859–870.

Lieberman, Robert C., and Greg M. Shaw. 2000. "Looking Inward, Looking Outward: The Politics of State Welfare Innovation Under Devolution." *Political Research Quarterly* 53:215–240.

Chapter One Discussion Questions

1. Which stage of the research process is most important? Why?

2. Kuhn states that when paradigm shifts occur, they are controversial and demand debate, each side presenting its evidence, sure of the accuracy of its findings, and rejecting as incomplete that of the other. This is possible because "no paradigm ever solves all the problems it defines and since no two paradigms leave all the same problems unsolved, paradigm debates always involve the question: Which problem is it more significant to have solved?" (Kuhn 1970, 110).

Thinking about Kuhn's proposition, identify an area of public service or public policy (domestic violence, drug use, elections, economic development, education, housing, criminal justice, or another area) and discuss the paradigm that you believe defines the way that knowledge is understood in this area. What are the problems that this paradigm defines, and what are some of the problems that it does not? Are any of the unexamined problems more important than those that are incorporated into the paradigm? Are there other ways that we "should" look at this area of public service?

3. Why are double-blind peer-reviewed resources preferable to other types of information? Do you think it is possible for the double-blind process to be corrupted? How could this happen?

4. What ethical concerns might we encounter in conducting research focused on public administration or nonprofit management? What steps could we take to minimize risks associated with these types of projects?

Chapter One Practice Assignments

1. Look at sources published in the last three months. Using the *Chicago Manual of Style* author-date reference format (see http://www.chicagomanualofstyle.org), give bibliographic citations for each of the following categories:

   Peer-reviewed academic journals

   News magazines

   Newspapers

   Government reports

   Think tanks or interest groups

   Blogs

2. Using library resources, investigate and answer the following questions: When have there been paradigm shifts/scientific revolutions in public administration or nonprofit studies? How and why did they come about?

3. Read more about the Tuskegee experiment. Discuss how the principles of beneficence, respect for subjects, and justice were violated.

4. If your institution is a member, register for and complete CITI training for human subjects research for social and behavioral sciences (see https://www.citiprogram.org).

Chapter One Linked Assignments

Throughout the text, we include a series of "linked assignments." These have been developed to walk the research methods student through the entirety of the research process by developing a research project that includes each phase of both applied and basic research.

For Chapter One, make a list of three topics that you might be most interested in studying. For each, identify the subfield into which it best fits. Then, using your library, identify a few academic (peer-reviewed) articles or academic press books on the topic and read them. On the basis of your readings, refine your topics, thinking about what we know, what we do not know, and other possible ways the topic could be studied.

Chapter One Link to Online Assignments

Read the final report for the Alabama needs assessment study of women age sixty-five and older:

Brown, Mitchell, and Kathleen Hale. 2011. *State-Wide Assessment of Alabama Women 65+: Organizations, Practices, and Participant Perspectives. Final Report to the Alabama Women's Commission.* Auburn, AL: Auburn University.

Following the research process outlined in Chapter One, lay out the components in the worksheet in Figure 1.7.

1. For "Ideas and Questions," what is the research question or problem that motivated the study?

2. For "Theory Development," identify the focus and types of literature used early in the report to describe the problems.

3. For "Research Design," summarize the design decisions made by the authors.

4. For "Conducting Research," lay out where the primary data came from and how they were collected.

5. For "Data Analysis," describe how the data were analyzed.

6. For "Conclusions and Reflections," summarize the overarching findings and implications of the study.

Figure 1.7
Research Process Outline Worksheet

Ideas and Questions	
Theory Development	
Research Design	
Conducting Research	
Data Analysis	
Conclusions and Reflections	

Applied Research Questions, Literature, and Theory

I n this chapter, we take up three linked components that are integral to a quality research design: asking research questions, using existing scholarship to develop an empirical theory about the question, and developing research expectations to test that theory. We begin the chapter with a discussion of research questions and how those fit in generally to the basic research process. In the second section of the chapter, we turn to the process of developing theory for applied research in community settings, which typically present challenges associated with complex and interconnected problems. Applied research projects are often concerned with identifying, defining, and solving contemporary problems. In applied research, we conduct literature reviews and develop hypotheses as in basic research, but we also take the additional steps of identifying the problem, defining the parameters of possible interventions to address the problem, and considering how these interventions ought to work. Doing this permits us as researchers a way to think through how to create a research design that captures the logic of a program as well as any anticipated or unanticipated consequences we can measure. In this way, the logic model for a program becomes a road map for its study. The logic model establishes relationships between concepts and is undergirded by a theory of change that addresses the interdependencies between policy areas and public service jurisdictions, as such interdependencies are the norm in today's public service environment.

ASKING GOOD RESEARCH QUESTIONS

We begin by considering research questions. Good research questions have several important qualities. First and foremost, good research questions are interesting. In general terms, this means that the question resonates within a discipline to pass the "Who cares?" or "Why does it matter?" test. Related, we need to be certain that we are asking a question for which there is not already a definitive answer. Good research questions are also **testable**. This means that it is possible, given available resources—including skills and time constraints—to collect and analyze data to attempt to answer the question. Last, writing good research questions is an iterative process. This means that we start with a question we are interested in and then refine it multiple times after examining it through various lenses. We discuss the research question with others to better understand its importance and to clarify terminology. We review the relevant literature to determine what others have found about similar issues or approaches. We reflect on our question and what it will add to those findings, if anything. We consider the available resources and what is actually possible in terms of time, money, staff, and access to data. Typically, we further refine our question after we consider these factors. Our questions are rarely, if ever, just right the first time we ask them.

In applied research, research questions are interesting to practitioners and stakeholders; the questions typically come from the field. The iterative process therefore is at its best when we engage practitioners and stakeholders in thinking about our questions, approaches, and possible solutions. This interaction between the research community and communities of practice can proceed in varying degrees of engagement. At one end of a continuum, we may read about practical issues or gather data from public administrators or nonprofit executives about problems and concerns. At the least, this approach gives us systematic information about perspectives other than our own. At the other end of the continuum, researchers and stakeholders are engaged in the coproduction of knowledge by defining together the problems that exist and the possible solution sets that should be considered. Coproduction exemplifies the nonlinear aspects of applied research. Stakeholders typically have divergent opinions, and the process of defining problems or interventions is rarely formulaic. Research about community-based issues requires sensitivity to context, community values, and culture as well.

Within the social sciences and humanities, the concept of engaged scholarship has gained currency as a way to describe this reciprocal relationship between researchers and stakeholders and the community (Ellison and Eatman

2008). At its most limited, applied research is research conducted *on* a community and its constituencies rather than as a reciprocal enterprise (Brown 2013). At its best, research about community issues is research that creates knowledge *about* a problem and also creates knowledge *with* and *in* the community that is served (Hale and Hankins 2013).

Applied research questions are generated from several contexts that intersect with the practical world of public administration and nonprofit studies. The literature that we consult will extend beyond the academic literature to include reports by government offices and nonprofit organizations; we are explicitly seeking practitioner explanations of conditions and concerns. Questions are prompted by changes in existing policy or practice. These changes can be national in scope, or they can be locally driven; these policy changes can also reflect external or internal decisions. Questions can also be prompted by communities and stakeholders.

Each of these potential sources of information and experience shape the kinds of questions that we ask, and provide us with a different degree of latitude about how to frame our questions. Questions provoked by changes in policy tend to be directed at where and how the policy will be implemented, the process by which the policy will work, whether the policy will achieve its desired result, and whether the policy will produce unintended consequences. Policy changes also prompt questions about whether other alternatives would be preferred, and why that might be the case. Questions provoked by changes in policy may also involve considerable interaction with stakeholder communities, but that is not always guaranteed. Questions spurred by communities and stakeholders tend to be broader and perhaps less tied to continuing an existing policy, particularly if that policy is not getting to the heart of what the community believes should be done. Thus community and stakeholder questions tend to be broader, and are often directed at assessing the current state of affairs, expressing needs or desires for change, identifying changes that would be desirable, and identifying resources and strategies to bring about those changes.

Case Illustrations of Research Questions

The following are examples of the types of questions that were posed in the cases presented in the Introduction.

- How can a community best engage in sustainability?
- What is the status of elderly women in Alabama?

- How has the national election equipment certification program affected local elections offices?

- How well does a federal domestic violence intermediary model work?

- Do faith-based and community organizations have the capacity to carry out federal policy initiatives?

- What tools can be used to enhance the possibility of success for policy innovations that involve nonprofit organizations working alongside multiple layers of government, whether in criminal justice reform or another policy area?

All of these questions are typical general applied research questions. The answers have considerable practical application, and research to explore or address these questions can proceed in many different directions. As our case studies illustrate, the initial conversation about a research question is only the beginning of a dialogue that continues throughout the entire research process.

The community needs assessment around sustainability ideas is a particularly good illustration of an open-ended applied research question. The question began with the idea that leaders in the community wanted to do something around sustainability that would also promote civic engagement, and wondered what specifically could be done and how to go about it. Our research questions became honed through a series of discussions with two community representatives. These discussions were open ended and could have turned in any number of directions. The common themes of community supported agriculture (CSA) and community gardens kept recurring, so we were able to focus the idea of sustainability around those two concepts. The research question became more focused at this point: Could the community develop and sustain a CSA initiative in the form of a community garden?

Our study of the changing election equipment landscape illustrates another way in which research questions develop. Here, our study evolved out of a long-standing relationship with election officials in a program to professionalize the conduct of elections. Over a period of years, as we spent time with practicing public administrators who conduct elections, we learned in greater detail about their challenges in implementing local elections given continuing and changing federal policy initiatives. In our attendance at various national conferences of election practitioners, we listened to many discussions of the issues facing election administrators and voter registrars. These challenges were not framed as research questions; they were framed in the everyday language of the practice of election administration. Increasingly, these discussions focused on technology. Election administrators asked questions of each other along the following lines: How will I be able to afford new equipment? How can I get new equipment that will be based on technology that doesn't require continual upgrades? How can I service the equipment that I have? Why are my choices in equipment so limited? How can off-the-shelf technology help me and help voters? These were not the only questions that election administrators had, but when we heard a significant number of the same types of questions over a few months, we knew that we were hearing about a problem that needed to be researched.

In both cases, further discussion with practitioners and our reviews of the literature led to a series of other questions, which in turn framed the research project. We considered what we heard in combination with what we already knew and what others had found through their research. It is also important to note that although the questions in these cases were directed at particular problems or programs, it is easy to see how these questions can be applied to many other situations. For example, the questions listed at the beginning of this section could be rewritten as follows:

- How could we launch a new initiative in our community?
- What are the conditions that affect a particular group in our state?
- How are public officials coping with technological change?
- How well does this program work?
- Do we have the capacity to undertake a new idea?
- What tools can we use to promote innovation?

Sometimes applied research questions are determined entirely by the researcher, although the results have strong implications for practitioners. The study of criminal justice policy reform is an example of this type of applied research. The study was initiated to explore how and why a policy innovation took hold in cities and counties across the country, in the face of considerable political and social opposition. The study was guided by theories about how ideas and information are transferred between public administrators and nonprofit leaders through networks of relationships and organizational structures. The results demonstrated that national professional associations were particularly valuable in spreading information, and that certain kinds of information were more likely to be useful to practitioners when considering new ideas and establishing new programs. Professional associations that were prominently involved in this policy innovation were particularly interested in the outcome of the study after results were published.

Research Questions and Sponsored Research

A significant proportion of applied research is conducted in response to requests from funding sources. This type of applied research is typically referred to as **sponsored research** or **funded research** because it has a sponsor who provides financial support. Typically this support is in the form of a grant or contract that pays the researchers for some (though usually not all) of their expenses to collect and analyze data and write a report. Funding sources can be government agencies or nonprofit organizations or foundations; these groups typically pose specific questions in **requests for proposals (RFPs)** that guide the research that follows. As sponsors, these groups have questions in mind and seek researchers to conduct studies to answer those questions. In some cases, sponsored research allows researchers very little control over the research questions; questions are specified in a grant application or RFP.

For example, a municipality interested in the efficiency of a housing voucher program that it has implemented may be interested in program mechanics. For example, How many vouchers were issued? Were any benefits extended to persons not eligible for the service? and What is the cost of operating the program? However, the response to the RFP may provide the researchers with some degree of latitude in terms of what data to collect, how to collect them, or how to analyze them. If, for example, the municipality is interested in how effective its voucher program has been, we may be able to refine the research question to look at the contextual issues surrounding the program to better understand the results of the program.

Case Illustrations of Research Questions in Sponsored Research

Our case studies include two sponsored studies. These two different RFPs illustrate several comparisons in terms of the latitude that researchers have in crafting responses to RFPs and how their responses shape research questions. In both cases, the research questions were derived from a blend of the funder's interests and our experience as researchers.

Statewide Needs Assessment In this case, the RFP issued by the Alabama Women's Commission was very broad, asking only for an assessment of the status of women in Alabama, with a focus on women age sixty-five and older. The RFP itself posed no particular questions. We proposed a three-part strategy that looked at organizations, women in this age group, and best practices for meeting needs. We chose a broad approach that would allow us to examine Alabama as a system. Our questions were, broadly: What is the capacity of organizations that serve women in this age group? What are the needs of women in this age group? What are the best practices currently in use? When making these choices, we were guided by studies about organizational and system capacity that we had done in other areas; our interest in responding was to have an opportunity to bring our past research experience to bear on these general questions.

It is important to note that we could have taken many other routes in responding to this RFP, and the Alabama Women's Commission may well have been receptive to other ideas. We approached the design of the research questions for this study from two perspectives. One perspective came from the literature. We began by consulting the public administration and nonprofit literatures to identify major questions affecting public service. One significant contemporary issue is whether public systems (networks of public agencies and nonprofit organizations) actually have the ability to deliver the services that legislative and executive bodies approve. This broad issue of capacity—whether public systems have the ability to do what is intended—runs throughout analysis of every policy area. Related to the issue of capacity is the issue of intergovernmental power and administration—whether particular arrangements of government agencies and nonprofit organizations are optimal for tackling particular problems or for generating new ideas. Our other perspective came from observations of the environment around us. In particular, we noted the increasing proportion of the population at or beyond retirement age, the higher proportion of women in that group, and the differences in earnings between men and women during their working lives. Together, these factors and the literature caused us to wonder how the Alabama public service system would cope with a rapidly growing population in need of services. We felt that the best way to begin was essentially to map the Alabama terrain; thus we responded with a proposal to describe the services currently in place and identify the challenges that providers and recipients were experiencing.

National Program Evaluation Study   In this case, the RFP noted that the funder was interested in organizational capacity. The expectation among the policymakers who created the faith-based initiative was that the types of organizations they wanted to target for assistance in human service provision would not have the basic organizational capacity to apply for federal grants (federal grant applications being notoriously complicated and long), nor to engage in required reporting if funded. Indeed, there was some sense that these organizations would not qualify to apply because they had not met the basic application requirement of 501(c)(3) nonprofit tax status. This lack of basic infrastructure was part of the impetus for using an intermediary model: if intermediary organizations received the federal grants, these groups could use their own RFP processes. The intermediaries' RFPs were shorter and less complicated, did not require that participating organizations have 501(c)(3) status, and had easier reporting requirements. The government was interested, then, in knowing whether its expectations were accurate and whether the capacity of the applicant organizations could be raised through the interactions with the intermediaries. Our job as researchers was to translate these interest areas into workable research questions.

USING LITERATURE AND BUILDING THEORY

As we mentioned in Chapter One in our overview of the research process, while we develop our research questions we simultaneously develop theories, referred to as middle-range theories, which are explanations for behavior or phenomena we plan to study. We develop these theories in order to produce useful, testable expectations, or **hypotheses**. Hypotheses represent our best guesses about how and why the phenomena we investigate operate the way they do. These hypotheses then help us develop the best possible research designs in order to gather data to test our research questions. We will focus specifically on the integration of hypotheses into research designs in Chapter Three. In the following sections, we focus first on the methods we use to access published literature, and second on the interrelationship between literature about a problem or phenomenon and theory building.

The Literature Review

Once we have determined generally what we want to study, our next step is to read about what other people have discovered about the topic. Our end goal is to compile references and write a literature review. The literature itself tells us two important things: the first is the state of the field; the second is the questions that remain. The literature review amounts to a synthesis and analysis of the relevant literature that tells us where we are; it can also provide guidance about where we want to go. It acquaints us with the field and evaluates the state of research and analysis. Important, the literature review also suggests new directions for research, which can be in the form of gaps in the literature or of emerging questions.

Literature Sources

In Chapter One, we discussed many and various types of literature that can be used in the applied research process. We saw that there are many different sources of information and that sources differ in terms of purpose, approach, and quality. Here, we consider these differences across three primary sources of published material: popular press sources, trade and professional sources, and scholarly sources.

Popular press sources include national newspapers such as the *New York Times* or the *Washington Post*, news magazines such as *Newsweek* or *Time*, and any number of special interest publications. An editor or board of the publication chooses the material for publication. The purpose of the publication is to provide general information and/or entertainment and to report ideas in the general public conversation. Material is presented in a nontechnical manner and is typically written at about the eighth-grade reading level. These sources include material written by staff writers employed by the press; often the author is not identified. Articles are brief and rarely cite sources. Popular press material usually includes color photographs and graphics. Pieces cover a broad range of issues and news content. Publications contain paid advertisements.

In contrast, **trade and professional sources** focus on specialty issues with technical coverage and ads for specialized services and products for the trade or professional area that is the focus of the sources. Staff writers account for a significant portion of the writing, with contributions made by practitioners in the field. For example, public administrators and nonprofit staff interested in workforce development, including employment and training issues, can turn to the *Employment & Training Reporter*, published by MII Publications, for information on current legislation, government programs, reviews of research and evaluation reports, and highlights of new and/or successful programs. Most, if not all, of the substantive and administrative areas of government service and the areas in which we provide human services have similar publications. Sometimes these are free, and in other cases are available only in a fee-for-service format.

Finally, **scholarly sources** include peer-reviewed journals and university press books. These typically present a lengthy text with formal or scientific writing about specialized topics. Journal articles are not written by journal staff; instead, articles are written by researchers from institutions located anywhere in the world. Journal staff serve as editors for these pieces; the topical focus of the journal is determined by its editorial board, which comprises academics in the field. Advertisements are also typically not included; an exception is an ad placed by another scholarly source, such as a university book publisher. University press books are written by researchers. The press itself is aligned with a major university; for example, Oxford University Press is aligned with Oxford University, and Georgetown University Press is aligned with Georgetown University. The press typically employs editorial staff dedicated to the acquisition and editing of manuscripts, as well as to marketing and distribution. These presses also rely on academic editors either to oversee books developed around particular themes or as governing boards, or both. Editorial boards are chosen in a variety of ways; new members may be invited by current academic members, the press staff, or both. The printed material is typically black-and-white and limited to text, charts, and graphs. Lengthy bibliographies accompany every scholarly journal article or university press book.

Popular press and trade and professional sources are often easy to read. Scholarly sources, including academic journal articles and university press books, are more difficult to wade through when using them for the first time. Typically, however, these forms of writing follow a specific pattern. Knowing and using this pattern will guide users in the most efficient manner to the desired information. Academic journal articles usually consist of

- An abstract, which summarizes the purpose and findings of the article
- An introduction, which poses the research question, establishes why it is interesting and/or important, and provides an overview of the rest of the article
- A literature review and empirical theory section, which summarizes what we know about the phenomenon from other researchers and presents the authors' expectations, or hypotheses, about the results of their own research

- A methods section, which includes information on what data were used, how they were collected, and how they were analyzed

- A findings section, which presents what the researchers found when they analyzed their data

- A conclusions/implications section, which summarizes the purpose and findings of the study and then discusses the substantive meaning and possible implications of the findings

University press books follow a similar format—both forms of scholarly writing are reporting the results of the research process, so this is not surprising. Books, however, are not structured quite so tightly. Books begin with an introduction that explains the problem under study and discusses why it is an important topic, and an outline of the book that follows. The interior or "body" chapters establish the literature and discuss findings, typically in a manner that is more integrated than in journal articles. Conclusions and implications for further study and policy recommendations are included in the last one or two chapters.

Literature Searches

The literature review begins with a literature search, which is a search of the published literature on our topic. As a first step, we typically conduct a keyword search of relevant computer databases for journal articles and books about our topic. Google Scholar and JSTOR are typical starting points, as are the other sources of quality information described in Chapter One. In applied research, it is important to look for professional and trade publications as well as popular press articles; our studies have implications for the practical world, and it is important that we know how the questions are framed and discussed by publications that speak to both general and professional audiences. We cannot limit our search to those sources, of course, and must also seek out the relevant scholarly journals and books on our topic as well as government sources of information.

It is not possible to list all the scholarly sources that address applied research concerns; in Figure 2.1, we list several widely known journals in the general field of public administration, nonprofit studies, and public policy that tend to regularly include a relatively significant number of articles that reflect applied research principles. Many substantive subfields of public service have journals

Figure 2.1

Figure 2.1
List of Selected Scholarly Journals for Applied Research
in Public Service

American Review of Public Administration

International Journal of Public Administration

International Review of Public Administration

Journal of Nonprofit Education and Leadership

Journal of Policy Analysis and Management

Journal of Public Administration Research and Theory

Nonprofit and Voluntary Sector Quarterly

Nonprofit Management and Leadership

Policy Studies Journal

Public Administration Review

also, including those that focus on organizational functions (human resource management, budgeting, planning, and evaluation, for example) as well as those devoted to particular policy areas (economic development, emergency management, criminal justice, and social and human services, for example). In Figure 2.2, we list a sample of the source documents we used in some of the cases that we focus on in this book, as examples of the types of journals, government documents, and books that are typical in applied research.

Our objective in conducting the literature search is to build an **annotated bibliography** of the articles and books we have found that turn out to be relevant to our purposes. An annotated bibliography provides a paragraph-level summary of each work listed within it. The paragraph typically comprises a full bibliographic reference to the work, a summary of the research question, the importance of the question, the hypotheses tested, design considerations, and findings. In writing entries for an annotated bibliography, researchers keep three things in mind: first, what other researchers have found to be important; second, the data collection and analysis approaches that worked well and those that did not; and third, summary notes of ideas that arise while reading the article or book that help to shape the research under way.

Figure 2.2

Examples of Scholarly Sources Used in Case Studies

American Politics Research articles

Government Accountability Office (GAO) reports

Inter-university Consortium for Political and Social Science Research (ICPSR) data

Nonprofit and Voluntary Sector Quarterly articles

Nonprofit Management and Leadership articles

Policy Studies Journal articles

Political Research Quarterly articles

Public Administration Review articles

Public Management and Change series, Georgetown University Press books

U.S. Census data

U.S. Department of Justice reports

U.S. Department of Health and Human Services reports

An example of a typical annotated bibliography is shown in Figure 2.3. As our research experience in a particular area increases, our familiarity with a topic may tempt us to shortcut and reduce the level of detail in the bibliography, focusing only on one item of particular interest for the current project (such as theory, data collection methods, or datasets used). We recommend avoiding that temptation; it is preferable to preserve the full information set in order to be able to address changes that may occur in the current project and for future work. Questions that seem settled today may be open research questions tomorrow.

When complete, the annotated bibliography should provide us with a comprehensive picture of the work that has been conducted that is relevant to our question. How we use this bibliography is up to us. At the least, it will become the basis of the bibliography of our research study. More broadly, the annotated bibliography is synthesized into the writing that becomes the literature review. The literature review also shapes our views about viable and important research questions and about how to frame those questions.

Figure 2.3
Journal Article Worksheet

Bibliographic Information	Tolbert, Caroline J., and Ramona S. McNeal. 2003. "Unraveling the Effects of the Internet on Political Participation?" *Political Research Quarterly* 56:175–185
Research Question	What effect does Internet use and exposure to online election news have on voter turnout?
Theory	Behavioral theories of voter participation—socioeconomic characteristics of voters—are best predictors of voter turnout. These models are underspecified and need to take into account the impact of advances in communication technology, despite what some current research suggests. To understand why that might be wrong, we need to look to media system dependency theory, which "suggests that the difference between those forms of media. . . [that] have a direct impact on the public and those that do not is based on needs and resources" (175). Using this theory, the authors "hypothesize that the variety of information sources on the Internet (about candidates and elections), combined with the speed and flexibility in obtaining information online, may stimulate increased participation. . . [We] draw on mass communications theory to further explore how telecommunication technology may increase participation through increasing the availability of political information" (175).
Methods (type and source of data, variables, and data analysis techniques)	Use ANES data from the 1996, 1998, and 2000 elections; dependent variable is whether or not the person voted; main explanatory variables are Internet access and observing online political information; use control variables for SES, partisanship, race and ethnicity, age, reading newspaper, watching TV news, efficacy; ballot initiatives; state diversity. Used logistic regression for analysis, then constructed predicted probabilities, and finished with two-stage least squares regression.
Findings	"We find individuals with access to the Internet and online elections news were significantly more likely to vote in the 1996 and 2000 elections, overcoming concerns about over-reporting voting in survey data. Simulations indicate that individuals with Internet access were on average 12.5 percent more likely to vote, and those that viewed online political information were 7.5 percent more likely to vote, all else equal in the 2000 elections. Unlike traditional mass media, such as television and newspaper, the data suggests the mobilizing potential of the Internet during elections" (184).
Conclusions and Implications	These types of technologies may be very important for increasing political information and turnout.

The writing aspect of the literature review is discussed in more detail in Chapter Seven. Here, we note simply that the process of synthesizing the annotated bibliography will also further hone our research questions. For the cases in this book, we organized the literature that we found around the major themes of capacity, power, and administrative arrangements.

The final bibliography of our study includes citations of all the sources used in the articles or books or reports that we prepare that stem from this research. Properly citing other people's work is essential. While writing summary notes in the development of annotated bibliographies, it is critical that we properly attribute quotations and paraphrasing to the appropriate author and location in the text. Typically, the location is a page or pages, but can include charts, figures, and tables. It is also critical at this stage to include all the information needed for full and accurate attribution later in the writing process. As we construct the annotated bibliography, we have to consider in advance of other writing how we might want to reflect the ideas and words of others. This means that preparing the bibliography is more than a mechanical exercise; it requires synthesis and critical thinking about the material and how it contributes to current research and perhaps future projects. In writing the annotated bibliography, attribution can come in one of three forms: direct quotation of the author's words, paraphrasing or rephrasing the author's words, and simply attributing a finding or idea to the author. In all instances, we should make careful notes so that we can later verify exact quotations and page numbers.

A Note About Citations

As just noted, proper citation takes one of three forms: direct quotations, paraphrasing, and simply attributing a finding or idea to an author. There are several different styles of citing other people's work. In political science publications, we typically use the *Chicago Manual of Style* author-date system.

For example, we are writing a research paper on the effects of federal funding programs on nonprofit sustainability, and we want to use information from the conclusions of an article on a similar topic. We search through online databases and find the perfect article and corresponding paragraph:

Doe, Jane. 2010. "Federal Intermediaries and Sustainability: Enhanced Program Longevity or a New Form of Trickle-Down?" *Journal of Applied Government & Nonprofit Studies* 14:126–145.

"The federal government increased the use of intermediary organizations for funding non-profit human service delivery organizations significantly during the Bush administration through Bush's expanded faith-based initiative. The logic behind the use of intermediaries was that they would be able to reach out to small, faith-based organizations that would be daunted by federal requirements for achieving funding, from writing grant proposals to submitting activity and fiscal reports. The plan was that the intermediary organizations would be able to do more on-the-ground recruitment of these faith-based groups, would provide assistance in the process of writing grant applications, would be able to by-pass requirements for receiving federal grants (for example, having a tax status as a public charity), would be able to provide more hands-on assistance in filing reports, and further would be able to again by-pass normal federal reporting requirements with simpler forms. In turn, the support provided by these organizations would then enhance the capacity of the non-profit organizations, thereby also enhancing their long-term sustainability." From page 128.

If we wanted to provide a direct quote in our paper, we would write something along the lines of the following:

The logic of intermediaries as a way to enhance nonprofit sustainability is through one-on-one contact with faith-based groups. Doe (2010) writes that "the support provided by these organizations [intermediaries] would then enhance the capacity of the non-profit organizations, thereby also enhancing their long-term sustainability" (128).

However, if we wanted to paraphrase what was written, we could write:

Intermediary organizations used as pass-through vehicles to provide federal funding to small nonprofits have been found to support the development of skills and capacity in nonprofit organizations (Doe 2010).

Finally, if we simply wanted to acknowledge that an idea from the piece informs what we are writing, we would write:

The logic of intermediaries as a way to enhance nonprofit sustainability is through one-on-one contact with faith-based groups, and through that contact organizational capacity would be built, which would then influence sustainability (Doe 2010).

In all cases, we would include the full bibliographic citation at the end of our paper or report.

Theory Building

The annotated bibliography is also an important tool for building an empirical theory. The annotated bibliography provides a ready reference to the material that we have synthesized during the literature review. We use all of the sources in our annotated bibliography to develop our empirical theory. As we read the literature and think about our research questions, our next step is to start to develop a theory and, from that, hypotheses.

An **empirical theory** is simply a story that is developed based on our own observations, findings in the literature from other research, and logic about how the phenomenon we are studying ought to work. Empirical theories are explanations about why things work the way they do; for most social science research, we are not simply describing phenomena but are trying to explain why something works the way it does. Theories help us turn a series of facts and observations into causal arguments. They simplify complex social phenomena and, by extension, allow us to test our hypotheses or predictions. The tests of our predictions are important regardless of whether our predictions are correct or not. If our tests show that we were correct, that is good, and also somewhat rare—the research process always leaves some questions unanswered and raises new questions as well. However, if our tests show that we were not correct, or only partially correct, in explaining what we sought to explain (which is almost always the case), then we continue the iterative process, reviewing and revising our research questions, our theories, or both.

Empirical theories are middle-range theories and are typically grouped into two broad categories known as **inductive theories** (based on the process of induction) and **deductive theories** (based on the process of deduction). The two categories are actually processes that are mirror images of one another. Induction begins with facts and proceeds to develop theory; deduction begins with theory and predicts what will occur when the theory is applied to particular facts. Figure 2.4 illustrates the differences between induction and deduction, using broad elements of the research process. Figure 2.5 illustrates the mirror-image relationship between induction and deduction; both involve the same elements but address them by beginning at opposite points in the research process.

Most research on the political world begins with induction. Induction is based on empirical facts. We begin with observations, and we use what we observe—the facts and our interpretations of our observations—to talk, or theorize, about how similar things will act or how similar situations will occur. For

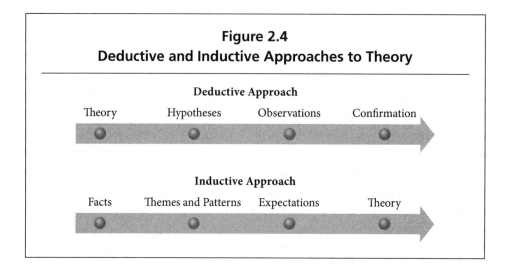

Figure 2.4
Deductive and Inductive Approaches to Theory

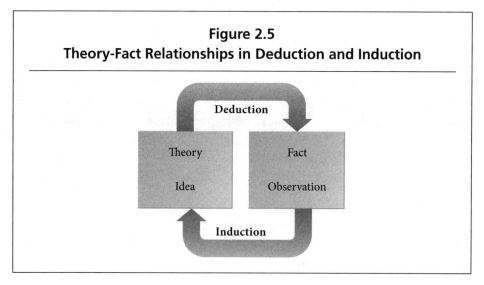

Figure 2.5
Theory-Fact Relationships in Deduction and Induction

example, the data we gather from interviews with elderly women in Alabama about their needs can help us theorize about the needs of elderly women in other states. Empirical theories may also include assumptions that are used to make predictions. In deduction, we start with a theory and predict empirical behavior on the basis of those assumptions. For example, in the study of public policy decision making, diffusion theory suggests that information is a resource, and that information which flows between organizations can improve the ability of organizations to accomplish certain tasks. From diffusion theory, we can hypothesize or expect that particular kinds of information exchanges between organizations will improve organizational performance on particular tasks or in specific areas.

Together, the methods of induction and deduction help us produce theories and hypotheses. Table 2.1 illustrates and compares the ways in which we linked theory, literature, and research questions to develop hypotheses in the case studies.

Following Manheim et al. (2007), the best theories and hypotheses have several elements. First, they are **testable**. Second, they are **generalizable** beyond the case or cases the researcher will study. Third, they are **parsimonious**, which means that the theory explains as many of the phenomena as much as possible using as few **concepts** (and, later, variables) as possible; in effect, the theory is the simplest explanation. Finally, good theories and hypotheses can link together concepts we are interested in studying, such that they form causal arguments.

Good **causal arguments** meet four specific conditions. For two concepts X and Y, where X is believed to cause Y, the following conditions are required before we can claim a causal relationship:

1. The two concepts must **co-vary**, meaning there must be an observable, empirical relationship between the two—changes in Y occur systematically along with changes in X.

2. Changes in X must precede changes in Y in time, which means that they demonstrate the proper **temporal order**.

3. There must be a specified **causal mechanism** that ties the two together (but this does not have to be observable—it can just be hypothetical).

4. The relationship between the two concepts cannot be **spurious**, meaning that it cannot be caused by a third unseen or unmeasured concept; in other words, there must be no plausible alternative explanation for changes in Y.

Table 2.1

Case Comparison of Approaches to Theory, Literature, and Hypotheses or Research Expectations

	Community Garden	Statewide Aging Assessment	Election Administration and Technology	National Program Evaluation	Criminal Justice Policy Reform
Gist of the Research Question	How can a local government best develop a CSA and sustainability initiative?	What are the current resources and needs in the state for this population?	What factors influence state compliance with suggested federal guidelines about voting equipment?	What is the organizational capacity of faith-based and community groups providing violence prevention services?	How do non-profits inform policy innovation through information diffusion?
Approach to Theory	Gather background information	Typical of an academic literature review with development of research expectations	Academic literature review with formal hypotheses for testing	Theory of change with typical academic literature review and development of research expectations	Academic literature review with formal hypotheses for testing
Type(s) of Literature Used to Develop Theory	Academic Government Professional	Academic Government	Academic	Academic Government Professional/ Practitioner	Academic Government Professional/ Practitioner
Example of Hypotheses and/or Research Expectations	None.	Wealthier areas will have greater and higher-quality community resources.	There will be no relationship between state-level factors and compliance with VVSG.	There will be significant differences between faith- versus community-based capacity.	Nonprofit information networks foster sustainable policy innovation.

Developing Research Expectations and Hypotheses

Research expectations and hypotheses reflect what we believe we can understand or learn as a result of the research process. Drawing on what we expect to find or explore from our literature-based empirical theory, we draft simple statements of expectations about what ought to be the results of our data collection and analysis. If we are testing existing theory using quantitative analysis, we think in terms of hypotheses. If we are exploring new ground or building theory, typically through qualitative methods, we think in terms of research expectations.

As a first step, we reduce our concepts to **variables**, or observable and measurable characteristics that represent our concepts or one or more aspects of our concepts. This process is called **operationalization**. All of the concepts that we are interested in studying through applied research have to be operationalized. This part of the research process is key in translating our ideas into something that we can actually study in a systematic way. For example, in studying questions that pertain to public administration and nonprofit organizations, we are frequently concerned with whether organizational arrangements are effective in meeting their missions. We want to study such concepts as the capacity to perform, effectiveness, efficiency, and program outcomes. We may want to study the configuration of organizational arrangements themselves, and determine whether different arrangements are more beneficial than others.

In order to use any concept as a variable, we must first operationalize it. This means that we define it and specify its boundaries. Our operationalization of any of these concepts can take many forms. What is most important is that we are explicit in our definition of the concept and that we communicate our definition and any assumptions and decision rules we use to anyone reading our research. Only by taking this step do we make it possible for others to replicate our studies. When we cannot measure a concept directly and exactly, we substitute a **proxy** as a substitute measure.

Several of the concepts that we used in the case studies are illustrated in Table 2.2, along with the way that these concepts were operationalized. Operationalization is a choice that all researchers make. This choice is always affected by available resources, including time, money, and whether or not data must be collected (and how easy or difficult that will be). This choice is also affected by the goal of the project and its relationship to prior research. In order to extend or compare findings, it can be important to follow convention and operationalize a concept in the same way as earlier researchers have done. It

Table 2.2
Case Comparison of Concepts and Operationalization

	Community Garden	Statewide Aging Assessment	Election Administration and Technology	National Program Evaluation	Criminal Justice Policy Reform
What Was the Concept?	Community resources	Personal need	Federal-state-local relationships	Evaluation capacity of organizations	National information network
What Was the Measure?	Interest	Actual daily activities compared to what we know about need	Adoption, adaptation, and opting out	What was measured and how it was measured	Information linkages
How Were Data Gathered?	Community meetings Survey	Follow-back calendar Interviews	State laws	Survey over time	Interviews Survey

may also be important to stake out a different definition for a concept, if the point of the project is to call attention to a gap in the literature around that definition.

The end product of operationalization is a variable. We commonly talk about two different types of variables: (1) the **dependent variable**, Y, the phenomena we are trying to explain; and, (2) one or more **independent variables**, X, what we believe will explain change in the dependent variable. We examine all of the variables in our empirical theory and the causality present to develop clear statements about how they ought to relate to each other. Our ideas about causality can be our own theoretical propositions or can come from the prior research of others that has been reported in the literature. These statements become our research expectations and hypotheses. We must be able to deduce expectations and hypotheses from the empirical theory.

The meaningful difference between a research expectation and a hypothesis is a technical one. A research expectation is typically associated with qualitative analysis, and formal hypothesis testing is typically associated with quantitative analysis. In qualitative analysis, we look for themes and trends to develop theory based on our own observations and experiences and the data we collect about the observations and experiences of others. In quantitative analysis, we use sample data to make inferences about the population. This is sometimes referred to as **inferential statistics**. When we do this, we describe characteristics of a population by talking about its **parameters**, such as the average age or weight of a population. It is usually not possible to identify data for an entire population, so we typically draw samples of the population instead. When we use sample data, we infer population parameters from estimated parameters based on those sample data.

We can safely say that we may infer the population parameters from the estimated parameters when we find **statistical significance** (see Chapter Six for more discussion). However, we start with the assumption that our sample data do not actually tell us anything about the population data—the expectation we have about the parameter is called the **null hypothesis**—which is what we believe in the absence of contradictory evidence. In hypothesis testing, what we are trying to do is reject the null hypothesis, but we do not say that we accept the alternative hypothesis, because there is a certain degree of error inherent in all inferential analysis. Remember: our research is about falsifying, not about proving things to be "true."

We can also do this by looking at two variables and whether or not there is a relationship between them. We start by constructing a hypothesis stating that there is no difference between two variables; this is the null hypothesis. It is expressed in a formula as follows, where the hypothesis H_0, is the difference between two parameters that we name variables π_1 and π_2 and the difference between the variables $= 0$.

$$H_0 = \pi_1 - \pi_2 = 0$$

Here we are saying that there are no differences between the two variables and that they are essentially the same thing. That there is no difference implies a natural alternative, which is that the variables are not the same or that there is a difference between them. This condition is represented in the following formula, in which the hypothesized difference between variable (parameter) 1 and variable (parameter) 2 is not equal to 0:

$$H_A = \pi_1 - \pi_2 \neq 0$$

We can establish criteria for believing that sufficient difference exists between our variables; on the basis of statistics from the sample, we determine that there is enough evidence to say that we can infer that a relationship in the sample data will also be present in the population, or not.

When engaging in hypothesis testing, we are concerned with two types of errors that can be made, and we design research and analyze data with the intent of minimizing the possibilities of making these errors. A **Type I error** occurs when we falsely reject the null hypothesis from sample statistics when in fact there is no population relationship. A **Type II error** occurs when we fail to reject the null hypothesis from sample statistics when there is a relationship in the population among two variables of interest. Otherwise put, we imagine that there is a truth about our variables of interest within a population, but we cannot measure that population, so instead we draw a sample and try to infer information about the hypothesized population relationships from the sample data. There are four possibilities:

1. In the population, there is no relationship among the variables, and we find that to be the case in the sample data—this is a correct finding.

2. In the population, there is no relationship among the variables, but we find one in the sample data—this is a Type I error

3. In the population, there is a relationship among the variables, and we find that to be the case in the sample data—this is a correct finding.

4. In the population, there is a relationship among the variables, and we do not find that to be the case in the sample data—this is a Type II error.

The challenge in applied research is first to determine which type of error, if made, would cause the greatest difficulty for a group of people, an organization, or a program and then to minimize the possibility of making that error through the design and analysis choices that follow in the research process.

THEORIES OF CHANGE AND LOGIC MODELS

Thus far we have been thinking in terms of empirical theory, which is simply a statement of how a particular phenomenon ought to work based on our reading of past research, personal observations, and logic. In these theories, we identify the major concepts, differentiate between the outcome (in variable terms, the dependent variable) and the factors that lead to that outcome (in variable terms, the independent variables). We also identify the linkages between outcomes and the factors that lead to them. These linkages are the logical causal mechanisms that we think of when considering whether we are able to articulate a causal relationship between concepts or whether we are limited to relationships that are simply correlations (which do not establish causation).

Theories of Change

In applied research, we also think in terms of the systems or environments within which these outcomes and factors exist; for example, when we look at programs that deliver human services typical of many government and nonprofit efforts, we look at them in the context of a system and in the context of the environment in which they are delivered. When looking at these systems or environments—typically, communities—we can develop an illustration that presents a unified view, or theory, of how policy and program interventions ought to work. In these cases, the theory that we develop is referred to as a theory of change.

A **theory of change** is simply a theoretical description of a problem, a program (or intervention) that will address the problem, and the expected outcomes of the program; it unifies these elements by identifying the links between them. The theory of change is based less on past research (though this is still important) and more on identifying practical problems as well as the appropriate interventions and the outcomes we expect to see from those interventions. Theories of change are frequently used in applied social sciences for designing programs and for evaluating their performance.

A theory of change can also be used to help develop a research design that can be used to examine program design, implementation, and/or outcomes, and to plan new programs. When used to evaluate, a theory of change is sometimes referred to as an **evaluation framework**. Another term in common use is **logic model**, which is simply a graphic representation of a theory of change.

What differentiates these efforts from studies of interventions seen in classic experimental designs (see Chapter Three for a discussion) is that we explicitly study human service programs or other public policy interventions in the context in which these interventions occur—as complex, messy, and interactive; it is essentially impossible to pinpoint specific causal factors because we cannot control for the environment.

A researcher who adopts a theory of change approach to research questions commits to a process in which the theory of change is articulated first, the research is designed with this theory in mind, the research study is then carried out, and the results are used to readjust the program to better achieve its desired ends. The assumption here is that the purpose and timing of the research process is such that results can (and ought to) be used to improve programs.

Most people who work in public service programs—whether in government agencies or in nonprofit organizations—work within a framework guided by some theory of change, or have a basic idea about how and why their work ought to produce a desired outcome. Theories of change are the normative basis for almost all public service activities. However, most public servants have not articulated this process and are likely to be unfamiliar with this term. In working with public service programs, it is often the job of researchers to listen to the people involved in the programs in order to gather data and to construct their values and beliefs about the program in a systematic way so that these values and beliefs can be used as a visual and written description of their theory of change.

Theories of change in today's world tend to be comprehensive. In applied research, we frequently encounter conditions in communities or other institutional systems that are interrelated to one another and that involve public agencies as well as nonprofit organizations. This is not particularly surprising, because today we understand the American government landscape as more than government agencies alone; rather, it is a collection of arrangements that involve government agencies and nonprofit organizations. Another element of our understanding of the problems facing communities is the interrelationship among the elements that make up community, including education, employment, crime, healthy families, violence prevention, and so on. Our appreciation of the interconnected nature of the forces that bear on communities has evolved significantly over the past twenty years and is reflected in the evolution of team-based problem-solving approaches across disciplines. Many nonprofit funding sources, in particular some foundations, are interested in a comprehensive, multidisciplinary approach to making a difference, and believe that this is best accomplished when all aspects of a community are included in policy change.

One illustration of this collective approach is the **comprehensive community change initiative (CCCI)**. A CCCI is used to describe community change initiatives that are focused on making broad-based improvements in stressed communities. CCCIs can come in the form of stand-alone programs, coalitions, or collaboratives, and focus on myriad issues like education, employment, healthy families, violence prevention, and so on, usually in combination, and guided by the philosophy that healthy communities require improvements in all of these areas.

CCCIs achieved popularity in the 1990s and remain relevant today. They have been designed and implemented by government agencies and by nonprofit organizations, and the typical CCCI involves organizations and individuals across public service. One standout example of a program undertaken by a nonprofit organization is the national, multisite Jobs Initiative designed and implemented by the Annie E. Casey Foundation. The Jobs Initiative was intended to improve conditions and outcomes for disadvantaged groups; here, the target group was disadvantaged young adults living in inner cities. A strong example of a government program is the Empowerment Zone/Enterprise Communities (EZ/EC) concept initiated by the U.S. Department of Housing and Urban Development. The EZ/EC program focused on community revitalization of the neediest urban and rural areas in America. Both programs were national in scope and involved multiple sites, multiple layers of government, and extensive interaction over a decade or more with communities, organizations, and leaders (Hebert and Anderson 1998).

A key feature of CCCIs generally, which we find in both the Jobs Initiative and EZ/EC, is the integration of local stakeholders into the design of change itself. Each CCCI initiative engages the target communities as full partners in identifying strategic goals as well as programs, opportunities, and partnerships that could assist in meeting the goals. Local stakeholders are also involved from the ground up in identifying outcomes and measures of success.

The concepts of collaboration and interdependence in theory building and in research design continue to be important today, as many federal grant programs require collaborative efforts of one form or another across organizations, communities, or regions. The theory of change approach to understanding complex systems is also relevant in contemporary studies of networked arrangements where there is program delivery or some kind of intervention as a part of the program. Across the analysis of public services, the theory of change approach is at work (whether explicitly or implicitly) in the way public administrators and nonprofit leaders define public problems and think about the range of possible public policy solutions that can be successful.

CCCIs also intend to engage problems through multiple levels at once—at the individual level, the institutional level, the community level, and, in some cases, the structural level. CCCIs value comprehensiveness; they also tend to be driven by a community-building and community-organizing approach as evidenced by the incorporation of stakeholder views into the design, implementation, and evaluation of the initiative. CCCIs encompass the essence of the challenges that researchers face in producing believable evaluation results and require smart thinking about how to design and evaluate programs.

Logic Models

Regardless of the theory employed to establish causal linkages, logic models can be used for any program or policy problem to identify the key elements of an issue and look at the linkages between them. Logic models are based on a series of components that differentiate between the problem or issue we are trying to address, the resources we have, the activities we pursue, and the results of those activities. In applied research, the logic model can be a valuable tool in research design generally, as the problems typically connect either to existing programs or to plans for new forms of intervention. More specifically, we talk about

- The problems or issues we are trying to address, which are also sometimes referred to as **challenges**.

- Resources that can be used, which are usually referred to as **inputs** and can include money, personnel, volunteers, organizations, in-kind donations, community interest, and positive public opinion.

- Activities that can be conducted, which are typically referred to as **outputs** and can include things like the development of materials, distributing those materials, holding information sessions or listening sessions, and holding trainings, among other activities.
- The results of these activities, which are typically referred to as **outcomes**. Outcomes can be short term, medium term, or long term. How we define each of these depends on the program and its activities.

Generally speaking, there are two time horizons for understanding outcomes. In the first time horizon, the short term is immediate; the medium term is within days, weeks, or months; and the longer term is more vague. In the second time horizon, the short term refers to occurrences that happen within a year; the medium term is one to five years; and the long term is around ten years. Another way to think about outcomes in either the short-term or longer-term time horizon is to think with respect to changes that are made (or expected). In the short term, the concern is to identify someone learning something. In the medium term, the outcome is a change in behavior of some kind. In the long term, the outcome is a greater or cumulative benefit of that behavioral change as it is repeated over time; in other words, the outcome is a positive change because of the cumulative effect of the changes made or actions taken. Figure 2.6 illustrates these different outcome concepts in the case of the community garden study. The short-term time horizon reflects outcomes directed at teaching community members about food that could be grown in a community garden. These outcomes include learning about healthy food (short-term outcome), taking action in the form of buying fresher foods (medium-term outcome), and achieving better nutrition and possible weight loss (long-term outcomes). The long-term horizon reflects outcomes that evolve from creating the community garden itself. Outcomes here include establishing the garden (short term), producing healthier food (medium term), and creating improved health outcomes (long term). The short- and long-term time horizons should complement each other; it is also possible and indeed advantageous that outcomes interact.

Consider another example in practice. We work in a nonprofit organization located in an area with low voter turnout. Local politicians have decided that this is indicative of low democratic functioning. As an organization, we could establish a goal of increasing turnout by sending out a nonpartisan reminder to all eligible voters. We would then have the following scenario:

- Problem/Challenge: low voter turnout
- Input: local political support to make a change; small budget for activity; human resources
- Output: creation of nonpartisan reminder; distribution of nonpartisan reminder
- Outcomes:
  - Short term: trigger intent to vote, which is indicated by voter turnout at the polls
  - Intermediate: voters get into the habit of voting and, in the aggregate, increase voter turnout
  - Long term: enhanced democratic functioning

The logic model for this scenario is displayed in Figure 2.7.

We gauge progress in each phase of the logic model with **benchmarks**. The process of benchmarking can be thought of in one of two ways. Organizations sometimes set standards for where they ought to be at each step of their process, and compare their actual progress to their projected progress. Another approach is to compare where they are against the performance of the highest-performing comparable organization or program in order to determine what else might be done to achieve excellence. In our democratic functioning example, we could establish benchmarks for the activity itself (how many reminder notices we provide) as well as the short-term, intermediate, and long-term outcomes. Short-term outcomes could be measured by changes in voter registration and actual ballots cast. We expect that these changes will be positive—that is, that voter registration and voting will increase. For intermediate outcomes, we expect that increased registration and voter turnout will endure over time. We could compare our community to others and note the trends in our registration and turnout relative to that in other communities. Long term, we could measure increased democratic functioning through additional measures of civic participation, such as participation in community planning activities and other aspects of civic life. How we define and measure these outcomes is up to us and is based on our theory of change. We could establish benchmarks

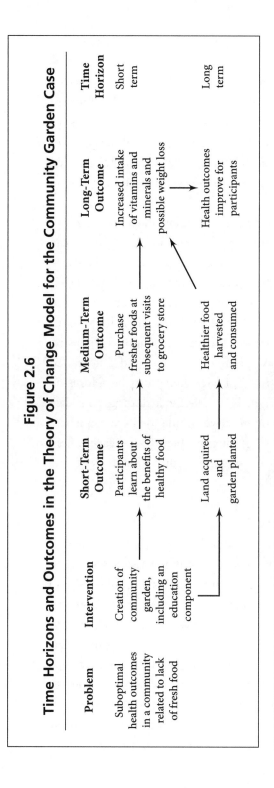

Figure 2.6

Time Horizons and Outcomes in the Theory of Change Model for the Community Garden Case

Problem	Intervention	Short-Term Outcome	Medium-Term Outcome	Long-Term Outcome	Time Horizon
Suboptimal health outcomes in a community related to lack of fresh food	Creation of community garden, including an education component	Participants learn about the benefits of healthy food	Purchase fresher foods at subsequent visits to grocery store	Increased intake of vitamins and minerals and possible weight loss	Short term
		Land acquired and garden planted	Healthier food harvested and consumed	Health outcomes improve for participants	Long term

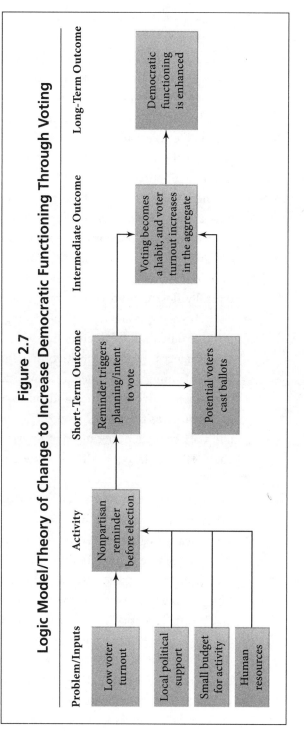

Figure 2.7

Logic Model/Theory of Change to Increase Democratic Functioning Through Voting

Problem/Inputs	Activity	Short-Term Outcome	Intermediate Outcome	Long-Term Outcome
Low voter turnout	Nonpartisan reminder before election	Reminder triggers planning/intent to vote	Voting becomes a habit, and voter turnout increases in the aggregate	Democratic functioning is enhanced
Local political support		Potential voters cast ballots		
Small budget for activity				
Human resources				

based on what we want to have happen, or on what has happened elsewhere in similar projects.

Together these elements of the logic model help us figure out what to measure and when to measure, and provide insights about how to measure. The utility of the logic model approach is twofold. First, it helps researchers address possible causal interactions under circumstances where causality is often difficult, if not impossible, to establish. Second, it helps researchers articulate from the planning phase of the research what the policy or program intervention actually is and how it is supposed to work.

There are several limitations to this approach, however. First, logic models capture intent to make change, not what actually happens. Second, logic models can reduce complex phenomena to simple concepts, but this reduction can also obscure causal factors. Third, if followed as prescriptions and without deviation, logic models can stifle creativity and spontaneity in the conversations that typically flow around community change initiatives. Finally, when logic models are used for evaluation, some people claim that because the models focus on positive outcomes, evaluators may overlook negative outcomes and unintended consequences, whether positive or negative. This deficiency can be addressed when planning the applied research design, by explicitly including consideration of negative outcomes and positive or negative unintended consequences along with positive outcomes. CCCIs pose particular problems for measurement and data collection, because long periods of time are required for the systemic change that is the typical focus of these initiatives.

Steps for Development of Theories of Change

When working with communities and programs to develop a theory of change, we typically begin with a simultaneous process of identifying issues and goals. As a part of one deliberate thought process, we think about the problem(s) and the ultimate outcome(s) we would like to achieve. We then trace our intervention and our processes back from the ultimate outcomes that we would like to see. We next identify intermediate outcomes and then immediate outcomes. This process is sometimes known as backward mapping. At this point, for each type of outcome we have identified, we identify the benchmarks we would expect to see in order to show that we are making progress. We then trace these benchmarks to the activities that will produce those outcomes, and then trace these back to the resources that are present. The gaps between resources and necessary activities are highlighted by this approach. At this point, we also identify the causal links that connect resources to programs and then to results.

This dimension of applied research offers a natural opportunity for extensive community and stakeholder involvement. This involvement can take many forms and can be directed by the researcher, by the community, or codirected by both together. The coproduction of knowledge that occurs when researchers and communities work together is a particularly important aspect of applied research. Through coproduction, we guard against conducting research in a vacuum and against imposing our values on the communities that we are studying (Baker, Hale, and Summerfield 2013; Brown 2013). Issues and goals emerge from the experience of each group. Virtually any of the tools used to gather qualitative data can be deployed in this setting (see Chapter Four for detail).

The logic model can be applied to many common activities conducted by public administrators and nonprofit leaders and managers, including program design and planning, policy implementation, and evaluation. The process of constructing a logic model and its information and conceptual relationships can be directed toward the "whole" of a problem or condition, and also to its constituent parts. Logic models tend to highlight gaps (and linkages) between resources and necessary activities and between necessary activities and desired outcomes or intended goals.

When we write the narrative that accompanies the logic model, it is critical to articulate the assumptions that we bring to the program. These are beliefs about the program, the people involved, and how the program will work. These assumptions can involve such higher-level issues as our views about how people learn and behave, various motivations for change, and the impact of external factors. These assumptions can also reflect our views on structuralism and agency. Our logic model will reflect our beliefs about the range of possible actions and the degree to which we feel that these actions are constrained by invisible processes, such as institutional arrangements or the economic arrangements in a given community. The logic model will also reflect our beliefs about the ability to overcome these structural and institutional constraints by activism, policy entrepreneurship, and other courses of action. It is important to note that the assumptions that underpin a logic model can be the subject of research as well. In subsequent chapters of this book, we discuss various approaches to gathering qualitative data on values, beliefs, and perceptions; these are at the heart of all models based on theories of change.

As an illustration, the national program evaluation study explicitly utilized a logic model approach for thinking through how the role of the intermediary organizations *ought* to enhance the capacity of the grantees. Figure 2.8 illustrates the logic model developed by the researchers. It includes intermediary activities and the possible outcomes at each stage of the process (differentiating between intermediate and ultimate outcomes), and ties these to possible benchmarks that could be used for measurement.

Developing the program logic model was critical because it established the foundation for what was expected to occur, which would then form the basis for evaluating whether what was expected to occur actually did happen. The proposal that was made in response to the RFP was based on assessing capacity with respect to the components that the researchers identified in the logic model.

The case is a typical illustration of the interplay that occurs between researchers and funders. Here, the funder wanted to assess capacity; the researchers provided a framework for identifying capacity in order to then assess it. This case also illustrates the significance of theoretical foundations in applied research; the researchers used their understanding of the literature to prepare a theory of change; this grounded their proposal in concepts and principles that are understood broadly within the discipline.

The concept of change is part and parcel of every policy initiative. Public policy decisions that are implemented by public administrators and addressed by nonprofit organizations (as part of the implementation process, as advocates, or as independent agents for change) are intended to change the status quo. An important aspect of thinking about change is to understand where the studied environment is located in relationship to ideas about change. Many times, we are involved in studying a program or policy that already exists. In other cases, we are involved in examining an environment to identify possible programs or policies that could bring about the changes that are desired.

The theory of change concept works slightly differently in each of these two circumstances. In the situation of an existing policy or program, the theory of change—or a normative view that is something close to a theory—has been initiated through the design of the policy intervention. In the perfect world of policy design, interventions are based on one or more theoretical propositions that have been vetted to produce particular results; in the real and imperfect world of public service, interventions are usually tied at least to some basic suppositions about what should happen as a result of the changes that have occurred.

Figure 2.8
Program Evaluation Logic Model for Study of Community Organizations

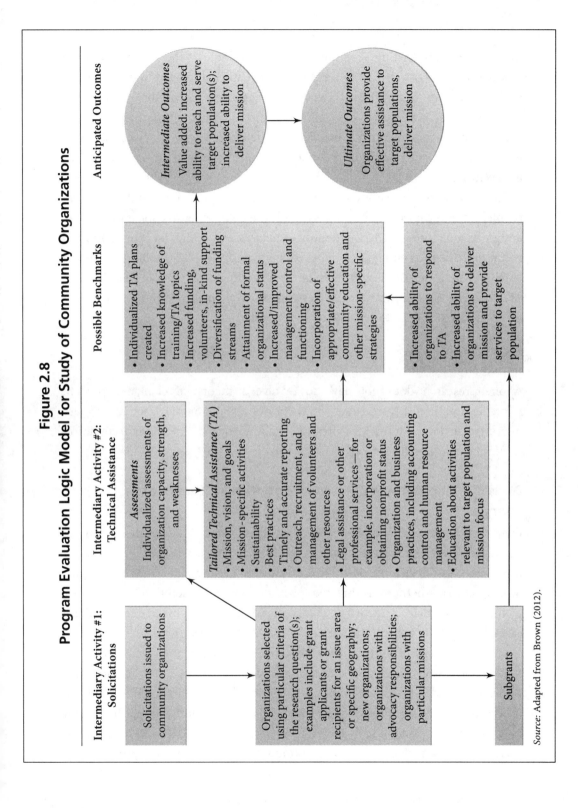

Source: Adapted from Brown (2012).

In the case of an existing program or policy, the logic of the theory of change model should focus on the intervention and whether it has led to the intended outcomes or not. In short, the intervention has already been determined, and our role as researchers is to determine whether the intervention has "worked." We may need to look to the literature to determine how to measure "what works" in a particular arena, or that may have been identified for us in the policy intervention.

In the case where we are examining a solution to a community or social problem, the theory of change takes on a more comprehensive meaning for the design for our study. Here, we identify outcomes and design an intervention to accomplish them. The logic of the theory of change model should lead to the outcomes that the community desires. In this latter case, we also identify possible benchmarks to track our progress. In short, we begin with the results that we seek, and look back to see how to accomplish them.

DECISION TREE

Applied research does not have to involve a theory of change approach. However, it is useful to consider the theory of change model whenever we are interested in longer-term measures of actual change in the human condition (typically measured by outcomes).

Decisions About Applied Research and Using a Theory of Change

Figure 2.9 illustrates the basic decisions we make when thinking about framing a study in terms of a theory of change. The first step is to analyze the purpose of the project and determine whether it is directed at studying an existing policy or program, or whether it is directed toward developing a solution to a social or community problem. A theory of change model can be applied in either of these cases, but does not apply if the project focuses on basic research.

If the research will study an existing policy or program, then we assume that the study is already operating with a theoretical framework or set of normative values that guided the intervention. A theory of change—or something close to it—has been initiated through the design of the policy intervention. This design may or may not include consideration of outcomes. Thus the first task is to review the relevant literature to determine whether outcomes are proposed for

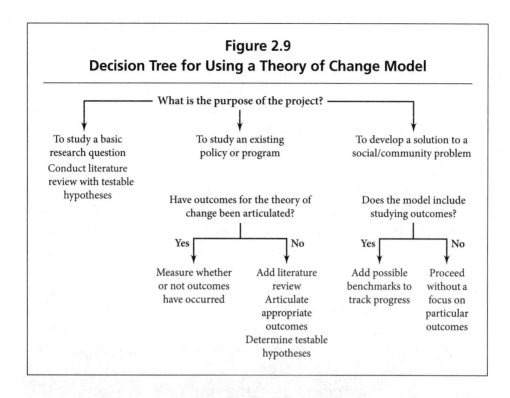

Figure 2.9
Decision Tree for Using a Theory of Change Model

What is the purpose of the project?

To study a basic research question
Conduct literature review with testable hypotheses

To study an existing policy or program

Have outcomes for the theory of change been articulated?

Yes — Measure whether or not outcomes have occurred

No — Add literature review
Articulate appropriate outcomes
Determine testable hypotheses

To develop a solution to a social/community problem

Does the model include studying outcomes?

Yes — Add possible benchmarks to track progress

No — Proceed without a focus on particular outcomes

this intervention. If so, the focus then turns to measuring whether or not those outcomes have occurred—in other words, we assess the degree to which the intervention was successful. If outcomes are not an aspect of this intervention, then we turn to the literature to determine testable hypotheses.

Research directed at developing a solution for a social or community issue can employ the theory of change approach in a more comprehensive manner than a study directed at an existing intervention. The desired outcomes are used to develop benchmarks to track progress toward those outcomes, using the backwards mapping process explained in this chapter.

CONCLUSION

In this chapter, we tackled two primary concepts. The first is the development of applied research questions, and how these questions fit into the research process. Researchers and practitioners frequently work together to develop good questions which reflect ideas that matter and which address problems that need to be resolved. This synergy between researchers and the administrative and policy environments is critical to an informed study, and is more likely to generate results that are meaningful to a community or an affected group. This chapter also highlighted the importance of finding and evaluating different sources of literature, and building an annotated bibliography that can guide a study so that it builds on existing information and contributes to our broader understanding. The basic conceptual building blocks of operationalization and variables discussed in this chapter will be used in subsequent chapters as we move through the stages of the research process.

The second key concept in this chapter is that of theories of change. Theories of change are particularly useful in applied research settings because these theories are directed at solving problems. In developing a theory of change, researchers typically work with community members to seek to understand the problem in the context of its environment, and develop outcomes measures linked to the solutions that researchers and communities seek. As the case studies illustrate, theories of change and logic models are powerful research tools that can be used to examine existing programs and to create new solutions. We build on these concepts in Chapter Three as we learn how to develop a research design.

CHAPTER SUPPORT MATERIALS

Chapter Two Relevant Articles

Doebbeling, Bradley N., Thomas E. Vaughn, Robert R. Woolson, Paul M. Peloso, Marcia M. Ward, Elena Letuchy, Bonnie J. BootsMiller, Toni Tripp-Reimer, and Laurence G. Branch. 2002. "Benchmarking Veterans Affairs Medical Centers in the Delivery of Preventive Health Services: Comparison of Methods." *Medical Care* 40:540–554.

Dwyer, John J. M., and Susan Makin. 1997. "Using a Program Logic Model That Focused on Performance Measurement to Develop a Program." *Canadian Journal of Public Health* 88:421–425.

Ellis, Robert A., and Roger R. Moore. 2006. "Learning Through Benchmarking: Developing a Relational, Prospective Approach to Benchmarking ICT in Learning and Teaching." *Higher Education* 51:351–371.

Lieberman, Robert C., and Greg M. Shaw. 2000. "Looking Inward, Looking Outward: The Politics of State Welfare Innovation Under Devolution." *Political Research Quarterly* 53:215–240.

Chapter Two Discussion Questions

1. Discuss the links between research questions, empirical theories, and research expectations or hypotheses.

2. What might the impact on research be if we did not include the step of developing empirical theories?

3. Is there really a difference between research expectations and hypotheses? Explain your answer.

4. Pick a concept that you would like to measure. Some examples are poverty, need, achievement, or accuracy. Operationalize this concept in six different ways; use secondary data sources for three, and original data for the remaining three. Identify and describe the strengths and weaknesses of each of your operationalization approaches. For each, also indicate whether the scheme can be replicated over time and whether that aspect is important.

5. Why would articulating assumptions about a theory of change be important?

Chapter Two Practice Assignments

1. Find the following article through your library and develop an annotated bibliography for it. Then write a one-paragraph summary of the article, including examples of direct quotes, paraphrasing, and acknowledgment.

Lieberman, Robert C., and Greg M. Shaw. 2000. "Looking Inward, Looking Outward: The Politics of State Welfare Innovation Under Devolution." *Political Research Quarterly* 53:215–240.

2. Select an article from both *Public Administration Review* and *Nonprofit and Voluntary Sector Quarterly*. Prepare an annotated bibliography entry using the blank form in Figure 2.10.

3. Read the following excerpt about the city of Greenburg and answer the questions that follow. Use the logic model worksheet in Figure 2.11 to complete this exercise.

The city of Greenburg has a population of 100,000, with another 45,000 people living in rural areas surrounding the city. The outlying areas consist of mainly older, white, poor farming communities. Greenburg itself has a long-standing African American community representing about 10 percent of the population, which has lived there for the last seventy years. Over the last ten years, there has been an influx of relatively young Latino and Asian families moving to the community, who now represent 15 percent of the population. The regional school-age population is about 55 percent youth of color, including approximately 10 percent for whom English is their second language.

Greenburg has historically experienced low rates of property and violent crime, but one weekend six months ago, five teens were killed with firearms. Following these tragedies, the Greenburg Youth Service Agency (GYSA) was barraged with phone calls from people expressing outrage and seeking answers. In response, the GYSA sponsored two community meetings with the goal of harnessing residents' energy and emotions into positive action. The group has been meeting at a local recreation center that has historically served youth under age thirteen years. At the second of these sessions, the concept for the Greenburg Coalition for Peace unfolded with the vision to reduce violence and build safe homes and peaceful communities. The mission of the Coalition is to prevent violence by strengthening and empowering families, communities, and neighborhoods and encouraging community pride and involvement through education, community organizing, development, and revitalization.

The Coalition has met once a month for six months, with most of the major sectors of the community involved. Those members who have been especially active include the school resource officer, a parent of one of the victims, and a youth worker who knew two of the victims. Activities considered so far in meetings have included improving the quality of public housing; opening recreation center activities to youth thirteen to eighteen, including their arts-and-crafts and dance classes, as well as offering access to the gym; working with police to clean up crime "hot spots"; and helping residents establish neighborhood associations.

Also during this time, Greenburg Community College was awarded a federal grant to address youth violence, and received $50,000 to plan a youth violence prevention program. One of the requirements of the grant is to create a logic model of the new program and to generate some ideas based on that logic model about how it might be evaluated.

Given this overview, build a logic model that represents this Coalition. After you have completed the model, answer the following questions:

a. Are there any planned activities that will *not* help them achieve their goals?

b. Are there other programs, activities, or interventions needed to achieve their goals?

c. How could the logic model be used to develop an evaluation?

4. For each of these listed items focused on election administration, identify the type of event (challenge, input, output, or outcome—specifying short, medium, and long term) and justify your answer.

a. Information about how to vote is placed in the newspaper.

b. Poll lines are long.

c. The public desires a change.

d. Voter registration cards are mailed out.

e. An interactive website is developed for voter information.

f. People learn that their polling place has been moved.

g. People who speak English as a second language turn out to vote at a higher rate than they did in the previous election.

h. Members of your organization attend a planning meeting with community groups.

i. You receive complaints about your election materials from groups that represent voters with vision impairments.

j. Poll worker volunteers are trained.

k. Poll workers fluidly respond to voter questions and needs on election day.

Chapter Two: Linked Assignment

Throughout the text, we include a series of "linked assignments." These have been developed to walk the research methods student through the entirety of the research process by developing a research project that includes each phase of both applied and basic research.

On the basis of your work on the Chapter One linked assignment, select the topic that best passes the "Who cares?" test and is testable. Develop a research question from the topic. Then identify at least ten academic, peer-reviewed resources on that (or a similar) topic. Create an annotated bibliography for these sources. Using what you have written in the annotated bibliography, attempt to develop an empirical theory for how the phenomenon you are studying ought to work, culminating in a hypothesis or statement of research expectations. Identify and operationalize at least one dependent variable and one independent variable, and explain how you will measure these. When this is complete, go back to the research question and make sure that the question, the empirical theory, and the hypothesis or hypotheses all fit together. Revise each component as necessary.

Chapter Two Link to Online Assignments

Thinking about your own community, identify an unsolved problem that you can imagine developing a program to solve. Then complete the following tasks:

1. Develop a logic model for that program using the Logic Model Worksheet in Figure 2.11.

2. Write a one- to two-page theory of change to accompany that logic model.

3. Discuss how you could then use that logic model and theory of change to advocate and organize for change.

Figure 2.10
Annotated Bibliography Entry Worksheet

Bibliographic Information	
Research Question	
Theory	
Methods (type and source of data, variables, data analysis techniques)	
Findings	
Conclusions and Implications	

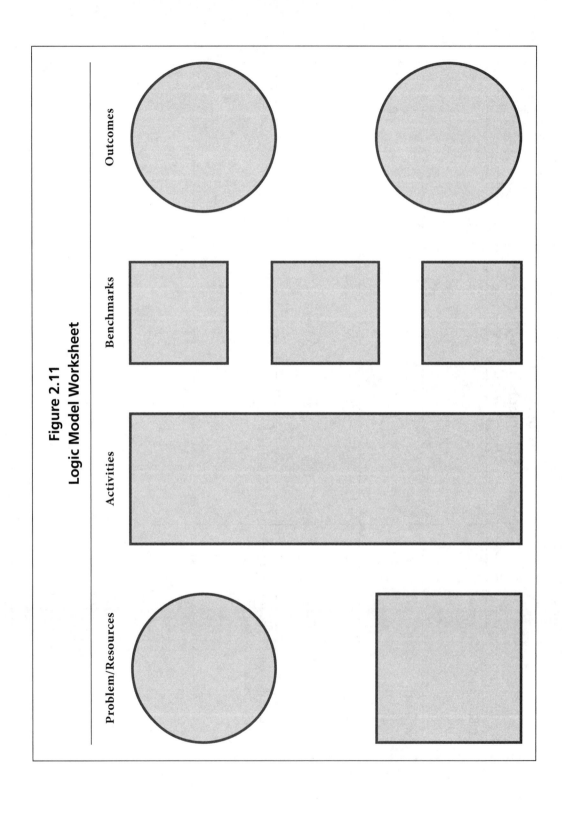

Figure 2.11
Logic Model Worksheet

Applied Research Designs

I n this chapter we discuss **research designs**, or plans to go about collecting data. We begin with a discussion of general design parameters and the major design types and their conditions and general principles. We discuss research designs that are best suited for applied research studies; although the concept of a research design describes a common set of principles and practices, there are some approaches that are more suitable to certain questions than others.

GENERAL PARAMETERS OF DESIGN

A main consideration in research design is the **degree of control** that exists over the conditions in and around the phenomena we wish to study. Ideally, we are interested in a design that will help rule out alternative explanations for the phenomena, so that we can focus only on one main hypothesis or explanation when we examine the results. This approach is driven by one of the conditions of causality—here, nonspuriousness. However, it is not possible for our main hypothesis to rule out all rival explanations. The world around us is full of complexity and unexpected events that may affect our best efforts at such designs. In practice, we design research studies along a continuum within two extremes. At one extreme, we strive for a research design in which we can control all conditions except the factors that we believe to be explanatory. At the other extreme, we design a study in which we can collect and analyze data reflecting all possible explanatory variables. Across this continuum, our research designs are also limited by finite resources and limitations regarding access to data.

Six other factors are also considered when selecting a research design. The first is our **unit of observation**, or the level at which we will locate our study. Common units of observation include individuals, political units (city, county, district, state, nation), organizations, and organizational arrangements (service delivery teams, collaborations, networks); these are also referred to as units of analysis at the analysis stage of the research process. The second factor is to determine where our data will come from, referred to as **sampling**. The third factor is referred to as **validity**; in its most simple form, this is the extent to which we are actually measuring what we think we are measuring. The fourth concern we have is **reliability**, which is the extent to which the tools we use to collect data, otherwise known as **research instruments**, are capable of yielding consistent results. Our fifth concern is about **bias** or **error** that is introduced into our study; this can also be thought of as the systematic difference between our sample characteristics and the population characteristics. Our final concern involves **ethical issues** and ensuring that our design selections do not in any way violate the established research standards of beneficence, respect for subjects, and justice. In this chapter, we outline each of these considerations in greater detail.

MAJOR DESIGN TYPES

Generally speaking, designs are classified by the degree of control embedded within the design over the factors that may impact the dependent variable, or the factor(s) in which we are interested. The more control we have over the features of our design, the greater our assurance that any relationships we find through our research are not caused by other factors. We classify research design types based on the degree of control that is possible. In descending order of control, we broadly classify design types as experimental, quasi-experimental, and non-experimental. Each of these design types is explored further here.

Experimental Design

The purpose of an **experimental design** is to study the effect of one specific variable in an environment that is sufficiently highly controlled that it rules out other possible explanations. In experimental design, an outside element that is referred to as a **treatment** or **intervention** is introduced in order to examine its effect on our variable of interest. As a simple example, we may want to know if the presence of religious icons at a polling place affects the opinions of voters and the votes that are cast in that location. In this example, the intervention or treatment would be the addition of a religious icon at the polling place.

Experimental design includes other components in addition to the treatment or intervention. An experiment requires an **experimental group** that receives the treatment and a **control group** that does not. In our example, the experimental group would vote at the polling place when the religious icon is present, and the control group would vote at the polling place without the presence of the religious icon. The subjects of the experiment are **randomly assigned** to one or the other of these groups, meaning that there is no systematic assignment to the groups, either conscious or unconscious. A measure of change is also involved. Typically this involves the use of **pretests** and **posttests**, which are administered to both the experimental and control groups before and after the intervention, respectively. We can determine that there is an effect from the intervention in one of two ways. One is if there is a statistically significant difference between the pretest and posttest; the other is if there is a statistically significant difference between the experimental and control groups on the posttest.

There are several variations within the category of experimental designs. The most common comprise randomized comparative change design; randomized comparative posttest design; multiple-pretest design; and multiple-posttest design. Each of these has in common several characteristics, including the presence of an experimental group and a control group, and random assignment. The key differences among these experimental design types are the point at which measurements are taken and how many measurements are taken. The various experimental design types are described here and shown in Table 3.1.

Randomized comparative change design. This approach utilizes both pretest and posttest measurements. Sometimes this design is referred to as a pretest-posttest control group design. This approach is considered to be the standard approach.

Randomized comparative posttest design. Randomized comparative posttest design takes only a posttest measurement. Sometimes this design approach is referred to as a posttest-only control group design. This approach minimizes the resources needed.

Multiple-pretest design. Multiple-pretest design utilizes multiple pretest measures and one posttest measure. This approach allows the researcher to better determine if any change between the pretests and the posttest is the result of the intervention or because of "learning" from the pretest.

Table 3.1
Measurement and Intervention Sequence for Major Forms of Experimental Design

Form/Name	Measurement	Measurement/ Intervention Sequence
Randomized comparative change design (or pretest-posttest control group design)	Pretest Posttest	Time 1–Intervention– Time 2
Randomized comparative posttest design (or posttest-only control group design)	Posttest	Intervention–Time 1
Multiple-pretest design	Pretest Pretest Posttest	Time 1–Time 2– Intervention–Time 3
Multiple-posttest design	Pretest Posttest Posttest	Time 1–Intervention– Time 2–Time 3

Note: Each form utilizes a control group, an experimental group, and random assignment.

Multiple-posttest design. Multiple-posttest design uses one pretest measure and multiple posttest measures, allowing the researcher to determine how lasting or sustainable the impacts from the intervention may be.

The strength of the experiment is determined by its ability to establish causality, which is also referred to as **internal validity**. A central aspect of achieving internal validity depends on randomness. Technically, experiments require that subjects be randomly assigned to the treatment and control groups. This means, generally, that the researchers do not use any sort of systematic manner of assigning subjects to these groups, and that subjects have the same chance of being assigned to one group as to another. It is this randomness in the execution of group assignment which assures that we can believe that the effects we observe are attributable to the intervention in the experiment. By randomly assigning subjects to control groups, we essentially remove the threat that spurious (outside) factors may have an effect on the difference between control and treatment group outcomes; the absence of spuriousness allows us to establish a strong causal argument.

When random assignment is not possible, the essential nature of randomness can be achieved in other ways. Randomness can be approached at the group level, rather than at the level of the individual; in other words, subjects can be assigned such that groups rather than individual members have the same characteristics on average. Randomness can also be achieved by random assignment of individuals to groups with similar conditions. Finally, randomness can be approached through the use of matching characteristics. For example, if we wanted an equal number of men and women as participants in both the experimental and control groups, we could randomly assign participants to groups while simultaneously ensuring that an equal number of men and women are assigned to each group. The number of characteristics that can be matched is limited by our resources (time and contact information in particular) and also by the pool of available participants; the more characteristics we choose on which to match, the more challenging it becomes to identify participants who possess all of the characteristics. It should also be noted that characteristics that are not matched may affect outcomes. These unmatched characteristics may be quantities of interest—specifically, independent variables. These unmatched characteristics may also be simply random or systematic characteristics. In any case, the method of assignment and its limitations should be clearly specified in the design and discussed in the findings.

Experiments are considered by some to be the most pure form of social science research. However, experiments have some real limitations that make them difficult to utilize in the social sciences. These limitations are sometimes referred to as bias or error.

Bias in experiments comes in several forms. First, **selection bias** comes from differences in groups that occur as a result either of a flaw in the group selection process or from **attrition**, meaning that over time, some of the subjects drop out of our studies. Second, we sometimes refer to bias in the form of **endogenous change**, meaning that subjects change during the life of the experiment regardless of exposure to the treatment, or because of the subject's "learning" from the testing. Third, we sometimes experience error because people are affected either by their **history** or by current **external events** that influence how they answer questions, even in the presence of the treatment. Fourth, in some cases, experiments may be affected by **contamination** of the control group by the treatment group. Contamination can occur in several different ways. Subjects may compensate when they know they are in the comparison group or think they are in the experimental group by changing their behavior accordingly; this is referred to as the **placebo effect**. Sometimes subjects work harder or differently simply because they are aware that they are part of a study, a phenomenon called the **Hawthorne effect**. Finally, another important limitation of experimental designs is that while they have high internal validity, they have correspondingly low **external validity**. This means that it is difficult to generalize from experimental studies to other situations because of the high level of control involved in the environment in which the experiments take place; similar control is difficult to achieve without replicating the original study, which defeats the goal of generalization.

Applications for Public Administration and Nonprofit Studies Utilizing experimental designs is generally difficult in social science research. This is because the topics we undertake for study are often inextricable from the world around us, and it is difficult, if not impossible, to take our research into a laboratory where spuriousness can be ruled out. However, there are some subtraditions of political science, public administration, and nonprofit studies that use this approach. These include (1) the growing area of field experiments, in which researchers try to isolate causal factors and implement interventions "in the field," or in natural settings; (2) some forms of program evaluation in which ethics permit random assignment or modification of a control group; (3) research on the effects of political communication (for example, the effect of particular crime scripts on viewers); and (4) research trying to show an empirical relationship to game theory (rational choice) findings.

The experiment is often talked about as the ultimate form, or gold standard, of research design. However, utilizing an experiment does not ensure that the conditions of causality have been met, except under the most highly controlled conditions. What is often most difficult to discern is the issue of nonspuriousness. Most policy research and evaluations that use experimental designs are subject to more effort than experiments in a lab setting. In social experiments, in particular, randomization does not necessarily lead to clearly delineated control and treatment groups. As noted earlier, **experimental contamination** occurs when (1) treatment is delivered accidentally to control group members, and (2) control group members believe that they received the treatment and, as a consequence, behave differently than they would have otherwise.

An example of experimental contamination comes from a social experiment in New Jersey (Camasso et al. 2002; Loeb et al. 2003). Before the Welfare Reform

Act of 1996 was passed, the federal government allowed states to apply for waivers to experiment with the Aid to Families with Dependent Children (AFDC) program, more generally known as public welfare. The state of New Jersey received a waiver for such a program, called the New Jersey FDP AFDC Section 115 Waiver welfare experiment.

The treatment in this study was a regulation that placed a family cap on payments for children born ten months and after AFDC payments began; the family cap limited monthly support based on family size and capped child support at the amount provided for a family with four children, and provided no additional support for larger families. The method used random assignment of new enrollees into AFDC either into the family cap option or the control group that had no cap on the number of children for whom the participant could expect support. The treatment group ($n = 5{,}501$) and the control group ($n = 2{,}892$) were statistically sufficiently large. Assignments were made on the basis of the last four digits of the primary caregiver's social security number. The researchers surveyed the women quarterly, and pooled these data for the time periods during which the cases received AFDC benefits over a four-year period across the state. They found that for the treatment group, the birthrate was 12 percent lower and the abortion rate 14 percent higher than the control group. This finding applied to new cases on the AFDC case rolls, not to women who had been in the system prior to the experiment. They also found that these results pertained primarily to African American women as compared to women of other racial and ethnic groups.

Some evaluators did not believe the results of the study and conducted an additional survey of study participants to gauge whether and how well participants understood whether they were in the control or treatment groups. Analysis of this subsequent survey (which had a response rate of 40 percent) found that study participants were confused about (1) what group they were in, and (2) the rules of the treatment. Other evaluations of state waiver experiments that examined whether cases were in treatment or control groups demonstrated that participant confusion was common in other welfare experiments. Although the authors of the original study were able to support their original conclusions, the concerns raised by other researchers signaled caution in interpreting results.

Quasi-Experimental Design

We next take up the classification of **quasi-experimental design**. For our purposes, quasi-experimental design means a research design that retains many of the components of an experiment but fails to qualify as a "pure" experiment because the conditions render a true experimental design impossible. Common situations in which pure experiments are not possible occur when a control group cannot be used for ethical or practical purposes, or because random assignment would be unethical.

One such instance that illustrates the limitations of true experimental design that result in a quasi-experimental design is a 1998 Substance Abuse and Mental Health Services Administration (SAMHSA) study examining housing arrangements for persons with severe mental illnesses. Researchers wanted to determine whether different combinations of housing and professional services would result in better long-term outcomes for clients. These combinations included comparison of a traditional residential group home option and a reform arrangement referred to as supportive housing. In the traditional residential group home option, clients lived in a controlled environment with twenty-four-hour supervision and utilized services provided within the home. In the supportive housing arrangement, clients used apartment vouchers to live essentially independently in the community and utilized services that were "wrapped around" them (meaning brought to them). It would be unethical to randomly assign participants to either of these different housing arrangements. Random assignment could hamper successful treatment both by placing high-functioning individuals in a twenty-four-hour supervised home setting that would limit and frustrate them and by placing low-functioning individuals in the community without adequate support and/or oversight. In this and similar situations, we turn to a quasi-experimental design in which some of the criteria of the full experiment are relaxed. Specifically, the condition of random assignment to control and treatment groups would not be used, and would be replaced with another method of assignment.

The major forms of quasi-experiments include nonequivalent control group designs, before-and-after designs, and factorial designs. These major forms of quasi-experimental design are summarized in Table 3.2. The key differences among these design types concern the presence of a control group, how group assignments are made, and variations in the points at which measurements are taken.

Nonequivalent control group designs utilize both a control and experimental group. Assignments to the control and experimental group are made on a case-by-case matching to each group where similar individuals are placed in one of the two groups as they become available, or by aggregate matching where the

Table 3.2

Major Forms of Quasi-Experimental Design

Form/Name	Control Group	Experimental Group	Assignment	Measurement
Nonequivalent Control Group Designs	Yes	Yes	Yes	(Pretest) Posttest
Before-and-After Designs	No	Yes	No	Pretest Posttest
Factorial Designs	Yes	Yes, but multiple treatments given to different groups	Yes, but multiple treatments given to different groups	Posttest

desire is to use some similar characteristics of the overall groups. These designs always utilize a posttest, and frequently include pretest measurement as well.

Before-and-after designs do not utilize control groups; therefore, there is no need for assignment decisions to be made. This type of design always includes a pretest and a posttest. A typical form of before-and-after design is intervention analysis. In **intervention analysis**, we examine the effects of a specific policy or program intervention on behavior over time, collecting data both before and after the intervention to determine those effects. Another form of a before-and-after approach is **time series analysis**, which includes observations of the phenomenon with measurements taken over time. The interval at which measurements are taken depends on the research question; the length of the overall study must be sufficiently long to allow patterns to emerge that relate to the question and to the behavior that is expected to change. For a long-term outcome, the periodic measurement might be in terms of years; for a short-term outcome, monthly (or weekly) measurement may be appropriate.

Factorial designs take a variety of different forms. Typically, a factorial design includes one control group and multiple experimental groups, and possibly some variation of assignments to these groups. Frequently these designs utilize only posttest measurements; however, at times these designs include pretest measurements as well.

There are trade-offs in the strengths and weaknesses of these quasi-experimental designs as compared to experimental designs. Quasi-experimental designs have lower internal validity because of the inability to place subjects into test groups in a purely random manner. However, some have much higher external validity, meaning that researchers are better able to generalize from the findings to other similar situations because they are not bound so tightly to unrealistic experimental conditions. Quasi-experimental designs are also subject to the same sources of bias and error that we see in experimental designs. Literature in the substantive area will serve as a guide to common approaches, benefits, and limitations.

Nonexperimental Design

Much research about public administration, nonprofit management, and politics in general has no experimental element to it. This is primarily for practical reasons. We are interested in understanding the communities around us, so experimental conditions are relatively expensive to establish, or cannot be created in a way that will ethically generate interesting, useful, or valuable data. As a consequence, much research about public service activities is conducted through nonexperimental designs. There are some who contend that nonexperimental designs should be used only for descriptive or exploratory research, and not for explanatory studies. However, when strict rules are established early on regarding data collection, and the concepts of interest are clearly operationalized and measured, nonexperimental research makes a significant contribution to our understanding of the social and political world. Thus, although we proceed in many cases to conduct research about public service without an actual experiment or quasi-experiment, we continue nevertheless to precisely specify the data that will be collected (what, how, when, why, and from where), and we precisely specify the key dependent, explanatory, and control variables. With strict adherence to these basic research precepts, nonexperimental research designs can greatly add to our understanding of social and political phenomena.

Nonexperimental designs are said to be reflexive, or to have the property of **reflexivity**, meaning that all parts of the research process occur simultaneously and influence or inform each other. Another way to think about this is that the research process is nonlinear and iterative, and the lessons learned from each iteration inform the next iteration. Frequently, nonexperimental research involves the collection of qualitative data.

Nonexperimental approaches to data collection take a variety of forms. Some of the key approaches are presented in Table 3.3 and outlined in the paragraphs that follow.

To one degree or another, nonexperimental approaches involve researcher interaction with those whom they are studying. On one hand, studies utilizing these approaches are sometimes criticized for a high degree of subjective interpretation, lack of validity, or limited generalizability; on the other hand, scholars

Table 3.3
Approaches to Nonexperimental Data Collection

Data Collection Approach	Overview	Strengths and Weaknesses
Direct Observation	Passive or active observation of phenomenon	(+) in-depth (−) highly subjective and often unstructured
Focus Groups	Small-group moderated conversation	(+) interactive and in-depth (−) reliability
Elite or Key Informant Interviews	Conversation with experts or key informants, with varying degrees of structure	(+) in-depth (−) reliability, validity
Case Studies	In-depth examination of a phenomenon or place, utilizing multiple data forms	(+) in-depth, causality (−) generalizability, reliability
Content Analysis	Systematic analysis of recorded materials	(+) in-depth (−) reliability
Surveys	Oral or written collection of information about beliefs and behaviors; demographics	(+) in-depth (−) validity, reliability, subjectiveness
Secondary Data Analysis	New or repeat analysis of data others have previously collected	(+) minimal effort/cost to obtain data (−) no control over operationalization or data collection

argue that subjective phenomena such as culture, personal perception, and political views cannot be fully understood without utilizing these approaches. Here, we introduce several key nonexperimental approaches. How and why we use these approaches are explained in more detail in Chapters Four and Five.

Direct observation involves watching people or events or processes. Approaches to direct observation vary in the degree to which the researcher is involved with participants, and the knowledge of those under observation about what is taking place. At one end of the continuum, direct observation can be **passive**, in which we as researchers simply observe participants and take notes on their behaviors. Moving along the continuum, we may choose to conduct our research as **participant observers**, in which we observe while taking part in the activities that we are studying. As a more in-depth form of participant observation, we may choose to engage in **ethnography**, in which researchers fully immerse themselves in a culture for an extended period of time.

Focus groups usually consist of a small group of people who are brought together for a moderated conversation. Focus groups are used in the research process in various ways. Among these are to augment surveys, conduct exploratory research, pilot and refine instruments, study group processes, and evaluate policy.

Elite or **key informant interviews** engage the people closest to an issue or phenomenon in a directed conversation that utilizes their expertise to help us better understand the issues. Elite or key informant interviews vary in the degree to which these conversations are structured around specific questions. Generally speaking, these interviews range from very open-ended, unstructured conversations to semistructured or structured discussions in which the topics of discussion are relatively limited. The reliability and validity of these interviews depend a great deal on the degree of structure in the interview questions (also referred to as the **interview protocol**).

Case studies involve an in-depth examination of an event, geographic area, or public problem. Case studies can be conducted on data drawn from a single case or from multiple cases. Case studies are used frequently in research that compares two or more units of analysis (for example, a city, program, country, state, or organization). Whether focused on one case or on multiple cases, the researcher gathers in-depth information about a particular event, place, or phenomenon through a variety of data collection techniques in order to produce what is referred to as **thick description**, or a detailed accounting of events and the context and processes that caused them to unfold. These studies often have high internal validity but low external validity.

Content analysis involves the systematic analysis of recorded materials for common themes using the application of a strict set of rules. These recorded materials are typically archived in some way. **Archival documents** are essentially historical documents and records of past actions. These include the standard records of government offices and nonprofit organizations as well as newspapers and other media. Today, it is easy to imagine that virtually any sort of medium can be used to create records of action and other information that will become archival records. Because of the nature of the data collected, these studies sometimes suffer from the biases of the sources used or from the unrepresentative nature of samples of materials. These studies are also susceptible to problems with reliability, particularly if more than one person is coding and interpreting the data.

Surveys involve oral or written data collection about individuals. Frequently the purpose of the survey is to collect information on their behavior, beliefs, or opinions. Additional data about **demographics**, or the personal characteristics of the people being studied, are included to determine if there are patterns between certain demographic characteristics and respondents' beliefs or actions.

In nonexperimental designs, we commonly use data that others have collected, called **secondary data**. Secondary data analysis refers to the use of these data. We use secondary data to conduct new analyses. We also use secondary data to reanalyze findings that have been published, which is a form of **replication** used to verify previous findings. Secondary data has many strengths and advantages. Many of these data are immediately available, which minimizes the time it takes to conduct research, as well as the cost. Many of these data are free, which also minimizes cost. Some types of data that we use frequently are far too expensive for us to collect on our own; the population data collected by the decennial census and released by the U.S. Census Bureau are a prime example. The use of secondary data also has some drawbacks, most notably related to quality and reliability. For data that originate from a high-quality and reputable source, such as the U.S. Census Bureau, we have information about the data collection processes, including design, sampling, instrument construction, collection, and reliability. Figure 3.1 presents a list of common sources of

Figure 3.1
Common Sources of Secondary Data

U.S. Bureau of the Census

Federal budget and federal agency budgets

Government Accountability Office reports

State statistical abstracts

State budgets and state agency budgets

Book of the States series

PEW General Social Survey

PEW subject-specific datasets including Center on the States

American National Election Survey

Roper polls

Gallup polls

Encyclopedias

Urban Institute publications

Internal Revenue Service Form 990s and other datasets

National Center for Charitable Statistics

Inter-University Consortium for Political Science Research (ICPSR)

United Way local-level data

National Conference of State Legislatures (NCSL)

National Governors Association (NGA)

National Association of Counties (NACo)

secondary data used in applied research; a common thread is the veracity of the information and our ability to consider it to be authoritative, as discussed in Chapter One.

To address concerns about reliability, we reflect on the concerns related to quality information and find the most appropriate source of data. It is also important to obtain the background information about how data were collected, as well as the codebook. Related, it is important to consider the limitations inherent in secondary data as data that already exist. We have no control over how questions were constructed nor the level of measurement used for response categories. As a consequence, we may not have the same information that we would obtain if we collected the data. At the least, we have to carefully consider the specifications of secondary data in our analysis (see Chapter Six for more discussion).

Case Illustrations of Research Design Approaches

Table 3.4 illustrates the different research design approaches taken in each of the cases illustrated in this book. Applied research design is often severely stymied by real-life considerations, including the design of the public program itself and the populations it is intended to serve. Applied research design is also limited by the specific agendas of research funders, which oftentimes reflect ideological objectives and sometimes reflect overt political agendas. Specific decisions, limitations, and circumstances for three of the cases are discussed in the next sections.

Statewide Needs Assessment   In the case of the statewide needs assessment regarding women age sixty-five and older, we made several broad design choices. One design choice was to examine the environment from two perspectives. One perspective was the capacity of government institutions and of nonprofit and for-profit organizations in Alabama to provide public services. The other perspective was that of the women receiving public services from the state of Alabama. This use of dual perspectives allowed us to explore the possibility that there might be gaps between need and service provision; these gaps could be important to the funder, and were certainly important to us from an applied research perspective.

A second design choice was to employ mixed methods, in which we collected and analyzed both qualitative and quantitative data. The mixed-method approach strengthened our study because it was not possible to survey or interview either of the populations of interest; these populations would include all women in the state age sixty-five and older, and all public and nonprofit organizations providing services to all women in this age group.

We also chose to limit our study to women. We made this choice because the mission and role of the funder relate specifically to women; however, men in this age group are also in need of services and support, and we found that many organizations that provide services to women in this age group also provide services to men.

Table 3.4
Case Comparison of Research Designs

	Community Garden	Statewide Needs Assessment	Election Administration and Technology	National Program Evaluation	Criminal Justice Policy Reform
What Was the Approach?	Nonexperimental	Nonexperimental	Nonexperimental	Nonexperimental and quasi-experimental	Nonexperimental and quasi-experimental
Why Was This Approach Selected?	Exploratory purpose	Exploratory purpose Met needs of funder	Looking at "why"	Quasi-experimental possible because of presence of unfunded applicants	Examining policy intervention
How Was This Approach Implemented?	Focus group SWOT analysis Elite interviews Resident interviews Secondary data analysis	Participant interviews Survey of providers Observation	Elite interviews Secondary data analysis	Surveys Interviews Document review Site visits Focus groups	Elite interviews Case studies Time-series analysis of secondary data
What Were the Strengths of This Approach?	Identification of local capacity gaps	Comprehensive statewide description	National trends Elite opinion leaders	Credibility of approach enhanced because of triangulation	Strength in multiple methods over time and in comprehensive view
What Were the Weaknesses of This Approach?	No information about some groups	No information about some groups	Design does not forecast new policy direction or resolve problem	Limited findings because of short time frame of study	Design cannot test elements of individual program success

National Program Evaluation In the national program evaluation, as we designed the research approach, we were given a few basic parameters about what the national program would look like, but were not provided with specific information. We knew that there would be intermediary organizations (though not how many), that there would be grantees (again, not how many), and that the grant periods would be for a year and all grants would begin and end at the same time. We had to proceed with our design based on assumptions. We developed a design assuming there would be about ten intermediaries (the idea being that the federal government would fund regional intermediaries covering about five states each), that there would be more than three hundred applicant organizations, and that at least one hundred of those would be funded. We also expected that these organizations would receive roughly the same amount of federal funding. Our design choices reflected these assumptions.

The capacity study was designed to minimize error and enhance validity and reliability by using triangulated data collection techniques. We included a natural quasi-experiment, comparing through surveys the capacity outcomes and sustainability of the funded versus unfunded organizations. We ran focus groups with all of the funded organizations about their experiences. And we included in-depth case studies of ten of the funded organizations (two per each of the expected regions) consisting of a site visit, document reviews, and monthly phone interviews.

The national program was not implemented exactly as anticipated. In fact, three intermediary organizations were funded, comprising one that covered a state, one that covered several counties in a different state, and one that covered the rest of the country. Approximately 150 organizations actually applied, and fewer than 60 were funded. Further, the intermediaries began dispensing funds at different times, so it was impossible to field surveys of organizations at one point in time and interpret the findings the same way across the grantees. The funded organizations also received very different levels of funding depending on their projects.

The consequence of these differences was largely practical, and adjustments to the design were required. We maintained all of the components of the original design, but reduced the number of case study organizations to eight (two for the statewide intermediary, two for the regional intermediary, and four for the national intermediary). We also added a third wave of the capacity survey to adjust to the differing funding periods. Doing so allowed us to expand our analysis of sustainability for the early-funded organizations.

This case illustration underscores the reflexive nature of the applied research process. We created a design, but had to make changes to that design midway through the data collection period in order to address the program as it actually existed. Doing so then allowed us to alter some of our research questions. As we have noted elsewhere, this process of iteration and reflection is typical of many applied research studies.

Election Administration and Technology In making our design choices, we were faced with several practical considerations. One was actually drawn from the sense of urgency that we heard expressed by practitioners. Election officials noted frequently and passionately that the rapid rate of technological change was quickly rendering election equipment obsolete. This suggested that our research design would be more valuable if it were implemented relatively quickly, so that our results could contribute to the current debate. The systemwide nature of our question suggested that we should compare data from multiple states. The intergovernmental nature of the election administration system suggested that we should examine national, state, and local factors. Not surprisingly, experimental designs were inappropriate; our research questions could not be answered by simulating an election condition or subjecting people to a range of different election conditions.

We chose a nonexperimental, mixed-methods approach in which we used quantitative analysis to compare the fifty states and qualitative analysis to understand interviews with national, state, and local election officials. The fifty-state comparative design compared state-level factors that influenced how states were responding to national opportunities (which could also be perceived as pressures) for voluntary certification. It is the case that election administration decisions have a strong local, county-level component; however, we did not pursue a county-level design that would allow us to compare counties across the country. Our choice was both practical and theoretical. Practically, the time required to compare counties was significantly greater than the time required to compare states. Theoretically, states would likely be more important than localities in our final analysis, because voting machines are simply too expensive for localities to purchase with local funds. We expected that state legislatures rather than county commissions would make most of the significant decisions about providing funding for new equipment. We chose to reflect on the intergovernmental dimension of the problem by conducting interviews with national, state, and local officials.

SAMPLING

The idea of sampling is relatively easy to comprehend, and it is very important in all applied research. This section identifies terminology and basic concepts that relate to sampling and its application to public administration and nonprofit research questions.

When we conduct research, it is very often the case that we do not have the time, resources, or ability to collect data on the population, or the universe of all of the possible units, instances, or observations of the phenomenon we are studying. We therefore select a **sample**, or subset, from the **population** we are studying. This sample is called a **census**. We then use the data from that sample to make inferences (and sometimes predictions) about the population. A **sampling unit** is a single member of the sample.

The first step in sampling is to define the population we are interested in studying. After that, we develop a **sampling frame**; this is simply the set of sampling units from which we select the sample for our study. In most cases, we want this frame to be either the population itself or representative of the population.

On its face, the concept of a sampling frame seems fairly straightforward. In practice, we face several obstacles. These arise in our interpretation of the existing data that we believe represent the population. One problem is making sure that all possible units in the population can actually be captured in the sampling frame. In other words, how can we know that the sampling frame encompasses the entirety of the population so that when we draw a sample, we are drawing it from the entire population?

For example, we may want to study nonprofit organizations in the state we live in, and we want to randomly assign five hundred organizations to our study. An easy way to obtain a sampling frame would be to turn to the *Encyclopedia of Associations* and draw a list of all the organizations included in the encyclopedia as our sampling frame. However, not all nonprofit organizations are listed in this publication, nor are some of the organizations profiled in it currently in operation. Thus we may inadvertently introduce error into our study by the selection of the sampling frame. Typically, these errors cannot be avoided entirely; even a list published very recently will be subject to some error because some items on the list no longer exist, and new items have arisen and are not yet included. What is critical, however, is to examine the sampling frame for systematic bias and to avoid frames that introduce systematic error.

Another problem is that we may include cases in the sampling frame that should not be there. A typical example from nonprofit studies might arise if researchers are attempting to study prohibited lobbying behavior undertaken by nonprofit organizations. If the sampling frame includes all types of nonprofits, it will include some types of nonprofit organizations that are permitted to engage in particular lobbying activities. In this case, the sampling frame error can be avoided by carefully specifying the question and by having an accurate understanding of the context of nonprofit activities. Another typical example involves the study of voter participation. Voter registration and voter turnout are two standard concepts in the study of voter participation and elections. A sampling frame that considers the voting-age population as the basis for calculating voter registration and voter turnout will include two groups of individuals who are not eligible to vote. Noncitizens are counted as part of the population, as are individuals with felony convictions. Members of the former group are not eligible to vote, and members of the latter group are not able to vote in all states and are subject to many restrictions that hinder both registration and voting.

Related, sampling frames may not include all the relevant cases. A famous case of sampling frame error comes from a poll of possible voters before the 1936 presidential election, which predicted that Governor Alf Landon would defeat Franklin Roosevelt. Roosevelt won the election. The reason for the error in prediction was simply that the sampling frame was not representative of the population. The researchers created the sampling frame using club memberships and phone directories. The problem with this approach was that the people who overwhelmingly supported Roosevelt did not have phones or belong to clubs—they were too poor and thus were not included in the survey; as a consequence, the survey results were biased.

There are two major groups of sample types, and within those two are different variations. The major groups are **random** or **probability samples**, in which each case within the population has an equal chance to be part of the sample, and **nonrandom** or **nonprobability samples**, in which this is not the case.

Random or Probability Sampling

Random sampling is based on the idea that each population unit has exactly the same chance of being included in the drawn sample as every other population unit. There are several forms of random sampling that can be used depending on how large a population we have and what access we have to lists of population units from which to draw our sampling frame.

Simple Random Sampling With the **simple random sample (SRS)**, each population unit, for our cases denoted by x, has the same probability (denoted as pr) of being selected into our sample from our population (denoted as N). In mathematical terms, the probability that each unit will be included in the population is

$$pr(x) = \frac{1}{N}$$

and thus for a given sample (denoted as n), each separate population unit has $pr(x_1) = pr(x_2) = \ldots = pr(x_n)$ of inclusion in the sample.

We are interested in the characteristics of the population, and we will learn them from our sample units. To understand the population based on the characteristics of the sample units, we can calculate **estimated parameters**, or descriptions, about the population from each sample we draw from a population. These estimated parameters include simple statistics like averages, standard deviations, percentages, and proportions. The estimated parameters are unique to each variable, and we calculate each independently of other variables. We calculate the estimated parameters for one variable at a time, and these results are therefore referred to as **univariate statistics**; sometimes these parameters are referred to as first-moments.

We sample to understand the population as a whole, which is of such significant size that we cannot examine each unit in the population directly. Thus we are interested in using techniques that will allow us to infer characteristics of the population from the sample. If we were to take an infinite repetition of samples and examine their **means** (denoted as μ for the population $\bar{X}$ and for the sample), or the mathematical average found by taking $\bar{X} = \sum_{i=1}^{n} X \frac{1}{n}$, we find that the **expected value**, or the average of all of the averages, will converge on, or approximate, the population mean, μ. Otherwise put, $E(\bar{X}) = \mu$, where E is the expected value. Therefore, any estimated parameters for any variable X calculated by using SRS techniques will approximate the population parameters.

This is a fundamental part of what is referred to as the **central limit theorem (CLT)**, also known as the **normal approximation rule**, which holds that for any SRS of size n, the sample mean will fluctuate around the population mean, and that as sample size increases, our **test statistics**, or estimated parameters, will look more and more like the population parameters. This is very useful because it means that so long as we have a sufficient sample size, we may infer that the relationships we see in our sample data will look like the relationships in the population data.

However, the CLT only holds for our test statistics if we follow the rules of the SRS. These rules include equal probability of selection and the assumption of **independence**, which states that some event A is independent of some other event B if the $pr(B|A) = pr(A)$; in other words, A is independent of B if the probability of event A does not change if B takes place. Independence means that we follow a procedure in which we replace each sampling unit back into the sampling frame after selection, in a process referred to as **sampling with replacement**. **Sampling without replacement** violates the assumption of independence. This is an important concept in inferential statistics, where we examine changes in one variable in the presence of another. If we do not utilize sampling with replacement, our estimation techniques will not work as intended.

Sometimes it is difficult to develop a representative sampling frame. In other cases, our sampling frame may come in forms that we can manipulate to make the SRS process easier. The following are techniques that we can use in constructing a sampling frame that will allow us to achieve relative randomness and independence without introducing significant error.

Sampling Intervals When our population is reasonably small, with a physical manifestation (like a list of units), and the population units are sequentially arranged, we can sample using a **sampling interval**, in which we predetermine the size of the sample, n, that we need, and use that to divide the population, N, providing us with each kth interval from which to sample. Otherwise put, $k = \frac{N}{n}$. We may use this technique if we are dealing with student files, audit files, voter registries, a series of complete public statements, and so forth. For example, if we have a list of 10,000 voter files, we could construct a sample of 1,000 files by selecting every 10th file. Here, $k = 10,000/1,000 = 10$. However, this method will introduce bias if the sampling units are arranged such that people or cases are systematically grouped. For example, if our voter list is arranged by political party or race or age, the intervals will reflect that bias, and the resulting sample will not be as representative of the population as a random sample. This error is called **periodicity**.

Stratified Sampling   If we are conducting research in which we know a lot about the population before we begin, and are certain that there are particular population characteristics that influence our variables of interest, we can break the population into components based on these characteristics, or **strata**. With this approach, we can then sort each population element on the basis of the relevant stratum, and then randomly sample within each stratum. In **proportionate random sampling**, we base our selection of each stratum sampling size on the size of each population stratum. However, there are times when it is important to oversample a particular stratum that is so small that we will not be able to accurately infer population parameters from the sample. This technique is called **disproportionate random sampling**. In these cases, in later statistical analysis, we weigh the observations to their actual proportion in the population in order to make more accurate comparisons to the other strata.

Cluster Sampling   In some cases, population elements are arranged in what are referred to as **clusters**, groups in which each element exists in one and only one cluster at a time. For example, houses are located in one particular block, town, or county at any given point, as are students enrolled in schools. In cases like these, we first develop a cluster-level sampling frame and then, for each cluster that falls into the sample, we build new sampling frames and then randomly sample within each cluster.

Nonrandom or Nonprobability Sampling

Sometimes it is impossible for us to take a random sample. In these cases, we need to select a **purposive sample** in which the sample is drawn with a particular purpose in mind. The best purposive sample accomplishes two objectives: it (1) maximizes our ability to generalize our findings from our study to other similar situations, and (2) minimizes the introduction of systematic bias that influences our interpretation of the effects of our independent variable(s) on the dependent variable. There are several approaches to nonrandom sampling, which we describe in the next sections.

Quota Sampling   In **quota sampling**, we determine in advance which characteristics of a population we want to focus on, and select a sample in proportion to those characteristics. What differentiates quota sampling from stratified sampling is that in our selection of cases, we may not have a sampling frame, so we select population units on the basis of availability. For example, we may want to survey people at a political rally about their political attitudes and may feel that there will be a difference of opinion based on gender. In this case, we would identify an equal number of men and women to approach to perform our survey.

Snowball Sampling In the case of **snowball sampling**, we are unable to obtain a sampling frame, but we know in advance that most of the elements in our population of interest are connected in some way. In this case, we identify sampling units—typically, people or organizations—through a process that begins with identifying a few units that fit our population criteria. We next use the process of data collection itself to identify additional sampling units. We begin by collecting data from the units that we identified initially. In the process of data collection, we also ask our initial units whether they can identify other units (people, organizations, and so on) that may share the characteristics we are interested in.

We obtain contact information for these new units, make contact with them, and continue the data collection process. During data collection, we ask the units to identify additional units. If our beliefs about the connections between the sampling units are correct and we continue this process indefinitely, we will eventually make contact with and exhaust all the possible sampling units in the population.

At this point, we will have conducted a census. In practice, resources do not permit research to continue indefinitely; we end sampling when we achieve saturation, which occurs when our contacts identify no or very few new units. The process introduces error because some sampling units are connected while others are not, and some are connected more extensively than others; both conditions bias our results.

Availability Sampling In **availability sampling**, we select population units based on their availability or ease of selection. This is also known as convenience sampling, and is seen as one of the least valid approaches to sampling because it lacks randomness. However, availability sampling is frequently used in applied research.

When we are selecting a sample for case studies, we often face limitations of time and other resources that constrain the number of cases that we can include in our study. We must therefore purposefully sample cases, such as states, cities, communities, organizations, or other units of analysis. We can take several different approaches to doing this. Some researchers follow a **convenience case selection** approach in which they select the easiest case to follow; this has the same drawbacks as availability sampling. In applied research, another common approach is to use a **best case** strategy as a particular type of convenience sampling. For example, we could examine the three states (or counties or organizations) that had the best performance on some particular outcome measures and use those units of analysis as cases to be evaluated in order to improve outcomes elsewhere. Another approach is to choose **contrasting cases**, in which we select several cases in order to contrast the variance in either the dependent variable or the explanatory variable of interest. If we know in advance what the most **typical cases** are that represent our phenomenon, we can select them on this basis. Finally, sometimes there are **critical cases** that must be included in order for others to accept our conclusions.

Sample Size

In addition to determining what and how to sample, we also have to determine how many samples to take. As a rule, the more sampling units (or cases) that we include in our study, the more able we are to infer from our sample to our population; generally speaking, a larger sample makes our results more accurate. However, a large sample is not always possible. A smaller sample size is acceptable when the population size is limited; for example, if we decided to study what are referred to as foreign terrorist organizations as identified by the U.S. Department of State, the population currently stands at fifty-two official organizations (http:// www.state.gov/j/ct/rls/other/des/123085.htm, accessed November 9, 2013). A smaller sample size is also acceptable when the population is largely homogenous.

Case Illustrations of Sampling Approaches

The following discussion compares our research cases in terms of the sampling approaches we used, why we made those decisions, and the strengths and weaknesses of the approaches we selected. A summary of the various sampling strategies we used is presented in Table 3.5.

Statewide Needs Assessment In the statewide needs assessment, we proposed to interview women age sixty-five and older who were receiving public services. Sampling was required because the population was both unknowable and out of reach in practical terms. Availability of interview subjects also mattered in terms of resources; we needed to be able to interview multiple women every day. Ultimately, we decided that we would interview women in locations

Table 3.5
Case Comparison of Sampling Strategies

	Community Garden	Statewide Needs Assessment	Election Administration and Technology	National Program Evaluation	Criminal Justice Policy Reform
What Was the Approach?	Convenience sampling of residents Snowball sampling of community leaders	Convenience sampling of participants Stratified sampling of facilities	Convenience sampling of elites Stratified sampling of state and local election offices	Case studies using matching characteristics by region	Snowball sampling to identify national network of elites
Why Was This Approach Selected?	Determined in conjunction with community leaders	Resource constraints Wanted to generalize results as much as possible	Resource constraints Access to elites Wanted to generalize results as much as possible	Driven by need to compare two categories but with limited resources	Exploratory research to identify parameters of unique national network
What Were the Strengths and Weaknesses of This Approach?	Inclusion of volunteers in interviews may have biased findings if the volunteers had common factors Resident interviews were limited to attendees at a community event	Inclusion of volunteers in individual interviews may have biased findings if the volunteers had common factors	Highly informed respondents at all levels of government were interviewed Extensive contextual information was collected Interviews had no predictive value	Regional comparisons aided in understanding context; possible that intentional selection may have been motivated by unconscious bias of researchers	Extensive contextual information was collected Participants all had unique motivations for answering questions

where they received services and where we could find groups of women as pools of potential interview subjects. Thus our first cut at sampling involved selecting facilities that provided services and where we would also have access to women. We used a list of facilities that was itself a sample of the service providers in the state; we used a variety of sources to develop this list, but could never be certain that it contained the entire population.

Because the needs assessment involved an entire state, we wanted our interview data to be representative of the state and to reflect as many different dimensions of the state as possible. We determined that the region of the state and the population density were important factors to consider, and that the potential acquisition of new resources could be connected to political factors. The combination of these decisions led us to select urban and rural locations in each of the state's seven U.S. congressional districts. Because our assessment included government, nonprofit, and private for-profit service providers, we constructed a list of interview locations that included multiple facilities of each of these types of organizations in urban and rural locations in each of the congressional districts. To conform to our proposal, the facilities included adult day centers, assisted living facilities, and community centers. At this point, the selection of interview locations from this list was based on availability of the facility director and our time for travel to these locations; we focused on distributing the facilities relatively equally across the three organizational categories of government, nonprofit, and for-profit service providers.

At each location, our sampling of individual women was also based on availability, which included the constraints of the facility's operating schedule and the interest of the women. We were typically allowed three hours to conduct our interviews, based on the facility schedules for various activities. To initiate the interview process, we introduced ourselves to the women as a group, explained our research study, and asked for volunteers. We conducted interviews until our allotted time had expired.

Several events occurred that bear special mention. The facility interview schedule changed several times and in significant ways. In one instance, a facility was destroyed by a tornado the week prior to our scheduled visit; in other instances, facility directors made changes to the activity schedules that changed the times during which our interviews could be conducted. In some cases, it became apparent that women were not clearly capable of giving consent, so these interviews were terminated. The point of these experiences in terms of sampling is that flexibility is an important dimension to consider. In all, the logistics of this type of data collection should not be underestimated.

Election Administration and Technology In the study of election administration and technology, we had several decisions to make around sampling in order to select the key informants. We wanted to be able to generalize the interview comments across the election equipment decision environment, which is an intergovernmental environment that includes local election jurisdictions, state election offices, national nonprofit organizations, and a national agency devoted to dissemination of information about election administration. The intergovernmental policy literature demonstrates that state administrative responses are influenced by their population, geography, and political makeup (see Berry and Berry 1990). At the local level, these decisions may also vary depending on whether the areas are more or less urban. Accordingly, we stratified our interviews to reflect diversity in jurisdiction across the intergovernmental system, geography, population, and urban/rural characteristics. The combinations that we chose gave us confidence that the data we gathered would be representative of the views of election administrators generally.

National Program Evaluation In the national program evaluation, we had three sampling decisions to make related to the different forms of data collection we were undertaking. Given the small number of organizations that applied for funding, the decision to undertake essentially a population study for the surveys and the focus groups was easy. The more difficult choice was in how to approach sampling for the case studies. Only organizations that received funding were included in the case studies. In the end, we decided to select case studies in such a way that we had representation from faith-based versus community-based grantees, newer as opposed to established organizations, and regions. We also had a resource consideration, as each of the case study sites was going to undergo a site visit, so we paired organizations that fit these criteria regionally (two per region) to minimize travel time and cost.

Criminal Justice Policy Reform In the case study around criminal justice innovation and reform, elites or key informants were selected using snowball sampling. This technique was ideal for identifying national nonprofit leaders who participated in a network with one another. It was a successful strategy because the national perspective held by leaders of national nonprofits is already broad; these leaders are aware of the national context for their issues and aware of other organizations with similar and opposing missions and views. This sampling strategy was also successful because the snowball sampling began with three very different and well-known organizations, with the expectation that these initial interviews would lead in very different directions, producing several lists of different organizations and individuals, and that these lists would eventually converge into a unified list. That is actually what happened.

Community Garden Initiative   Snowball sampling was also used to identify community leaders for interviews about resources available for the community garden project. In this case, snowball sampling led us to a network that was relatively insular. Interviewees continued to suggest the same names, so it appeared that we had achieved saturation. However, the end result of the study demonstrated very clearly that the community had interested leaders and resources that were unconnected to the elites we had interviewed. In fact, a new group emerged to explore further the ideas that the original leaders rejected. In this study, we also interviewed residents. The sampling was based on convenience and was also somewhat purposeful. The interviews were conducted at a community arts festival that included food and children's activities. The arts event is well known; however, the opinions we obtained were only those of attendees and not of the community as a whole.

DECISION TREES

Research designs take many forms, and researchers face an infinite number of choices. The strategy that we choose for sampling always relates back to our design and the purpose of our study. Both are influenced by a number of factors that include principles of research design and practical considerations. The following decision trees illustrate common questions.

Selecting a Research Design Type

To assist in conceptualizing the design process, we organize major choices made in research design into three major groups based on the purpose of the study we intend to conduct. We consider three primary purposes: to examine the effects of an intervention; to understand a contemporary problem; or to understand historical phenomena. These choices are illustrated in the decision tree example in Figure 3.2.

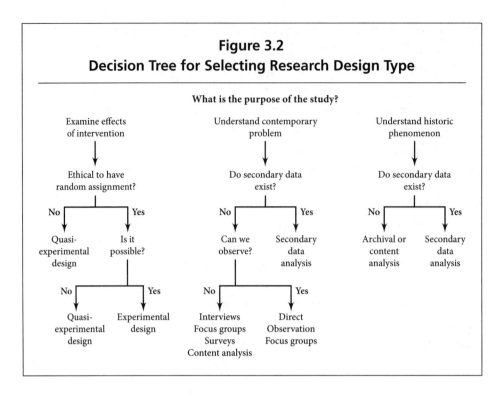

Figure 3.2
Decision Tree for Selecting Research Design Type

What is the purpose of the study?

| Examine effects of intervention | Understand contemporary problem | Understand historic phenomenon |

Examine effects of intervention → Ethical to have random assignment?
- No → Quasi-experimental design
- Yes → Is it possible?
  - No → Quasi-experimental design
  - Yes → Experimental design

Understand contemporary problem → Do secondary data exist?
- No → Can we observe?
  - No → Interviews / Focus groups / Surveys / Content analysis
  - Yes → Direct Observation / Focus groups
- Yes → Secondary data analysis

Understand historic phenomenon → Do secondary data exist?
- No → Archival or content analysis
- Yes → Secondary data analysis

If we are interested in the effects of an intervention, then we are essentially concerned with whether we can use an experimental design. A threshold question is whether it is ethical to use random assignment. If ethical considerations are not in play, the next question we ask is whether it is actually possible to accomplish random assignment. If so, then we can proceed with an experimental design. If it is not ethical, or if random assignment is not possible, then we are directed to consider one of the types of quasi-experimental design.

If we intend to study a contemporary problem, a threshold question is whether data exist. If not, our idea is at an end, and we must either stop our inquiry—because we have no data to collect and analyze—or we must rethink our strategy based on data that are available. If so, we ask next whether we can observe the data in some way. If that is possible, we consider using observational strategies, including direct observation and focus groups. If data exist but are not observable, then we collect through nonexperimental approaches.

If we intend to study historical phenomena, we ask again whether data exist. If not, our inquiry is at an end. If data exist, we next consider whether the data are available in a database. If so, we explore and analyze that secondary data. If data do not exist in a database, we proceed to review documents through archival analysis or content analysis methods.

Choosing a Sampling Strategy

Sampling strategy decisions are made for various reasons, ranging from the purest consideration of research principles to the relatively more pedestrian consideration of resource constraints. In our decision tree illustration in Figure 3.3, we present key decisions made when deciding on a sampling strategy. Here, we

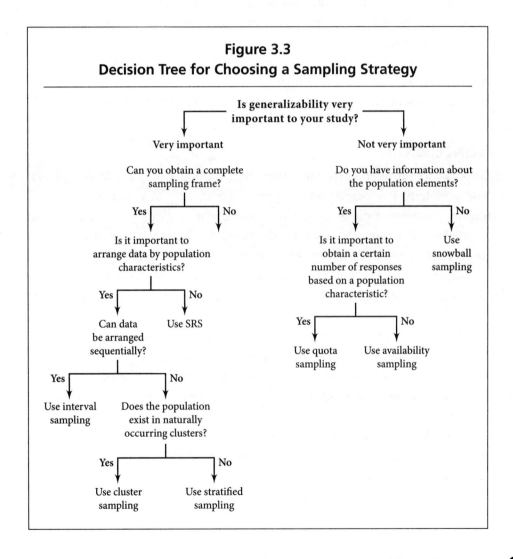

Figure 3.3
Decision Tree for Choosing a Sampling Strategy

focus on generalizability as one important dimension among others. Our decision tree is a combination of possibilities and priorities.

If generalizability is a very important objective of our study, we consider whether it is possible to construct a complete sampling frame. If arranging the data by population characteristics is important, we consider interval sampling, cluster sampling, or stratified sampling. We use interval sampling if data can be arranged in a sequence. We use cluster sampling if the population exists in naturally occurring clusters; we use stratified sampling if not. If population characteristics are not important, we consider simple random sampling.

If generalizability is not very important to our study, we consider other sampling strategies. If we do not have information about the population, we use snowball sampling. If we have information about the population elements, we can choose quota sampling or availability sampling. Between these two approaches, we choose quota sampling if we need to obtain responses from various subgroups of the population. If not, we use availability sampling.

CONCLUSION

This chapter provided an overall framework for comparing approaches to design and sampling. We focused on the general parameters of research design and major categories of design types. The most common forms of designs used in applied research typically vary from the pure experiments favored in the natural sciences. As a consequence, we access the rich variety of quasi-experimental and nonexperimental methods that were outlined in this chapter. We also considered sampling strategies and those particular appropriate for, and common in, applied research.

The strategies that we choose are guided by the research questions we ask and the literature that exists in our subject area. Each approach requires trade-offs; as we explain our work, it is incumbent upon us to make those trade-offs clear so that our work can be more clearly understood and can serve as a path for others. The decisions we make about a general design and sampling strategy are not the only decisions to make, and they do not exist in a vacuum; these decisions must also be integrated with decisions about how to conduct research in the field, which we consider in Chapter Four.

Chapter Three Relevant Articles

Camasso, Michael J., Radha Jagannathan, Carol Harvey, and Mark Killingsworth. 2002. "The Use of Client Surveys to Gauge the Threat of Contamination in Welfare Reform Experiments." *Journal of Policy Analysis and Management* 22:207–223.

Gerber, Alan S., and Donald P. Green. 2000. "The Effect of a Nonpartisan Get-Out-the-Vote Drive: An Experimental Study of Leafletting." *Journal of Politics* 62:846–857.

Gilliam, Franklin D., Jr., and Shanto Iyengar. 2000. "Prime Suspects: The Influence of Local Television News on the Viewing Public." *American Journal of Political Science* 44:560–573.

Loeb, Susanna, Bruce Fuller, Sharon Lynn Kagan, and Bidemi Carrol. 2003. "How Welfare Reform Affects Young Children: Experimental Findings from Connecticut—A Research Note." *Journal of Policy Analysis and Management* 22:537–550.

Miller, Daniel P., and Ronald B. Mincy. 2012. "Falling Further Behind? Child Support Arrears and Fathers' Labor Force Participation." *Social Science Review* 86:604–635.

Chapter Three Discussion Questions

1. What role does error or bias play in research? Why is it important?

2. Should nonexperimental research be used for purposes other than descriptive or exploratory research? Why or why not?

3. Think through the difference between the different forms of nonprobability sampling. Which form would produce more error or bias? Why?

4. Compare availability sampling to the other sampling strategies. Are the other strategies simply different justifications or rationalizations for an availability approach? Justify your response.

Chapter Three Practice Assignments

1. Using your library resources, access and read the following article:

> Gerber, Alan S., and Donald P. Green. 2000. "The Effect of a Nonpartisan Get-Out-the-Vote Drive: An Experimental Study of Leafletting." *Journal of Politics* 62:846–857.

Answer the following questions: (a) What was the intervention in this study? (b) How were the "subjects" in the study assigned to the treatment and control groups? (c) Of what did the pre- and posttests consist? (d) What did the study authors conclude about the effect of the intervention? (e) What were the strengths and weaknesses of this design?

2. Read more on the placebo effect and the Hawthorne effect. Describe each in detail, outlining how we learned about these possible effects. Then discuss what the difference between them is.

3. Roughly develop a research question that could be used for an experiment. Then identify the independent variable (or intervention/treatment), the dependent variable (or outcome), the most appropriate subject group, and how you would want to make assignments to groups; describe when and what you would measure.

4. Roughly develop a research question that could be used for a quasi-experiment. Then identify the independent variable (or intervention/treatment), the dependent variable (or outcome), the most appropriate subject group, and how you would want to make assignments to groups (if you have a control group); describe when and what you would measure.

5. Roughly develop a research question that could be used for a nonexperiment. Then identify the independent variable (or intervention/treatment), the dependent variable (or outcome), and the most appropriate subject group; describe when and what you would measure.

6. Read the following article and identify the sampling approach used by the researchers in each of the different phases of the study.

> Miller, Daniel P., and Ronald B. Mincy. 2012. "Falling Further Behind? Child Support Arrears and Fathers' Labor Force Participation." *Social Science Review* 86:604–635.

Chapter Three Linked Assignment

Throughout the text, we include a series of "linked assignments." These have been developed to walk the research methods student through the entirety of the research process by developing a research project that includes each phase of both applied and basic research.

Given your research question and hypotheses developed in the linked assignment from Chapter Two, develop a research design, keeping in mind that you will actually conduct this research. First, determine what approach makes the most sense—experimental, quasi-experimental, or nonexperimental. Identify the strengths and weaknesses of the approach that you select. Then identify how and what kinds of data will be collected. Next identify the unit of observation and the population. Then determine whether or not you can collect population data or if you need to collect sample data. If you need to draw a sample, determine whether or not you can take a random sampling approach. Then identify your sampling strategy and develop a plan that includes the number of observations on which you will collect data and the strengths and weaknesses of the sampling approach.

Chapter Three Link to Online Assignments

To complete this assignment, you will need to access the research design summary for the statewide needs assessment. Your assignment is to create a replication of this design that will focus on childhood obesity in your state.

The overarching questions that your study is intended to address for your state are the following:

1. Is there a problem? If so, how is it defined?

2. Is the problem more severe in some areas and not others?

3. Is the problem more severe for some demographic groups and not others?

4. What are the roots of the problem?

5. What is your research design? Your design will include research questions, concepts, and operationalization of variables, as well as a strategy for data collection.

PART TWO

Data Collection: Where and How Can We Gather Information?

chapter FOUR

Qualitative Data Collection in the Field

Qualitative data are most often associated with applied research questions for which the answers or explanations sought have to do with context, environment, and holistic assessment of a situation or problem. The goal is to obtain data that authentically reflect the perspectives of others and, through analysis, come to understand how people comprehend and interact with the particular phenomenon or process (or program or policy) that we are interested in. The need for qualitative data, as with any data, is guided by the research question(s) at hand. Researchers tend to collect qualitative data if they are interested in values, personal meaning, beliefs, context, tracing processes, and understanding causality for a particular event or phenomenon.

Methods of collecting qualitative data vary widely. However, all of these methods share some common features. One is that many data collection techniques involve sustained periods of time "in the field," or inside a research environment or context. Another common theme is that the researcher relies very little on standard instruments. Last but not least, qualitative data appear most often in the form of words. Generally speaking, we capture these words through conversations with others, through their oral or written responses to our questions, and through our observations of behavior, activities, and the environment around the people engaged in what we are studying. We also capture these words in response to images or writings. Wolcott (1994) observes that the words we examine as qualitative data are based on watching, asking, or examining. Miles and Huberman (1994) refer to these sources of qualitative data as observation, interviews, and documents.

Data about values and beliefs are integral to understanding public problems and the administration of policy solutions. Information related to expectations and opinions about responsibility, control, accountability, and performance run through the policymaking process and the administration of its results. Winning ideas and policy positions are political creations—whether determined formally in a legislative session or more informally in a community setting. Within the deliberative process, minority views persist, given the diverse nature of the American public and the guarantee of constant change in leadership across all levels of government.

VALIDITY, RELIABILITY, AND ERROR IN QUALITATIVE RESEARCH

As researchers, we ought to be concerned with obtaining the most valid and reliable information possible about the topics we are studying. **Validity** means that we are measuring what we intend to measure; put another way, valid data are those that accurately reflect the concept that we intend to measure. **Reliability** means that our measurement approach will capture the same data when repeated; reliable data are stable and consistently the same over multiple measurements. We can enhance validity and reliability by enhancing the amount of control we have through use of an experimental or quasi-experimental design. But this is not always practical or possible in applied research, and may not deliver the information on values and beliefs that we commonly seek. Instead, we address concerns about validity, reliability, and error through other means.

When developing a qualitative research design, a key decision to make at the outset addresses the degree of structure that will be built in to the design. Structure has both advantages and disadvantages. Greater structure produces more reliability; less structure promotes exploratory research. Highly structured qualitative designs involve making decisions before data collection begins, including identifying the specific data sources that will be examined, the variables that will be linked to each source, how those data will be collected, and how often. At the other end of the continuum, in contrast, loosely structured qualitative designs allow researchers to go into the field with some idea of the data that they might expect to find, but do not require prior decisions about what will be collected and from where.

The overall credibility of qualitative findings can be enhanced by considering types of error and taking those errors into account in the research process. There are two major types of errors that occur in conducting qualitative research. The first type of error is researcher bias. **Researcher bias** simply means that the assumptions a researcher brings to the research process may influence the outcomes of the research in a way that distorts reality. These biases can—and do—occur in the specification of the research question, the structure of the design, the process of data collection, or in analysis. The acknowledgment of bias is quite different in qualitative research approaches than in quantitative approaches. In quantitative approaches, the standard goal is to eliminate sources of bias through statistical specification. In qualitative research, the standard approach to addressing bias is for the researcher to understand those sources of bias and to be able to reflect on whether and how they might be influencing the research process, and to articulate this to the reader. In the statewide needs assessment, for example, it was important for us as researchers to reflect on our values and beliefs as essentially middle-class, white, and highly educated women before we entered into interviews with women who were, in some cases, utilizing public assistance. It is also important for researchers to be transparent about their views in their reporting. One approach is for researchers to keep a regular journal to reflect on the idea of bias and how it might be entering into the research they are conducting. Journal reflections are typically used to inform writing and other communication about research findings.

The second major form of bias is called **reactivity**, or the effect that researchers may have on the subjects of their research that would not have existed had the researcher not been there. Put another way, reactivity occurs if subjects alter their behavior (actions, responses to questions) because they are aware that they are being studied. One of our major tasks as researchers is to minimize the possibility that we might be directing the responses or data in one direction or another, or that our intervention into a situation produces change.

In our interviews with elderly women during the statewide needs assessment, our biases about education, family structure, or standards of daily living were all possible factors that could interfere with gathering reliable and valid data. We also have to recognize that we make an impact simply by being present. For example, in the statewide needs assessment, we conducted interviews with women in adult day centers in order to see how their needs were being addressed by the services of those facilities. In conducting our interviews, we interviewed a sample of women rather than all women in the facility. Our presence alone in the adult day center environment was not a typical event, and we may have created any number of effects on the women with whom we spoke—and on the women and men who were not interviewed—simply by conducting the interviews. We are obligated to consider our impact not only in designing and implementing our research, but also in our data analysis and as we draw conclusions.

The credibility of qualitative research can be enhanced in other ways in addition to the explicit consideration of bias. First, we can seek **respondent validation**. One way to do this is to provide respondents with the opportunity to read our reports before they are released to see if they agree with what we have captured. This does not mean that we allow respondents to dictate our findings. Respondent validation does recognize the possibility that we may not have completely absorbed or understood the phenomenon under investigation given the inherent complexity and nuance of qualitative data. For example, in the case involving election administration and technology, we wanted to know the opinions of elected and appointed election officials about new technology standards for voting equipment and the challenges they face in obtaining new electronic voting machines in their jurisdictions. The technological requirements are complex, and the acquisition process is fraught with competing demands. Moreover, the technology requirements and purchasing guidelines are established by state legislatures and are unique to each state. We chose to conduct a series of open-ended and wide-ranging discussions about election technology issues with election officials in order to understand their issues and concerns. We chose to do this using two-on-one interviews, in which one researcher guided the discussion and the other took notes. After each interview was concluded, we prepared a written summary of the notes, and both of us reviewed it. We then sent to each respondent our written summary of her interview for her review and clarification to make sure that we accurately captured her views, beliefs, and experiences. We made adjustments to our notes based on respondents' feedback.

A second approach that enhances the credibility of qualitative research is referred to as **triangulation**. This means collecting information on a single topic from a variety of sources using a variety of methods. We know we have a more believable study when there is convergence in the findings of these multiple sources, giving us a stronger case. The analysis of criminal justice policy innovation provides a comprehensive example of the use of triangulation. Interviews were used to identify a national network of nonprofit organizations and the perspectives of leaders of these organizations about the desirability and effectiveness of various policy changes that had occurred over the past several decades. These perceptions were explored in intensive case studies in six states, and through archival research of documents produced by these organizations covering a twenty-year period. The synthesis of data collected in each of these different ways provided a more complete picture than would data from any one alone; in addition, the convergence of findings from these different sources—as well as points of divergence—rendered the findings more influential than would have been the case otherwise.

Finally, to the extent possible, we do not limit data collection to a single case—**comparison cases** help improve the credibility of findings as well as our ability to transfer the findings to other settings. The statewide needs assessment, the national program evaluation, and the criminal justice policy innovation studies all made use of comparison cases, and in different ways. The statewide needs assessment compared facilities, the national program evaluation compared programs, and the criminal justice policy innovation study compared state administrative operations. Table 4.1 illustrates the approaches that we took in the various cases to reduce error and enhance reliability and validity.

Credibility is an essential component of quality research, and qualitative research is a common practice across public service. On the surface, qualitative research appears in some ways to be easier to conduct than research employing quantitative methods, perhaps because it does not obviously involve mathematical calculations that seem intimidating or beyond the normal routines of most public service operations. It is important to keep in mind that qualitative designs often involve data that are quite challenging to collect and analyze despite the lack of mathematical models. Because of the human interaction inherent in qualitative methods, it is always necessary to establish credibility for the findings by clearly specifying the research design and its limitations. Although these dimensions must be specified for quantitative approaches as well, it is particularly important to include this information for qualitative studies because of the lack of statistical controls and the inherently variable and subjective nature of the qualitative research process.

Table 4.1

Case Comparison of Case Selection Methods

	Statewide Needs Assessment	National Program Evaluation	Criminal Justice Policy Reform
What Was the Case Unit?	Facility	Organization	State Office of Court Administration
How Was It Chosen?	Convenience Most different geography (urban/rural)	Matched pairs by regions, identified by funding models used by intermediary organizations	Convenience Most different in terms of time of adoption (along a continuum)
What Sources of Evidence Were Used?	Semistructured interviews conducted on-site lasting about one hour Site visits Document review	Semistructured interviews conducted monthly over time Site visits Focus groups Document review	Semistructured interviews conducted during site visit of four to six hours Telephone follow-up
What Was the Degree of Control over the Process?	Flexible Script Open-ended protocol	Strict Script Closed-ended protocol	Flexible Script Open-ended protocol

THE PROCESS OF CONDUCTING FIELD RESEARCH

High-quality primary data collection from the field requires a great deal of planning and advance preparation. We engage in this preparation to enhance validity and reliability, as well as to minimize bias, as discussed in the previous section.

Advance preparation for field research begins with the design of our research **protocol**, which reflects our plans for data collection in the field. Advance preparation also encompasses the design of our **instruments** (the tools we use to collect data) and testing or piloting the protocol and instruments.

As we develop field data collection plans, or our research protocol, we have to be deliberate and thorough in documenting our planned processes. We do this to ensure reliability, which means here that other people could **replicate** our study by following our process, through which they would obtain (nearly) the same results. We clearly articulate our data collection process in the writing we produce about the research; this ensures transparency in the research process and is an assurance of quality because it facilitates public review.

Figure 4.1 illustrates the process we use for collecting data in the field. We start by determining exactly which data or information is needed in order to be able to answer our research question(s). We list these data and the sources we intend to use. For each source of data, we identify the necessary contact(s) who will give us access to individuals or organizations, and identify the steps we need to take to get the data. This becomes our data collection protocol.

In addition to drafting a data collection protocol, we also develop in advance of data collection a draft of every instrument we will use for data collection. This means that we develop draft surveys and questions for interviews and focus groups. If we are conducting a relatively structured qualitative investigation, we might also include instructions for **coding** and document analysis, and lists of possible themes that we think might emerge from observation. If we are proceeding into the field in a relatively unstructured study, we might choose not

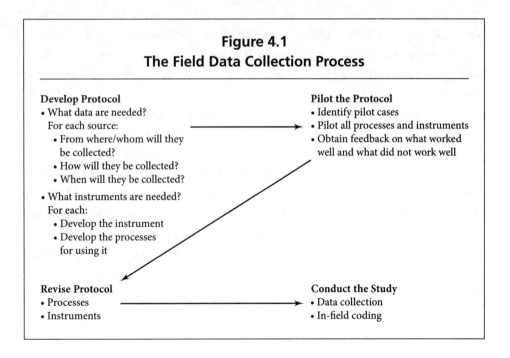

Figure 4.1
The Field Data Collection Process

Develop Protocol
- What data are needed?
  For each source:
  - From where/whom will they be collected?
  - How will they be collected?
  - When will they be collected?
- What instruments are needed?
  For each:
  - Develop the instrument
  - Develop the processes for using it

Pilot the Protocol
- Identify pilot cases
- Pilot all processes and instruments
- Obtain feedback on what worked well and what did not work well

Revise Protocol
- Processes
- Instruments

Conduct the Study
- Data collection
- In-field coding

to identify themes and coding schemes in advance, but rather to allow these to emerge from the data and the context of the field experience.

After we have created the study protocols and instruments, we then pilot the draft process and instruments. Piloting means that we test the process and the instruments to make sure that they achieve the types of results we are looking for in our research. Our overall goal is to identify any aspects of the protocol or the instruments that are not clear in the way that we intend. The number of respondents we use in order to pilot our study depends on the research design. For studies involving data collection from individuals, we pilot the protocol and instruments with at least two and up to four people. If our study targets a population with multiple subgroups, we should administer the pilot to at least one person from each subgroup, and preferably more. For example, if we intend to study differences between military veterans and nonveterans about drug use, we want to pilot our instruments with members of both groups. Note that the data collected during the pilot process are not included in the study; pilot subjects are removed from the final pool of subjects from which data are collected. When choosing pilot subjects, it is important also to keep the stakeholder community in mind. Every applied research study involves the community in one way or another; incorporating stakeholder perceptions and feedback into the design of instruments enhances reliability and deepens our knowledge as researchers about the ways in which problems are defined and understood.

Piloting data collection instruments is a two-step process. First, we administer the instrument and its instructions; next we obtain feedback about the subject's understanding of the questions and the instructions. The goal is to determine whether the questions can be understood by potential respondents in the way that we intend; otherwise put, we want to determine the validity of our instruments. After we have administered the instrument with each pilot subject, we review the subjects' responses with them to make sure we understand what they think we mean by our questions and why they answered the questions in the way that they did. This is sometimes referred to as a **cognitive interview**. Another way to gain feedback about our instruments is to observe respondents as they complete them. In our observations, we are interested in noting whether respondents struggle with any questions or instructions, and whether they need more time. If we observe this to be the case, we follow up on those items in particular during the cognitive interview.

For studies in which we rely on analyzing archival documents or making observations, we pilot our process by locating similar documents or places and proceed through each of our steps to determine whether they are complete and inclusive. Across all of these methods, if we are using coding rules in our design, we also examine the reliability of our coding strategy. Typically, this means we have at least two people code the same material. In its most simple form, we check for **intercoder reliability** across the coders by running a correlational analysis of their results, looking for a pairwise correlation of .90 or higher (see Chapter Six for more discussion).

After we have piloted our processes and instruments, we then identify the changes that need to be made and adjust our procedures and documents accordingly. The final instrument should reflect changes made as a result of the pilot study. As noted, the pilot respondents are not included in the study. However, the piloting process is described in our final papers, reports, and manuscripts. Pilot respondents are sometimes acknowledged by name; more commonly, they are identified by a designation which indicates that they are representative of the group(s) involved in the study. For example, in the state-wide needs assessment, we piloted the survey of organizations with individuals knowledgeable about the state's health care system. We piloted the individual interview protocol with individuals who had experience in providing nursing and nursing education and who had experience with health care services in home settings and in rural communities without ready access to institutions. We asked each of the pilot subjects whether he or she would be willing to be identified in our final report, and all agreed to allow us to use their names in connection with the project.

The following sections describe and discuss specific methods of qualitative data collection. In each section, we provide illustrations of the ways in which these methods were used in our example cases. We also identify strengths and weaknesses of the approaches we selected. As noted at the outset of this chapter, the common denominators for all of these methods is that they produce data in the form of words. However, the processes that we use to analyze these words remains essentially the same regardless of the method of collection or the form in which data are delivered. In our analysis, we are always looking for common themes and patterns; we discuss the process of qualitative data analysis in Chapter Six.

INTERVIEWS

In **interviews**, we select "experts" in whatever field we are studying and ask them a series of questions to get their perspective on our topic as the **key informants**, or sources of information. Who we identify as experts varies according to our research question. Experts can be political or organizational leaders, sometimes referred to as **elites**. They can also be everyday people who know a lot about our topic of interest.

There are three major approaches to conducting interviews. These approaches range along a continuum according to the degree of freedom that respondents have in providing information in response to the questions. From the least to the greatest degree of freedom, these approaches comprise structured, unstructured, and semistructured interviews.

In **structured interviews**, we seek simply to identify the numbers of responses that fall into predetermined categories. To do this, we pose **closed-ended questions** to respondents. Closed-ended questions are those in which respondents choose from among a set of predetermined responses. One example of such a closed-ended question is, "What is your political affiliation?" paired with responses "Democrat," Republican," and "Other." This approach is most appropriately used when we believe that we have sufficient information about the subject—here, political affiliation—that we know all of the possible outcomes (or categories of response) for any given question. A major problem with the structured interview is that we might not have identified the correct answers to the questions (response categories). An even more significant problem with this approach is that we may fail to identify the correct questions to ask.

In **unstructured interviews**, we are open to virtually anything the respondent has to offer about a general subject. We pose broad, **open-ended questions** that allow the respondents to talk unrestrictedly about the topic. As an example of an open-ended question related to political affiliation, we might ask, "What do you think about the two major political parties in America?" This method is used in a variety of instances. We use this approach, which is sometimes called the "soak and poke method," when we do not have much information about a subject. We may also use this approach to gain context about a phenomenon without suggesting any particular answer or beliefs. As an example of the latter, we might ask a local United Way board member, "How do you feel about the community-based process of allocating United Way funds?"

A major aspect of this approach is that the results are not very reliable. Responses can vary widely and far from the information we are seeking. The information gained may be quite valuable in guiding our research, however. For example, in our interviews with election administration elites about voting equipment, we asked an open-ended question about their views on state control of the equipment testing process. We expected that states would be eager to take control of the national process because we knew already that states felt that this process was not working well and took far too long to complete. The replies to this question were divergent; many states were not interested in assuming new administrative and technical burdens. Some respondents felt that this role could be filled in large part by off-the-shelf technology (using cell phones to download or cast ballots, for example); others disagreed. Although the responses to this question were quite unexpected, the line of inquiry was very fruitful and led the interviews in directions that we did not anticipate at the outset.

A third and common approach is the **semistructured interview**, which strikes a balance between the limitations of structured and unstructured interviews. In using this method, we believe that we are well informed about our topic and have a good idea about the right questions. However, we want to acknowledge the possibility that the respondents know more than we do about the subject. In this approach, we develop an interview protocol that establishes a series of general questions that we want to ask, and we arrange the questions in the general order in which we think the interview is likely to proceed. We also include **prompts** in our protocol, which are follow-up questions that help respondents understand what we are interested in learning or that can help them get back on track if they start discussing subjects that are off topic. Depending on the flow of the interview, we may skip around in the planned order of questions, add questions, or skip some questions altogether if they prove to be irrelevant. Essentially what we have in this approach is a common framework that provides a great deal of flexibility in design and execution in the field and that can be used for most types of interviews.

As with all forms of data collection, interviews have some major strengths and weaknesses. The strengths of the interview are that we get information about our subject directly from the people most involved and are able to probe them for in-depth information. A major weakness of the interview is related to these strengths, which is that the interview includes the values and biases of the respondent. Personal beliefs and values are exactly what we should be seeking through interviews. However, we have to be aware that our respondents may be advocating for particular views; have vested interests of one kind or another, including protecting their personal reputations; and in some cases may mislead us or lie to us. Another major weakness of the interview is that our data may not be reliable, depending on the form of interview we pursue; the unstructured protocol is the least reliable approach.

In developing an interview approach to collecting data, we follow some clear steps, which we outline here. These steps apply regardless of the structured or unstructured nature of the questions we ask.

1. Identify potential respondents whom we would like to interview.

2. Decide on the level of structure to be used in the approach.

3. Develop the documents for the interview; these include any instruments (the questions we want to ask and any prompts that we need) and any scripts we will use to contact respondents and to schedule the interviews, begin them, and conclude them.

4. Pilot the process and instrument and then make any necessary changes.

5. Follow the script to contact potential interviewees and to schedule interview times.

6. Conduct the interviews.

7. Immediately following each interview, review the interview and record impressions, including the setting, the disposition of the interviewee, and our thoughts about the process itself; allow thirty minutes to an hour for each interview.

8. After all of the interviews are complete, analyze the data.

Writing Interview Questions

The process for writing interview questions is iterative, as is every other aspect of the research process. One approach is to first brainstorm a list of all the possible topics we want to cover during questioning. We then break these topics into similar issue areas and arrange them so that we can proceed from topic to topic in an orderly manner. We develop questions around these topic areas, and we develop follow-up questions and prompts.

As a central organizing principle for collecting data through interviews, we do not ask for information that can be collected elsewhere. We frame each question to gather views about a single topic. We do not ask **double-barreled questions** (questions that have two or more parts and should instead be split into two or more questions). For example, imagine we are interviewing the director of a homeless assistance program, and we are interested in their partnerships with and support from local government. A double-barreled question would be, "What kinds of support do you get from the city, and is this adequate to meet your shelter needs?" Instead, we would break these questions up as, "What kinds of support do you get from the city?" and "Are these adequate?" with time in between each question for the program director to respond and explain each answer. This approach ensures that each of the questions are addressed.

Putting Respondents at Ease

Research is not possible without the voluntary participation of others in the world around us. However, in spite of the importance of research for gaining insight into public service decisions, it is important to remember that this process is not an everyday occurrence for most people. Our goal in the interview is to ask questions in an environment, in a manner, and in a context that puts respondents at ease with both the content of the information they are providing and the manner in which we will use the information.

In terms of environment, we ought to conduct interviews in a location convenient to the subject and where the subject is comfortable. The location of the interview is typically established at the time of scheduling and should be flexible. If we are conducting interviews in person, we can conduct interviews in an office, public place, or private place. We can also consider conducting interviews by telephone. Telephone interviews, historically, have been hampered by the disadvantage that researchers cannot observe the respondent, as they would be able to do if conducting the interviews in person. Today's technology (Skype, for example) reduces this limitation somewhat. However, telephone interviews do not typically provide the rich environment that comes with the in-person interview.

We can also put respondents at ease by disclosing to them the options that are available to them for attribution of their information in any publications that result from the research. Subjects can provide comments for **full attribution** to themselves. This means that their identity is included in the reports that we write. Respondents can provide comments on a **confidential** basis. This means that our reports will list something about them to identify them as people with whom we have spoken, such as a general level of administrative experience or subject matter expertise, but we do not attribute information gathered from them to them or to an organization that can be identified with them. Respondents can also provide comments **anonymously**. This means that in our reports, we do not disclose from whom we have gathered our data. The level of disclosure that respondents desire is typically included in documents approved by institutional review boards (IRBs) and is included in consent forms signed by respondents before the interviews begin (see Chapter One for more discussion).

In terms of how we present ourselves to respondents during the interview process, we want to begin the interview with an introduction of our research and encourage their participation by explaining the significance of the research and their role in it. We may also restate the critical nature of our research during the interview before we ask particularly sensitive or essential questions. During the interview, we should appear to be nonjudgmental no matter what the topic may be and no matter what we hear in the responses that are given. It is also critical that we allow respondents the opportunity to think about the questions and reflect on them before answering. Interruptions are not appropriate, and the good interviewer learns to be comfortable with silence.

The overall approach to our questions is also important. We typically begin with general questions before moving to specific or sensitive questions, if we have those types of questions to ask. A common approach is to begin an interview with what Leech (2002) refers to as a **grand tour question**. This is a broad question about the topic that is designed to be easy to answer, interesting to the subject, and not controversial or confrontational. Such questions get the subject warmed up and ready to talk with the interviewer. For example, if we are interviewing someone who holds some kind of leadership position in government or a nonprofit organization, we might start by asking the respondent to tell us about his or her successes, or about the successes of his or her organization. Another common starting point for interviews is to ask respondents how they came to hold their current position or about the aspects of their work that they find most rewarding.

We also know that the technology we use to collect data impacts the comfort level of respondents and how forthcoming they will be. Recording devices certainly are beneficial in terms of accuracy. However, subjects tend to be most comfortable and most forthcoming when we neither record nor take any notes during the interview. The clear challenge of not recording or taking notes is that we often forget important information and are not able to use any direct quotes in our reports. If our recording instruments are unobtrusive, subjects may get used to their presence and become more comfortable after a while. Still, typing transcripts of these recordings is resource-intensive, whether we do this ourselves or hire others to do it for us. A compromise position is to take notes during the interviews but not to use visual or audio recordings. The note-taking approach works best if two researchers are involved; one asks questions and provides prompts while the other takes detailed notes. After each interview, the two researchers review the notes and reconcile any differences before asking the respondent to review the notes. We used this dual-interviewer approach in collecting interview data for most of the case studies discussed in this book.

FOCUS GROUPS

Focus group research involves a small group of people brought together for a moderated conversation. This technique is used for many reasons, including to augment surveys, conduct exploratory research, refine instruments, study group processes, understand public opinion, and test marketing and campaign messages. It is a common tool in public service where collaborative efforts are involved. It is also commonly used to gather information about public administration and public policy decisions, including problem definition, policy design options, implementation strategies, and program evaluation. Nonprofit organizations may conduct focus groups to understand the influence of their programs and services and to identify and understand community needs.

Focus groups have between six and twelve participants, though this may vary with the number of constituencies and subgroups that are involved. The focus group form of data collection is different from interviewing because of the dynamic and interactive nature of the process that comes with having multiple respondents involved simultaneously in answering questions. The dynamic and interactive nature of the group process has both positive and negative aspects. On one hand, it can produce lively conversations in which one person's thoughts and ideas are sparked and influenced by others. On the other hand, sometimes people hesitate to fully share their perspectives because they fear what others may think. In addition, some people may dominate group conversations and consequently limit others' involvement. To address these typical (and unavoidable) group dynamics, it is common to use an accomplished facilitator to run focus groups. The ideal individual is someone who can think on his or her feet and politely, but effectively, draw out the more reticent participants while limiting the participation of those who want to dominate the conversation.

During the focus group itself, we are interested in collecting the same data that we collect in face-to-face interviews. We are interested in both verbal and nonverbal responses and make note of these throughout. We may also note physical reactions to different parts of conversations or terms that are used. For example, we can explore whether people appear uncomfortable talking about certain topics and note other emotional reactions, such as whether individuals appear happy, sad, interested, or ambivalent.

Conducting a focus group requires multiple researchers; it is impossible for one person to both facilitate a focus group and record responses. When we are fortunate, we have funding to permit the use of technology to capture the focus group data through audiovisual methods so that we can return to watch, listen, and better capture responses. Other technologies are also used during focus groups to capture responses. For example, participants can watch and/or listen to a presentation and use a dial to indicate how positive or negative they feel about what they are hearing. The focus group moderators watch these changes in responses and are then able to follow up with questions to gather more detail. Follow-up questions can target the average response or extreme responses, or both, depending on the research questions.

The typical outline for a focus group process is similar to that for conducting interviews:

1. Identify participants.
2. Develop the approach for recording information.
3. Develop appropriate questions and prompts.
4. Secure the location for the focus group.
5. Invite participants.
6. Conduct the focus group.
7. Analyze the data.

DIRECT OBSERVATION

Another method of collecting data in the field is through observation. **Direct observation** approaches involve a distinction about whether or not the researcher interacts with the phenomenon under observation. As a **passive observer**, the researcher watches, listens, and takes notes but does not interact with the phenomenon. As a **participant observer**, the researcher interacts with the phenomenon under investigation as a participant and as a collector of data at the same time. In addition to this distinction, observers can disclose to subjects of their observation the fact that they are being studied, or can go into the field as unobtrusively as possible without the subjects' knowledge and consent. Collecting data by observation without knowledge and consent is desirable if we believe that the **Hawthorne effect** will distort our findings, which occurs when people change their behavior because they know they are being observed.

Observational studies are subject to a major limitation in the form of researcher bias. Researcher bias always influences what we choose to study, when we choose to study it, and how we interpret what we see and hear; and each of these dimensions of research are always open to interpretation. In an absolute sense, researcher bias cannot be eliminated so long as humans are conducting research. A way to mitigate researcher bias is to be systematic in putting together a data collection protocol that identifies and ensures balance in the times, groups, and other activities of observation that cut across the range of possibilities. Replication is another limitation. Observation research of significant events is not replicable unless the event is recorded. Even with recording, limitations exist because the time period and surrounding context cannot be recreated exactly.

Observational research includes taking notes on the context in which phenomena occur (aspects such as the physical setting), the people (who they are, their similarities and differences, how they dress, how they interact with one another), the types of events (including their purpose, content, and conduct), and things that seem out of place. Sometimes we take pictures of what we see or recordings of what we hear. In addition, we often collect and analyze recorded materials to augment our observations. Finally, some researchers include an informal form of interviewing with the people who are being observed.

A more expansive form of direct observation is known as **ethnography**. Ethnography is an in-depth approach to data collection and analysis that is guided by what we call **thick description**. Thick description refers to the process of reporting about phenomena by including extensive background information that we believe will help explain what we are observing. Ethnographic studies are often written from the perspective of the subjects of the study and situated within the context and culture of the subjects. Ethnographic research often involves several months and even years of data collection in the field; data collection and analysis occur simultaneously.

Ethnography usually involves significant data collection from a variety of sources and combines both primary and secondary data. Ethnographic field-work tools used to collect primary data include interviews, surveys, participant observation, and collection and/or analysis of cultural artifacts including documents and other forms of expression. In conducting fieldwork, ethnographers look at the social structure of groups, relations among group members, social distance between people, body language, and the use of symbolism and rituals. Ethnographers examine physical settings to see if they find what they refer to as **outcroppings**, or significant physical arrangements, traits, or markers that are meaningful to the group in some way. Examples could include buildings, statues, religious icons, worship sites, and community gathering places. Outcroppings provide a strong indication of particular values or beliefs; these may be associated with the present or with historical events or times past. Outcroppings also show marks of change over time that help explain current events. Secondary data sources are also used to develop history and context.

Ethnography presents the same limitations and concerns that are found in direct observation and participant observation, but to a much greater degree. Ethnographers spend extensive time in the field; researchers are essentially embedded with their subject(s). Some question the ethical nature of this approach and argue that ethnographic study triggers cultural change that would not occur otherwise, and should be avoided for that reason alone. However, there are many excellent ethnographic studies. For an understanding of the ethical concerns we mention here, see the classic study of the Peruvian community of Vicos conducted in the 1950s and 1960s through the Cornell-Peru project (Dobyns, Doughty, and Lasswell 1971).

CONTENT ANALYSIS

Materials that contain any form of written, audio, or visual content can be systematically analyzed using an approach called **content analysis**. As the name suggests, content analysis is actually a form of analysis, but is commonly treated as a method of data collection. The contents of print hard copy materials such as journals, letters, and newspapers are common vehicles for content analysis, as are organizational documents and reports. New electronic media forms—for example, blogs, websites, Twitter feeds, and other similar e-delivery methods—are also appropriate for this form of analysis. Because electronic content is constantly changed and updated, care must be taken when using electronic media to establish a fixed time frame for capturing the content that will be analyzed and reported. True replication of changeable electronic content is problematic at best, so reliability is limited.

The heart of content analysis is a coding scheme, which we construct to identify and analyze themes and patterns. There are seven steps in the content analysis process:

1. Develop an appropriate research question.

2. Identify a population and source materials.

3. Obtain the source materials.

4. Create rules for the coding scheme, including identification of the smallest unit to be examined (recording unit), the general categories we will search for, and the specific search terms or events that we will code.

5. Create a form or database for tracking the materials and capturing the codes.

6. Pilot the process and make changes as necessary.

7. Execute the research and analysis.

The content analysis process is iterative and typically proceeds through several rounds of review. In each successive round, the quantity of content under review is reduced. This practice facilitates ready comparison of content across documents and promotes synthesis of meaning.

Consider as an example a research project that explores innovative practices in election administration. One aspect of the project considers innovative methods of providing required information to voters in advance of an election. All election jurisdictions must provide information about election issues, voter eligibility, and election practices—this is typically done through a document known as a voter guide. Periodically, election administrators make changes to their voter guide practices and write reports about those changes. Thus the documents that we can review include the voter guides and the reports written about changes made. The voter guides are extensively long; in some jurisdictions, voter guides look like the telephone books of small cities. The reports are also long (fifty to one hundred pages each), but shorter than the full voter guide and more accessible because they focus on the changes made, which suits the nature of our exploratory research project.

Table 4.2 presents an example of the content analysis strategy used to examine the reports. The raw data are the reports themselves, which are not reprinted

Table 4.2

Illustration of Content Analysis Strategy for Examining Innovations in Voter Guides

Number	State	Abstract (First Round)	Possible Second Round	Themes
1	A	County X wanted to find a low-cost method of providing people with visual impairments an easy way to access the local voter guide, which contained information on candidates, issues, polling locations, voter registration, absentee ballots, and local jurisdictions. County X collaborated with City D to produce the audio version of the pamphlet by utilizing City Y's interactive phone system. The information normally provided in the local voter guide, such as a statement from each candidate, was recorded into the general election audio voter guide, and it could be accessed through the audio menu by anyone using a touchtone phone. The general election audio guide was available for 30 days prior to the election. This report also details the number of calls and the cost of the system.	Guide to address visual impairment, local voters; list of information includes candidates, issues, polling locations, voter registration, absentee ballots, and local information; collaboration; interactive phone system, touchtone phone system; recordings of written voter guide; audio content; available in advance of election; assessment of efficiency	Visual impairment Interactive phone system County-city collaboration List of contents (list #1a) Audio contents (list #1b) Advance availability Assessment of efficiency
2	B	County Y produces a comprehensive voter guide prior to each major election. The guide is distributed to media, elected officials, political party headquarters, community organizations, and other identified citizens interested in this information. The objective of the guide is to provide each entity with all the information it needs to know about the upcoming	Comprehensive voter guide, distributed widely; distributed 3–4 weeks in advance of election; list of information on candidates and issues; trends in registration and turnout; new items for this election; technology; getting	Comprehensive Wide distribution Advance availability List of contents (list #2)

	election results; certification of elections; FAQs		Responses to voter concerns List of contents (list #3) Online guide Virtual ballot
3	C	County Z faced the following questions concerning elections: "Where is my polling place?" and "How do I find out more information about the candidates running for office?" To reduce the dilemmas caused by these questions, County Z developed an elections website. The site consists of an online voter guide, a virtual ballot, and a polling place finder. To enhance the online voter guide, candidates were asked to write a 400-word statement that detailed their qualifications, background, and positions on issues. The virtual ballot allows voters the opportunity to familiarize themselves with the candidates who will be on their polling place ballot. The polling place finder connects voters to polling places based on street addresses.	Voter guide in response to voter question; online guide; virtual ballot; polling place finder; candidate information

election. The guide is produced and distributed 3–4 weeks before the election. Content includes candidate and ballot propositions; historical trend information regarding voter registration and turnout for past similar elections; description of what is unique or newly instituted for this election; what type(s) of technology is used to conduct the election; how to get voting results on election night; when the election results will be certified as official; and answers to most frequently asked questions regarding election administration.

here due to length. The first step in document review is to read each report in full. From this first round of review we generate an abstract of each report. Table 4.2 presents composite examples of three such reports; the abstracts are shown as the first round of review. Each abstract is approximately 150 words to ensure a measure of consistency of review across documents.

The second round of review focuses on the abstract and pulls out key concepts and key words that are related to our research question, which here is to explore innovative changes in voter guides. Specifically, we are interested in the mechanics of voter guides that election administrators have found to be useful and where they have seen the need to innovate through the development of these practices. A different approach might be to wonder about the possible ways that advocacy organizations have influenced best practices in election administration—advocates for voters with disabilities, as one example; in that case, we would code and interpret these data in a different manner. The third round of review focuses on the key words from the previous round; here, we look for similarities and differences across the key words to develop themes that will be the basis of our analysis. Note also that the themes that appear to be the conclusion of this review actually form another layer of concepts that can be further coded by subtheme. As one example, each voter guide has a list of contents, and one guide has two such lists. From the first review, each list appears to be different; an exploration of these differences may be fruitful. We cannot know the outcome until we conduct the exploration, and we may not undertake such as a step in the current project. However, it is important to capture this level of detail across the review process for complete understanding as well as for future use.

It is important to note that these steps are those taken for conducting a manual content analysis. Computer software (SPSS and Atlas.ti among many others) is available that will generate a content analysis based on counts and position of words and phrases in documents. However, using such software requires that we identify key words and phrases in advance for search purposes. The key words and phrases essentially become the coding scheme; decisions about these codes and any changes to them should be tracked closely as the research process proceeds. Literature review can suggest particular themes that guide our exploration, or we may want to let the data "speak" without imposing any preconceived notions on our analysis.

Content analysis has several strengths. First, it can be used for many purposes, with many types of materials, and we can use it to review significant amounts of information. Second, it allows us to perform an in-depth examination of dense material. Third, depending on the material analyzed, the results of content analysis are usually highly generalizable. Content analysis also has some weaknesses. In particular, bias can be introduced if the sample of materials is not representative. Second, low reliability can result if the coding rules are not clearly and explicitly communicated to coders and reliability across multiple coders is not established.

CASE STUDIES

Another common form of qualitative research is the **case study**, which is an in-depth examination of an event, area, or organization. More formally defined, "a case study is an empirical inquiry that investigates a contemporary phenomenon within its real-life context, when the boundaries between phenomenon and context are not clearly evident, and in which multiple sources of evidence are used" (Yin 1984, 23). Case studies also use thick description to detail findings.

When we use case studies, we are generally trying to answer "how" and "why" questions. Case studies are used to build theory, identify the conditions that produce results or outcomes of interest, and understand the origin and genesis of critical cases. As with other qualitative methods, case study research has strengths and weaknesses. Case studies enhance our ability to trace processes, allow us to use a great deal of in-depth information to understand phenomena, and increase our understanding of outlier cases. However, this approach to data collection has limitations. Case study analysis does not utilize the statistical controls that we employ in the typical large-sample quantitative study or in designing the typical experiment. Because we use the case study method to study problems within their unique contexts and in great depth, we are not typically concerned about generalizability; in fact, generalizability is not an appropriate consideration for this method. We suggest that the concept of transferability is a more appropriate concept for the case study method; from one case, we may learn principles, theories, relationships, or solutions that we can transfer to other similar contexts. We are limited in our ability to transfer or generalize broadly from a single case; if that is our goal, we can mitigate that limitation by engaging in comparison across multiple cases through the process known as **comparative case study research**.

In case studies, we remain concerned with validity and reliability. There are three forms of validity that are critical elements of support for our research findings; these comprise construct, internal, and external validity (Yin 1984). **Construct validity** means that we have established correct operational measures for the concepts being studied. In other words, we can report our operationalizations with confidence. To do this, the researcher needs to be careful in the data collection stage to use multiple sources of evidence, establish a chain of evidence, and have key informants review the draft case study report. **Internal validity** means that we have established a causal relationship whereby certain conditions are shown to lead to other conditions, as distinguished from spurious relationships. To ensure this, the researcher can use pattern matching, build explanations for causality, and conduct analyses at separate points in time when possible. Finally, **external validity** means that we have established transferability (or generalizability). To do so, we use multiple cases.

To enhance case study reliability, the researcher should utilize a case study protocol and maintain what Yin (1984) refers to as a case study database. This database includes documentation of every step of the research process. It begins with a description of the research project's purpose and importance, including references to any relevant literature. It includes documentation of all processes and instruments used, along with lists of sources of data and when and how they were collected. It also includes the raw data collected, as well as files of any analyses conducted. The final report or product from the study may also be included.

In case study research, one of the key issues that we have to grapple with is our definition of the case itself. The case definition is essential in case study research because the case is actually the unit of analysis. The boundaries of a case are seemingly endless; cases can be policies, programs, organizations, networks, cities, counties, states, countries, or regions. Our definition of the case also depends on our research question. If we are comparing cases on one or more dimensions, we must also make a decision about our basis of comparison in terms of the key explanatory variables and the characteristics of the cases that we believe are (un)likely to be significant in our research question.

Most often, cases are selected on the basis of likeness to or difference from one another, using the labels introduced by John Stuart Mill (1884). With the **method of difference** approach, we select cases that possess similar characteristics in many respects but exhibit different values of the key explanatory variable. With the **method of agreement** approach, we select cases with different characteristics overall, but that exhibit the same values of the key explanatory variables. For example, we may be interested in how counties choose to deliver public health programs, and our supposition is that wealth and political party dominance will affect this choice. To study the effects of these two explanatory factors, we may choose to select counties with different wealth and political conditions, or we may choose counties with similar conditions on one or both of these factors.

CASE ILLUSTRATIONS OF DATA COLLECTION

Data collection in the field presents numerous challenges. The process is always evolving, and each setting is different. The following illustrations from the cases highlight common issues that arise in the field and in using qualitative approaches to applied research.

Statewide Needs Assessment

In the statewide needs assessment, the personal interviews posed several issues common to the interview method of data collection. The responses to our questions were based on personal recall. Memory and recall tend to decline as people age; however, recall is always an issue in human response. We relied on our personal observations of the interview subjects to help us assess the veracity of the information provided. For some, our presence in the adult day care setting may have been a grand diversion in an otherwise routine day; some women were very willing to talk about personal topics that ranged far from the subject of the interview, and they seemed simply glad to have the attention of a dedicated listener. To others, perhaps we were seen as interlopers; it may be the case that few of our interview subjects viewed us in this way, but we cannot be certain.

In these interviews, we also had to consider the possible effects of race/ethnicity and class. Approximately half the women we interviewed were women of color; we are not. To the extent that difference in race/ethnicity between interviewers and respondents was a factor for any of the respondents or potential respondents, our study cannot account for this. The potential effect of racial/ethnic difference could have been mitigated by having a multiracial interview team. Difference in socioeconomic class may also have been a factor in the interviews. The women we interviewed in adult day centers were all of relatively limited means, although women in assisted living facilities were relatively more well off or had family members willing to provide relatively generous financial support. Compared to the interviewers, these women had relatively limited education; the average was less than high school graduate. These differences in race/ethnicity or socioeconomic status may have influenced whether individuals chose to participate, what they would say, and whether they would be completely forthcoming or fabricate or embellish information.

Election Administration and Technology

In this case, our decisions about which data to collect, and how to collect them, were based on practical considerations. Our access to these particular public officials was easy because of our relationships within the election administration profession and with particular leaders in the field. Through these relationships, which were gained through applied research projects and other professional endeavors, we were relatively confident that we could identify individuals who would be willing to talk to us and could serve as key informants because of their considerable expertise on the subject. Public officials are not always so willing. Had we been studying a different aspect of public administration, we might well have faced challenges in identifying the correct interview subjects and/or gaining access to the specific individuals whom we wished to interview. At the least, we would have needed to build in additional time to the research process to account for the time that might be needed in order to gain access. In this case, we were able to contact particular individuals with confidence that we would be granted an interview that could occur within a specific time frame.

The interview method was also an appropriate approach given the data we wanted to gather. The subject of election equipment selection is multifaceted, and we wanted to gather a range of data from key informants, including their practical knowledge and their political expertise on this issue. Although some election officials are elected, here we were not examining partisan allegiance or ideology; we were interested in their assessment of the power relationships and political landscape surrounding equipment selection. We wanted respondents to talk about their experiences and take the interview in any direction that they felt relevant. These considerations suggested strongly that we would not be able to rely on memory, and that there could likely be new topics that were introduced in the interviews. We were able to conduct several interviews in person at various conferences; many of the interviews were conducted by telephone using speaker-phone capability. Although we were not able to observe the behavior of respondents over the phone, we had spoken in person to each of them on several occasions over several years, and used those experiences to gauge the emotional reaction of the respondents as we listened to them speak.

National Program Evaluation

In the national program evaluation, we used several forms of qualitative data collection, including focus groups, content analysis of archival data, organizational site visits, and interviews, and in doing so made both good and challenging choices. We structured the site visits and interviews to be consistent across all of the cases, which yielded valuable and insightful information. We discovered the amount and availability of archival data to be different across the organizations, depending on administrative choices about how much to save and how much to share; these differences rendered this approach to data collection inconsistent.

Perhaps the worst choice made was in the conduct of the focus groups. Using evaluation funds, we flew leaders of all the funded organizations to Denver, Colorado, for a three-day research meeting, during which we held general sessions as well as breakout focus groups on various topics. Because the research team was small, we held simultaneous focus group sessions and assigned one researcher to each group. We also chose not to record the sessions. The consequence of this approach was interesting conversation, but little of it was recorded in a systematic way. If we were to do this again, we would certainly have made different choices about how to lead the focus groups and capture the data; for example, we would either record them or hire a local temporary assistant to take minutes from the sessions while they were in progress.

DECISION TREE

Data collection can be approached in many ways, as is the case with other key aspects of the design and execution of applied research. Iteration is also inherent across every stage of the process, as we have noted. This aspect of the research process bears close attention from the initial stages. Planning for collection requires that we already have a great deal of information about what we intend to collect and that we are aware of the resources that will be needed.

Data Collection Strategy

Figure 4.2 illustrates the major questions that will confront the researcher in thinking about which data collection strategy to use. It may be useful to think of these decisions as a guide to conducting research about the data that exist and the data that can be collected. The priorities of the study and the constraints of the research environment play a role in how the researcher addresses the questions.

We begin our decision tree illustration by asking whether data currently exist in written or archival form. If they do, then content analysis is the approach. If

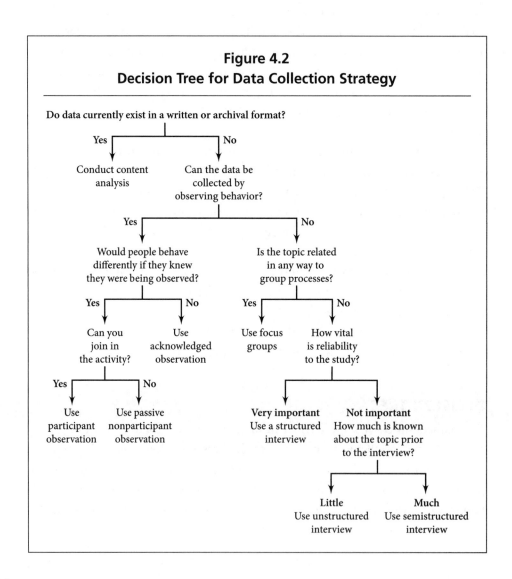

Figure 4.2
Decision Tree for Data Collection Strategy

Do data currently exist in a written or archival format?

Yes — Conduct content analysis

No — Can the data be collected by observing behavior?

Yes — Would people behave differently if they knew they were being observed?

Yes — Can you join in the activity?

Yes — Use participant observation

No — Use passive nonparticipant observation

No — Use acknowledged observation

No — Is the topic related in any way to group processes?

Yes — Use focus groups

No — How vital is reliability to the study?

Very important — Use a structured interview

Not important — How much is known about the topic prior to the interview?

Little — Use unstructured interview

Much — Use semistructured interview

not, then collection is appropriate, and can proceed along a number of paths, depending on our priorities for the study and what is possible both in terms of the environment and within our resource constraints.

For data that can be collected by observing behavior, we consider whether individuals would behave differently (and thus yield different data) and whether we can participate. The result of our consideration of these factors leads us to one form of observation or another. For data that is related to group process, we consider focus groups. When observation and group process are not important, we turn to interviews. Our priorities and preferences about reliability and our prior knowledge about the topic lead us to consider one form of interview over another.

CONCLUSION

In this chapter, we considered qualitative data collection in the field. The chapter established the central importance of values and beliefs in the American political process and, related, the unique role of qualitative data in the study of public service questions. The chapter examined in detail the benefits and limitations of qualitative data generally, as well as the primary methods of qualitative data collection used in the field. We also explored the process of conducting field research, including the common tools that researchers use and the benefits and limitations of various methodological strategies.

The qualitative methods toolbox is quite powerful and is commonly combined with quantitative analysis of secondary data to produce mixed-methods research designs, which are prevalent in the study of public concerns. Qualitative methods also link researchers to the communities that they study; these links often foster greater understanding for all involved. In the next chapter, we turn to examine the survey, a research tool that can be used in the field and that lends itself to the collection of both quantitative and qualitative data.

CHAPTER SUPPORT MATERIALS

Chapter Four Relevant Articles

Becker, Howard S. 1958. "Problems of Inference and Proof in Participant Observation." *American Sociological Review* 23:652–660.

Harklau, Linda, and Rachel Norwood. 2005. "Negotiating Researcher Roles in Ethnographic Program Evaluation: A Postmodern Lens." *Anthropology & Education Quarterly* 36:278–288.

Ospina, Sonia, and Jennifer Dodge. 2005. "It's About Time—Catching Up Method to Meaning: The Usefulness of Narrative Inquiry in Public Administration Research." *Public Administration Review* 62:143–157.

Perry, James L., and Kenneth L. Kraemer. 1986. "Research Methodology in the Public Administration Review 1975–1984." *Public Administration Review* 46:215–226.

Chapter Four Discussion Questions

1. Do you think that the concerns about biased knowledge production in a society in which there is a hegemonic group are founded? Why or why not?

2. Of the data collection approaches described in this chapter, which has the most validity? Reliability? Why? Which has the greatest potential for bias? Why?

3. Can the data collected through any of the approaches in this chapter be used for quantitative analysis? Why or why not? If yes, which?

4. Do you think it is possible to replicate any of these data collection methods in a meaningful way? Why or why not?

Chapter Four Practice Assignments

1. Imagine you want to interview leaders of national organizations to find out what their successes and failures have been, how they know, and what led to these outcomes. You will have one hour for the interviews. Develop an interview protocol, including a grand tour question. Pilot this protocol with another member of the class and then discuss the questions. Determine which questions worked, which needed to be changed and why, and how you would change them. Then think about your interview protocol and what type of information you would obtain from it. Answer the following questions: What information should you be suspect of? Why? Where else might you obtain this information from a less biased source? Turn in (a) the interview protocol; (b) a summary of your piloting process and the results; (c) a description of which questions you kept, which you changed, why, and how; and (d) the answers to the final questions above about suspect information.

2. Using your library resources, access and read the following article:

> Brown, Mitchell. 2012. "Enhancing and Sustaining Organizational Capacity." *Public Administration Review* 72:506–515.

In this study, there were approximately 150 applicant organizations (the organization was the unit of analysis), over 50 were funded, and case studies were conducted on 8 of them, matching them regionally; and within each region, a pair were selected, comprising a faith-based organization and a community-based organization. Describe and discuss the basis on which the cases were selected and whether this case selection procedure introduced any bias, and identify alternative ways cases could have been selected.

3. You are interested in studying the fifty states by case study method. In particular, you are interested in understanding the variations in reproductive health policies and what produces those differences. You believe that differences may be explained by some combination of the presence of women in state legislatures, state political culture, the strength of partisanship, and the status of women as the primary source of income for families. Select one of these variables as the key explanatory variable, then develop a case study design that will establish the causality between the variable and the various policy outcomes. Do this by answering the following questions: (a) What might your research questions be? (b) What cases might you use? (c) What sources of evidence might you use? and (d) What is your dependent variable? Your main explanatory variable? Why? Design a case study protocol and any necessary instruments to collect data from the relevant sources of evidence.

4. Imagine that you work for your local county government, and a county official has decided that the county should be more responsive to the needs of the clients who use the Public Health Department. You already have data about what services people currently access and how often. What you are not sure about is why they use the health department, what other services they might need, how useful the current services are, and what barriers to service exist for them. You have decided that to get this information, you want to collect qualitative data. Develop a research protocol by answering the following questions: What information do you need? For each type of intervention: Where can you find the information? How can you obtain it? From whom? What is your timeline for acquisition? What kinds of instruments might you need to develop?

5. You are going to try to be an ethnographer, with a focus on being either an observer or a participant observer. Your research question is: What are the values and priorities of college students? Go to a specific location on campus (for example, the library, the student center where people are eating, a computer lab), and observe/participate in whatever activities are going on for two blocks of at least one hour each. Take extensive notes during your observation/participation. You may also want to conduct informal interviews with people and collect documents. Using your observations and notes, write up your findings: (a) What are the values and priorities of college students? (b) How do you know? For this part of the question, provide narrative that answers the following questions: What did you observe? Did you see outcroppings? Did you collect documents? Did you interview people? Did you observe relationships, symbols, and/or rituals?

Note to instructors: This exercise can be cast in any setting that permits people to remain in place for at least an hour. Typical examples not necessarily connected to a college campus environment include a shopping mall, coffee shops, museums, parks, and gyms.

6. You work in city government, and the mayor has decided that the police department of the city is suffering from a crisis of confidence among the citizens and, as a consequence, has a demoralized workforce. You have been asked to design a study to address both of these problems. Answer the following questions: (a) What is your research question or questions? (b) How would you study this? What data would you want to collect? Why? Where would you get those data? (c) If you were going to include interviews, whom would you interview and why? What questions would you ask?

Chapter Four Linked Assignments

Throughout the text, we include a series of "linked assignments." These have been developed to walk the research methods student through the entirety of the research process by developing a research project that includes each phase of both applied and basic research.

Note: If your design includes primary data collection excepting survey research, you will complete this linked assignment.

You should begin this linked assignment by reflecting on and refining your research design. First, identify how you will collect data, and identify the strengths and weaknesses of your selected approach. Second, develop a protocol for data collection, including detailed plans about what data will be collected, from where and whom, when, and how. If any processes need to be followed (approaching people, observing a phenomenon, recording information, and so on), list those processes in chronological order. If any questions need to be asked of people, draft these. Next, pilot these processes and questions with one to two cases. When the pilot is completed, write up what you did and what the results were. Then modify the processes and instruments as needed. Finally, collect the data.

Chapter Four Link to Online Assignments

Imagine that you are conducting a study of drug courts today. In the study, you want to explore, identify, and compare the perspectives of former offenders who have participated in drug court programs and those of former offenders who have faced similar charges but did not go through a drug court program.

1. Design a study that collects data using focus groups and interviews.

2. Produce a protocol for each component of the study.

3. Identify the challenges that you expect to face, and outline your plan for resolving these.

Survey Research

I n this chapter, we provide an overview of survey research in terms of the process, practical concerns, and applications to public and organizational studies. Surveys are a mainstay of data collection generally. They are also used extensively in all areas of public service. They are seen as a relatively low-cost method of gathering information and are familiar and accessible to most everyone. Surveys produce data that can be analyzed using either qualitative or quantitative methods, or both. Surveys also offer increased opportunities for randomness, which may increase representation.

Today, we encounter surveys in many aspects of our daily life. These surveys come in various forms. We are asked to take paper-based surveys on campus, and we find them mailed to our homes. We receive requests on our phones to answer survey questions. We receive requests to answer surveys in our email or as we are browsing the Internet. The questions we are asked range from our opinions about teachers and politicians to our preferences for products and services. Sometimes we are asked to respond to various choices of answers, and sometimes we are asked to tell researchers in an unrestricted manner what we think and why; in this way, survey research is similar to interviews, discussed in Chapter Four.

Survey research is used when we want to gather direct evidence from many people about their beliefs, opinions, perceptions, attitudes, practices, and backgrounds. Surveys are particularly useful for gathering this type of information, particularly because we cannot observe most behavior directly. Most commonly, survey research is conducted by drawing a sample from a population as opposed to studying the population as a whole.

THE SURVEY RESEARCH PROCESS

Generally speaking, conducting survey research follows a process that involves eleven distinct steps, similar to those used in other types of data collection and analysis. The steps are listed here and are followed by further description and discussion of each step. Throughout the process, we reflect on resources and data availability to make sure that we can accomplish our research goals, and we then make adjustments as necessary.

1. Develop a research question and theory.
2. Identify the population and develop a sampling approach.
3. Develop survey questions, instructions, and coding scheme if any.
4. Determine the method of administration and the design and layout.
5. Develop an introduction of survey and researcher credentials.
6. Identify incentives for participation, if any.
7. Pilot the instrument and process, and revise accordingly.
8. Train survey administrators.
9. Administer the survey.
10. Code data and/or identify patterns.
11. Conduct analysis.

First, as in all research, we begin with research questions and connection to theory. Second, we clearly specify the population of interest in order to construct a sampling frame. Within our general research question, we have in mind an idea of the population of interest for our study. We develop the sampling frame, select an approach to sampling, and draw the sample.

Third, we develop questions by first identifying concepts and then turning them into questions. Here, the process is the same as that used in designing questions for other forms of data collection, such as interviews and focus groups. We decide whether to pose **closed-ended questions**, in which we provide fixed lists of possible responses, or **open-ended questions**, in which we do not propose any sort of response options and do not limit the information that respondents choose to provide. We also make decisions at this point about **coding** schemes. In particular, we decide whether to predetermine the value or meaning of any particular response by assigning codes to responses as we design the survey, or whether to develop coding schemes after the data are gathered. If we determine that we will develop codes in advance of administering the survey, we also construct a **codebook** at this point. Our approach to the issue of coding is guided by our larger conceptual approach to research design for each particular study.

Fourth, we make decisions about whether the survey will be self-administered or administered by a person. In either case, we have additional decisions to make about the form in which the survey will be provided to potential respondents. If we decide that the survey will be self-administered, we also must decide whether to send it by mail or to use an electronic survey platform. If we determine that the survey will be administered by a person, we also decide whether to administer the survey by telephone or in person. If the survey will be administered by a person, we also must determine the location(s) and whether more than one person will be present. After deciding on the method of delivery, we also determine how the survey will look. We determine the physical layout of the survey and determine the appearance of any material that the respondent will see.

Fifth, we develop an appropriate introduction for the survey that identifies the researcher and his or her credibility, the purpose of the survey, how long it will take to respond, and the basis on which information will be collected (anonymous, not-for-attribution, or for attribution; see Chapter Four for more discussion). Consideration of the ethical issues involved for protection of human subjects may require that we develop a consent form and follow other IRB procedures in order to gain appropriate permissions to administer the survey.

Sixth, we decide whether to offer any incentives for participation. For well-financed research, this may include financial compensation for all participants. Typically, however, compensation offers are designed as a raffle that people can opt into in exchange for participation. Raffle prizes range from gift certificates to larger items. Compensation for participation has several pros and cons. The obvious pro for incentivizing participation is that response rates are often low, and there is evidence that compensation increases participation. One downside to compensation is that it is costly. Another is that compensation may appear to be coercive for some; a sticking point in our research is the perception of IRBs looking at compensation for students in faculty studies. Providing compensation is also a resource issue; incentives require an extra step in survey administration that could be devoted more directly to the purpose of the study. Whether or not an incentive is involved, if we are conducting a paper-based mail survey, in this stage we also order supplies to include a self-addressed stamped envelope for the return of surveys.

Seventh, we **pilot** or pretest the questions and the process of administering the survey. This helps us make sure that the questions are understandable to subjects and that we are gathering the data we intend to gather. In particular, if we have predetermined **response categories** for any of the questions, we want to verify that the response categories are **exhaustive** (all possible responses are included) and **mutually exclusive** (the response categories do not overlap). There are a variety of ways to pilot data collection methods, as we discussed in Chapter Four. Universally, we pilot our studies by recruiting people who are similar to our target subjects, following the same process we plan to follow with our study in terms of recruiting participants and administering the survey. In addition to these steps, a few additional techniques are often used in piloting surveys. **Focus groups** with pilot subjects allow us to speak with them as a group. **Cognitive interviews** may also be used, in which the researcher follows up with questions about how the respondent understood the questions and response categories, whether they were confusing, or whether anything should be added. We sometimes engage in **behavioral coding** while subjects are taking the surveys, in which we observe respondents taking the surveys and watch for questions that take longer to answer or appear more difficult. Regardless of the process that we use to collect interpretive data from pilot participants, we conclude the pilot process by making any revisions to the questions, response categories, and layout of the survey as well as the process by which the survey will be administered.

In the eighth step, we train interviewers if the survey is going to be conducted by phone or in person and if there will be more than one interviewer present. We want to ensure that questions are asked in the same way to all people. If we are using computers or other technology to administer the survey, it is important to pretest the links in advance of fielding the survey to ensure that the survey is operable on (most of) the different types of devices that respondents may use to take the surveys, such as PCs, Macs, tablets, and smartphones. It is also wise to develop, in advance, an alternative method of delivery or alternative connectivity for those instances in which technology fails. The most common failures, in our experience, occur when respondents are unable to open an email link to the survey. We hope that these instances will be few and far between, but we have never fielded an electronic survey for which we did not have to consider and use alternatives.

Ninth, we administer the survey. Frequently, this involves two stages. We contact possible respondents in advance to let them know that the survey will be coming. A few days to a couple of weeks later, we send out the survey and/or interviewer. It is typical to distribute a survey more than once in order to try to capture the information of nonrespondents. This is increasingly true as we turn toward Internet-based surveys that have notoriously low response rates. It is common to distribute a survey and follow up with one or two additional distributions to the same potential respondents; these additional distributions might occur at two- or three-week intervals after the survey was first fielded. These multiple distributions of the same survey should not be confused with what are referred to as multiple **waves** of a survey, which are used to capture change over time among the same subjects. In such **longitudinal studies**, survey waves are sent out at successive intervals of months or years after the original distribution; the intervals are determined as a part of the research design.

In the tenth step, we code data and analyze patterns. Data are input into a database if we have collected information from paper surveys (see discussion of coding and data entry in Chapter Six). If we have used Internet-based survey software, like Survey Monkey or Qualtrics, we simply download the data into the appropriate file format required for the software we are using. In the eleventh step, we analyze the data and consider the conclusions and implications of our findings.

SURVEY DESIGN

A few general guidelines are important for survey construction. These guidelines are intended to render the survey easy to read and understand overall, thus enhancing validity. One readability issue is survey length. How long should a survey be? The most appropriate length for a survey depends on the audience and the method that is used to engage potential respondents. As a general guide, shorter surveys are better, but the survey must still contain enough questions to allow collection of all the information we need. Related, we need to ensure that all questions included in the survey are relevant to the purpose of the survey. Further, as a general rule, readability is enhanced by using shorter words rather than longer words and by avoiding technical terms, slang, or jargon. Readability is improved if we limit the total number of words per question to less than twenty, and limit the number of commas to three or fewer when possible. The next sections address some of the primary concerns that arise when writing survey questions.

Crafting Quality Questions

In addition to overall survey design, a critical aspect of survey research is the construction of survey questions. In fact, one of the most cost-effective ways to reduce error in survey research is to enhance the quality of the questions and response categories. Following Fowler and Cosenga (2009), quality questions are guided by four general principles:

1. Respondents need to be able to understand the questions that we ask of them.

2. Respondents need to possess the information that is being asked of them.

3. Respondents need to be willing to provide the information being asked of them.

4. Response possibilities must capture what respondents will want to report.

The quality of the survey questions is reflected in their psychometrics. **Psychometrics** are the measures of reliability and validity of our instruments. In survey research, **reliability** is a measure of the ability of questions to yield consistent answers; **validity** is the extent to which we are measuring what we think we are measuring with our questions and response categories. One method of gaining strong psychometrics is to rely on existing surveys for which psychometrics have already been established. This means that research studies have determined that the concepts and ideas that particular survey questions are meant to elicit are actually achieved by the survey questions. However, this is not always possible or realistic. If we are exploring new fields and new ideas, it is quite likely that our particular questions have not yet been posed in other research. When psychometric measures do not exist for the questions we want to ask, we have to focus on how to write good questions.

Writing good questions is difficult, and in some ways is as much an art as it is a science. In addition to the principles just listed, questions should be carefully constructed to collect the data we are seeking. This means that the questions must be crafted around the concepts we are attempting to understand. These concepts are the elements of interest in our study, also understood as the variables that we have included in our research design. In practice, the relationship between concepts and questions can be achieved in two ways. It may be possible to capture each concept in a single question. An alternative is to capture the concept through a series of questions; the answers are aggregated to form an **index** that then becomes the measure of the concept. Regardless of which approach a researcher selects, it is important to tie each survey question to variables or concepts, and it is critical that each question collect information on a single point—whether that point stands alone as a concept or whether it is aggregated with other responses in the form of an index. We explore the mechanics of indices and scales later in this chapter.

In writing survey questions, it is important to consider several common errors in question construction. When present, these errors diminish the utility of the answers to our questions. Generally speaking, these errors confuse respondents and allow the responses to stray away from the variable or concept of interest. These concerns are illustrated through the examples presented in Figure 5.1 and discussed in the next paragraphs.

It is important to minimize **ambiguity** and avoid confusing phrases. For example, if we ask respondents how they "feel" about a particular group of people, the term "feel" may not be precise enough to capture our intention. As another illustration, if we ask respondents whether they have been victims of a crime, the question can have many interpretations. The concepts of crime and victim can be interpreted in various ways and have different meanings to different people. Instead, it is more useful if we break down these concepts into component parts and ask a series of questions about different categories of crime and various types of victimization.

It is also essential that each question address only one topic. We avoid **double-barreled questions**. These are questions that actually pose two questions but allow only one answer. In the illustration in Figure 5.1, the double-barreled question asks at least two questions: whether homelessness is a problem in the respondent's community, and how it should be solved. Another example is the question "Did you vote in the last election, and for whom did you vote?" which also asks two questions. To avoid this condition, we ask what are called **filter questions** that address threshold concepts that are essential to our research questions. We use these filter questions as gatekeepers for subsequent questions. Respondents answer particular questions only if they respond to the earlier filter question(s) in a particular manner. The use of filter questions allows us to develop clusters of questions in a logical sequence in which entire groups of questions are

Figure 5.1
Approaches to Question Wording

Issue	Problematic Question Wording	Better Question Wording
Question Length	Because many periods of economic prosperity have occurred under the leadership of Democrats and Republicans, and many Democrats and Republicans agree on steps that we need to take in order to keep our nation strong and also agree on domestic public policy positions, and in addition individual members may disagree or agree across the partisan aisle, do you think there are any important differences between the parties in terms of what they stand for?	Do you think there are any important differences in the views of Republicans and Democrats?
Ambiguity	How do you feel about homeless people?	*Problem:* "feel" is ambiguous—this could indicate a variety of feelings, including individual-level fear of homeless individuals and seeing homelessness as a social issue that should be solved. A better question might be: Do you think homeless people are a threat to public safety?
Double-Barreled Question	Do you think homelessness is a problem in your community, and how should it be solved?	Do you think homelessness is a problem in your community? IF YES, How should it be solved? IF NO, Why not?

Emotional Bias	Should tax dollars be spent to address filthy, dirty homeless people?
	Should public policy address hygiene for the homeless?
Response Set Bias	On a scale from 1 to 3, how big a problem is homelessness in your community?
	1 = significant problem
	2 = somewhat of a problem
	3 = minor problem
	On a scale from 1 to 3, how big a problem is homelessness in your community?
	1 = significant problem
	2 = somewhat of a problem
	3 = not a problem
Social Desirability Effect	What sorts of public policy options should be developed to address homelessness?
	Problem: a respondent might feel that taxpayer dollars should not be used to deal with homelessness, and that instead it is an individual problem. However, because of the presumption of help in the question, he or she may suppress this response. A better question might be: Should the government address issues of homelessness?
	IF YES, What sorts of public policy options should be developed to do this?
Argumentativeness	Don't you agree that the Democrat party has done more to help address homelessness than the Republican party?
	Do you think that one of the major political parties has done more than the other to address homelessness?
	IF YES, which party?

either answered or skipped, depending on the responses provided to the filter questions. If the respondent answers no to the filter question, he or she skips the entire cluster of questions to which the filter question applies, and moves along in the survey to the next set of questions. For example, instead of asking, "Did you vote in the last election, and for whom did you vote?" we ask "Did you vote in the last election?" If the respondent answers no, the respondent skips the remaining questions in the cluster. If the respondent answers yes, he or she proceeds to the rest of the questions in the cluster; here, that question is "For whom?"

Another critical dimension of creating survey questions is avoiding words that trigger bias. Several forms of bias exist. Question bias falls into two categories: the use of words that evoke emotional responses, and the selection of response possibilities. In Figure 5.1, the word "filthy" in the problematic question is provocative and introduces **emotional bias**, conjuring up negative images that are not associated with the term "hygiene." The **response set bias** concern is different. Here, bias is introduced because the range of responses is skewed toward one viewpoint. In the example, responses to the problematic question are limited to choices that indicate some level of concern with homelessness; the problematic question does not allow for the possibility that respondents do not view homelessness as a problem.

It is also important to keep in mind that question design relates to the social context of some topics. Some respondents may want their answers to present a positive association with a particular topic, regardless of their true beliefs. We call this condition the **social desirability** effect. Topics that are associated with socially desirable responses include those pertaining to private behavior or behavior that may have a negative connotation or invoke social taboos (for example, criminal activity, mental illness, drug and alcohol use, some infections and diseases). The concept of social desirability can arise around other behaviors that have a particular value in a given social context—gang behavior, for example. In order to elicit a more accurate response in these cases, it is important to use words that do not condemn the behavior. To minimize the likelihood of social desirability influencing responses, it is important to carefully consider the question wording. As the example in Figure 5.1 illustrates, the social desirability effect can be quite subtle.

The pilot process should reveal hidden meaning or social context that may not be known to the researcher. In addition, there are steps that we can take in the administration of the instrument that may reduce responses driven by social desirability. First, we can ensure the confidentiality of respondents before asking these types of questions. Second, we can emphasize to respondents the importance of honest answers when introducing the survey. Third, we can provide respondents with additional information about why particular questions are critical, so that they will have a greater appreciation for the significance of their responses. Finally, if we pose sensitive questions, we use a self-administered survey rather than one administered by an interviewer, to the extent possible.

We also try to avoid **argumentativeness**. When developing survey instruments, researchers must keep in mind that they are trying to elicit honest, accurate, and complete information from respondents, as opposed to trying to convince people that a particular perspective is right. Questions that attempt to persuade respondents about a particular point of view are deceptive. This latter form of surveying is known as **push polling** when undertaken during a political campaign. In political campaigns, one candidate may develop a "poll" that is really used to disparage the other candidate. For example, a push poll question in this situation might ask, "Would you still be willing to vote for Candidate B if you knew that she had been married four times and was able to pay to have it covered up?" Although most push polls are not this obvious, they have been shown to be effective in persuading undecided voters in one direction or another. Similar questions are used in issue-oriented campaigns, and the responses to such questions can present a distorted view of public interests and desires.

Response Categories

Response options are also important in survey question design. Response options are typically not considered when researchers use open-ended questions; the point of open-ended questions is to allow respondents free rein. When researchers elect to use closed-ended questions, a few rules should guide their work. As noted earlier, categories of responses must be exhaustive, which means that the response categories include all possible alternatives, and also must be mutually exclusive, meaning that each category does not overlap with any other. These response categories should also be balanced, meaning that the categories are evenly distributed across the continuum of the concept that they are exploring and provide equal opportunity for respondents to select positive or negative responses.

The number of response categories that we choose tends to vary according to the method used to present the survey. In surveys conducted over the phone, it is important to minimize the number of response categories because respondents often lose track of categories and tend to become confused. In cases in which the respondent can see the survey in written form (whether on paper or electronically), the number of response categories is frequently higher. In the case of oral surveys administered in person (similar to a structured interview), the interviewer can provide cards to respondents that indicate the range of response categories, so that respondents can keep the categories in mind during questioning.

It is also important to consider the labels of response categories. Response categories that include "neutral" answers allow people to choose not to take positions. This may be acceptable, or even preferable, if we think that it is possible for the public or a respondent to be truly neutral about an issue. Further, the absence of an opinion may actually be of interest and an indicator of something important. However, if we want respondents to take a position on an issue, particularly a controversial issue, we should not include a neutral category as a possibility for response. Related, if we care about whether or not people understand questions or options, we can add a "Don't know" response category. However, we do not include "Don't know" or "No opinion" if we think it is possible that people will have opinions that they do not want to share. Figure 5.2 illustrates two similar response sets that gather different information about the same question.

If we are asking respondents whether they agree or disagree, **agreement bias** occurs because, in general, people want to appear positive (agreeable) and not negative (disagreeable), regardless of how they actually feel about the idea, proposal, or decision that is the subject of the question. We also have to be aware of response set bias, also known as **context effect**, where the order of statements and questions together affect the answers given.

Another common method of designing response categories is the use of ordered scales. A **scale** is a set of responses ordered from lowest to highest that allows respondents to express how they feel about something. Response scales are common survey response options when we want to ask similar questions about a range of services or programs. In addition, all of the ordered scale options allow us to capture a relatively large amount of detail about individual questions and concepts. As a simple illustration, imagine that we are interested in gathering data about customer perceptions of their experiences around a common public service: obtaining a motor vehicle license at a typical Department of Motor Vehicles (DMV). A survey question might ask, "On a 1–5 scale where 1 is the lowest and 5 is the highest, how would you rate your overall

Figure 5.2
The Influence of Word Order and Response Set Choices

Problematic Response Choices	Better Response Choices
Some people believe that our armed forces are already powerful enough and that we should spend less money for defense. Others feel that military spending should at least continue at the present level. How do you feel—should military spending be cut, or should it continue at the present level?	Some people believe that our armed forces are already powerful enough and that we should spend less money for defense. Others feel that military spending should at least continue at the present level. How do you feel—should military spending be cut, or should it continue at the present level?
Response choices:	*Response choices:*
Cut	Cut
Keep at least the same	Continue at the present level
	Don't know
	No opinion

Source: Adapted from surveys in the American National Election Studies collection, http://www.electionstudies.org

experience today at the Department of Motor Vehicles (DMV)?" The ordered response categories could be phrased in terms of satisfaction and range from very unsatisfied (1) to very satisfied (5).

There are a few general principles to follow when using scales. We typically use an odd number of categories (3, 5, 7) across the range of a continuum from low to high; the odd number allows for a neutral midpoint. We also take care to consider the distance between categories and strive to keep that distance equal so that we do not skew the scale to one end of the continuum or the other. The continuum itself is labeled to reflect our research question. Typical examples of concepts that are captured through the use of ordered scales include agreement, satisfaction, importance, favorability, and frequency. Figure 5.3 illustrates several typical ordered scales. In the illustration, we also include a typical coding scheme ranging from 1 for one end of the continuum up to 5 or 7 for the other end. It is not necessary to include the coding row on the survey; we show it here to clarify the connection between data collection and coding.

Figure 5.3
Illustration of Ordered Scales

How satisfied are you with the adult care services currently provided by At Home with You at its community center?

Very Dissatisfied	Dissatisfied	Neither Satisfied nor Dissatisfied	Satisfied	Very Satisfied
1	2	3	4	5

How important is it for you to receive in-home assistance from At Home with You?

Very Unimportant	Unimportant	Somewhat Unimportant	Neither Important nor Unimportant	Somewhat Important	Important	Very Important
1	2	3	4	5	6	7

A particular type of ordered scale known as the **Likert scale** employs multiple questions with ordered, equidistant response options arranged in numbered order. Figure 5.4 illustrates a typical Likert scale similar to those used in the criminal justice reform study.

This Likert scale was designed to gather data on the different types of information that state administrators sought out during the initial phases of a new program to provide jobs for recovering drug addicts seeking to reintegrate into the community. This particular illustration does not provide any prompts about the meaning of the category labels; for example, the meaning of "Never/Vary Rarely" is left to the individual interpretation of the respondent. To provide a measure of

Figure 5.4
Illustration of Likert Scale

As a program manager, how frequently do you look for the following types of information in your responsibilities related to WorkFirst, the state's new workforce development policy initiative?

	Never/Very Rarely	Rarely	Sometimes	Frequently/ Often	Very Frequently
State grant requirements	1	2	3	4	5
Local workforce development office information	1	2	3	4	5
Best practices from national nonprofit organizations	1	2	3	4	5
Program evaluation information from research groups or think tanks	1	2	3	4	5
WorkFirst software support	1	2	3	4	5

consistency in interpretation of frequency, we could add explanatory information about what each label means. The need for this type of clarification, or lack of it, is one of the aspects of the survey that is clarified during the pilot process.

As noted earlier in this chapter, it is critical that survey questions relate directly to our variables or concepts of interest. It is also essential that each question contain only one topic. However, many concepts that we study (and, by extension, many variables) cannot be reduced to the answer to a single question. In survey research language, this multifaceted concept is known as a **construct**. To gather data about a construct, we develop a series of questions that capture the construct (also a variable); we then use the composite responses to these questions to create an index.

Imagine that we believe that the experience at the DMV is more nuanced than a simple satisfaction scale could determine. We believe that the experience has several components, including cost, wait time, physical environment, interaction with the government worker, and ease in filling out forms. To capture the construct of customer perception of this experience, we develop a series of questions about each of these items and then create an index. If we believe that all factors are equally valuable, we can average the values for all of the answers to create an overall index of customer perception of experience.

Alternatively, we can create a weighted index if we believe that these items have different levels of importance in determining the experience. Our beliefs in this regard come from the literature, or may be the basis of our hypotheses or research expectations. The index can be developed by taking a simple average of the answers, or it can be designed as a **weighted index** if some questions are more important than others in understanding the construct.

Before we calculate an index value in Excel or SPSS, it is important to note whether each of the items in the index consistently point in the same direction; this can be done by eye for a random sample of the responses. If one (or more) of the index components is consistently different from the others, this may mean that the aberrant component is actually measuring another concept. When all of the index components vary in similar fashion, we have an indication that we have operationalized the construct correctly.

The following example illustrates the variation that is possible in constructing an index. In the statewide needs assessment, we interviewed sixty women about their lives, needs, and sources of support. Part of each interview included a follow-back calendar of the past week of each woman's life in which she described her daily activities. Many of these activities were indicators of engaged, healthy living. We created a list of all the topics mentioned by the respondents and created a variable for each topic as a positive indicator of healthy living. When we entered this information into the database, variables were coded 1 if the respondent had engaged in the activity at least once during the week, and 0 if not. The exception was nutrition; this variable was coded as the average number of meals per day. The positive indicators included twenty separate variables, and we were interested in the possible effect of each. In addition, we were also interested in the additive effect of these possible activities as a measure of overall health. Accordingly, we developed an additive index that included the activities listed in Table 5.1.

Table 5.1
Index of Engaged Healthy Living Activities

Index Activity	Activity Value
Average number of meals/day	2–5*
Doing yard work	1
Cleaning house	1
Grocery shopping	1
Running other errands	1
Attending church service	1
Attending other church group activity	1
Volunteering	1
Attending community activities	1
Employment	1
Attending a class	1
Helping someone else	1
Visiting a friend	1
Reading	1
Exercising	1
Talking with family/friends on the phone	1
Going out for entertainment (movies, concerts, etc.)	1
Traveling within the county/region	1
Traveling outside the county/region	1
Other activities	1

*Women interviewed reported a range of 2–5 meals per day.

The index was a single variable with a range of 3 to 16 (out of a possible 2 to 24), a mean of 11.25, and a median of 11.5. We were able to examine the relationship between this additive index and other factors that may be related to healthy, engaged living for this age group and circumstances. As one example, we found that the level of engagement with these activities is related to age, with the number of activities declining over time. As another example, we found no relationship between the index and educational attainment or income.

Demographic Questions

In studying the world of public service, we want to understand more about people's opinions, beliefs, perspectives, and behaviors. It is important also to be able to understand whether these views and behaviors differ according to the various social, ethnic, and economic groupings, or **strata**, to which respondents belong. In order to conduct these types of analyses, we usually include a set of demographic questions in our surveys. These typically include questions that give us information about gender, age, race/ethnicity, education level, employment type, and income. In addition, we sometimes ask questions about marital status, sexual preference, where people grew up, religion, and political party affiliation, among other aspects of life.

Respondents can be nervous about providing information that can personally identify them and connect them with their responses. Whether or not our pilot respondents exhibit any concerns about particular questions, we should be sensitive to this general concern. For this reason, these types of questions are typically positioned at the end of the survey. Before asking demographic questions, we also reassure respondents that their answers will remain anonymous or confidential. Another approach that puts respondents at ease is to provide categories of ranges of values as opposed to asking for raw figures and information. This approach is commonly used when gathering information about income and age. For example, a question that asks "What is your annual income?" may be ignored by a respondent as too intrusive; by comparison, a question that offers income ranges as response categories may be more palatable. One negative dimension of this approach is that the information within each category cannot be disaggregated for more nuanced data analysis. If we construct categories of age ranges—for example, age 18–24, age 25–54, and age 55 and older—we are limited in our conclusions to those age groups and will not be able to draw any conclusions about specific ages or about other different age ranges.

When using categories for gathering demographic information, it is important to consider carefully the category boundaries in terms of the information that we believe will be most important for our study and in terms of the common ways that demographic information is reported. For example, in the case of the study of women age sixty-five and older in Alabama, we decided to stratify our interview sample into three age bands: age 65–74, age 75–84, and age 85 and older. This approach allowed us to examine whether there were differences in views and experiences based on age within the often-generalized category of "elderly" or "over 65." These three categories are also commonly used in government reports and other scholarly literature on aging. We would have selected different age bands if the point of our study was to try to challenge these groupings as insufficient in some way, or to understand specific phenomena related to a particular age. If we did not have evidence to suggest that differences in age mattered within this age group, we would have omitted the stratification altogether.

PROBLEMS AND CONTROVERSIES IN SURVEY RESEARCH

There are several major sources of error associated with survey research. These comprise error due to poor measurement, the sampling approach, and lack of response. The first source of error is poor measurement, which occurs for a variety of reasons. One is the use of questions that contain one or more of the errors discussed in this chapter. Another is the use of response categories that are either incomplete or incorrectly specified, or both. Following the rules for writing good questions and properly piloting our survey mitigates this type of error.

Error due to the lack of response is known as **nonresponse error**; this error occurs when a low percentage of the sample actually completes and returns a survey. Response rates in survey research are very important. The greater the response rate from a random sample, the more information we have and the more faith we have in that information. Historically, a response rate of 70 percent or more was considered the norm. However, response rates have been steadily decreasing over the past forty years, and today many researchers are content with a return rate of about 30 percent. This percentage drops even lower for Internet-based surveys; response rates of 10 percent and less are not uncommon. The error that is associated with low response rates is bias, which limits the ability to generalize. If there is a systematic element either in who responds or in who does not respond, we may be recording information for particular types of people and not others, even if we have used random sampling techniques.

It is also important to keep in mind that lack of response is open to multiple interpretations. One interpretation is refusal; respondents received the survey and refused to respond. Another interpretation is that individuals received the survey but were not eligible to complete it and so did not; an age requirement is a simple example. Last, potential respondents may simply be unreachable. Each reason for lack of response suggests a solution for boosting response rates; all of these reasons should be considered in advance of deploying the survey in order to minimize the possibility that surveys will not be completed. It is also worth noting that we have individual-level information about nonresponses for some survey distribution approaches and not others. We can identify refusals and ineligibles when we conduct surveys in person and by telephone. We cannot typically do this for mail or Web-based surveys. Although we can identify refusals when using some approaches to survey distribution, a significant number of refusals may suggest that we should consider another method of data collection; this consideration is particularly important if the potential recipients may have reason to refuse to participate. Ineligibles can be encouraged to return the survey or to indicate that they have received the instrument and are ineligible. This process adds cost and administrative oversight. Unreachable respondents present a different dynamic; here, the effort can be improved by spending time on building lists of accurate contact information and verifying that information (to the extent possible) before deploying the survey.

The increase in low response rates across the range of survey distribution approaches is a consequence of several factors. First, potential respondents are subject to what we might term "survey fatigue." This fatigue is related to modern technology and our ability to inundate one another with requests for information, given the ease with which almost anyone can generate and disseminate a survey via the Internet. The common use of cell phones and the use of technological innovations such as caller ID and do-not-call lists make it increasingly difficult to engage potential respondents in telephone surveys. It may also be the case that people are more wary about providing information to strangers.

We also introduce error when there is inadequate coverage of the population. This can be the result of a poor sampling frame, as in the case of the polling conducted during the Roosevelt-Landon election (see Chapter Three). This may also be the result of systematic bias in who does and does not respond to our surveys. Finally, it is possible that we may produce a sample that is in some way not reflective of the population even when using high-quality instruments under conditions of properly executed random sampling. We mitigate this type of error by ensuring that we have a large sample size and by employing appropriate tools in our analysis (see Chapter Six for more discussion).

Unrelated to error considerations, another limitation of survey research is that it provides only **subjective** information; that is, the data that we gather come only from the perspective of the respondent. We place a high value on personal perspectives in the study of public service; however, personal perspectives may also have characteristics that distort information and can divert us from learning about the topic of interest. For example, we know from studying survey research that people often exaggerate, have imperfect memories, and possess information and beliefs that they want to hide. We can take some steps to improve on these possible limitations, such as carefully following the precepts of good question construction and ensuring respondents' anonymity; however, it is impossible to completely remove these dimensions of human nature. This is an inherent problem in all survey research, and thus interpretations of results from survey data are always subject to question.

CASE ILLUSTRATIONS OF SURVEY USE

The following cases illustrate several approaches to survey use and common issues that may arise.

Statewide Needs Assessment

The statewide needs assessment utilized a paper survey mailed to government offices, nonprofits, and for-profit service providers. The survey was designed to elicit organizational data about structure and operations, as well as views about future trends and challenges. We piloted the survey with several practitioners who had experience working in and with organizations that were on our list of potential respondents. These practitioners gave us advice to ensure that the questions were clear and easy to read.

Several typical issues arose that are common across survey research. The response rate for the mailed survey was low, which required follow-up in the form of additional distributions; as a result, we conducted a second and third round of distributions after the initial deployment. The second round was conducted by email when email addresses were available and by telephone call if not; the third and final round was done by telephone. Our response rate may also have been low because we faced challenges in identifying the correct organizational representative or did not target the survey to the proper office. This is likely to be an issue when trying to obtain responses from larger organizations for which we do not have specific contact information. It also suggests that time would be well spent early in the research process to identify particular individuals with appropriate knowledge and administrative responsibilities who would be receptive to the survey. By targeting respondents, however, we limit randomness, so it is important to balance these considerations in each research design.

Related, another limitation has to do with the medium, which here is the Internet. The Internet is an imperfect catalogue of any population. Our search for organizations that provided services to women in our target age group could only discover organizations that had chosen to place information online. In addition, we had no control over the accuracy and completeness of the information; phone numbers, addresses, and email contact information were not always current.

Criminal Justice Policy Reform

In the case of criminal justice policy reform, state court administrators responsible for drug court operations in each of the fifty states were surveyed by email using a common electronic survey platform. Telephone follow-ups were conducted in two rounds. The response rate was 100 percent, which is unusually high; perhaps this is attributable to the culture of this innovation and the strong desire among those involved to share information about it. In addition, a national professional association maintained a list of state contacts; this list was nearly complete, with the exception of a few updates. Here, in contrast to the statewide needs assessment, randomness was not a concern—the point of the survey was to obtain information from each state.

National Program Evaluation

In the national program evaluation, we were interested in three questions that survey research could answer. First, were there systematic differences between the organizations that were funded versus those that were not? Second, was there a change in capacity over the life of the grant for funded organizations versus those that were not funded? Third, to the extent that funded organizations experienced capacity changes, were these sustained after funding ended? To answer these questions, we developed a self-administered capacity study that measured capacity in six areas: management and operations, board of directors and governance, key allies, resources, program planning and implementation, and evaluation. We validated the survey using the capacity findings from the site visits and monthly interviews in five of the six areas. We fielded each wave of the survey via mail. The response rate was 100 percent in the first round, 80 percent in the second, and below 70 percent in the third round.

The only area in which we could not validate the survey was in evaluation. According to survey results, organizational evaluation capacity dropped over the life of the grant. In fact, what we discovered from the validation process was that capacity increased. The difficulty was that respondents did not understand the evaluation questions in the first wave of the survey. The fault for this lies in the piloting process. We piloted the survey using leaders of similar human service organizations in the local area where we were working at the time, Washington, D.C. Although it should have been intuitive that knowledge about evaluation terms and practices would likely be higher for those running human service organizations in Washington, D.C., than in rural areas around the country, this possibility was overlooked, thus producing discrepant results. This underscores an important lesson: selecting subjects for pilot studies is important and requires thoughtful consideration.

DECISION TREE

A common question in survey research is how to distribute the instrument. Each research project calls for a different approach. As with other elements of the applied research process, the approach should be considered carefully and justified by the goals of the study.

Decisions About Methods of Survey Distribution

Here, we compare the use of paper and Web-based surveys. Paper surveys can be used in person and also mailed to potential respondents. Web-based surveys typically involve the use of email and links to surveys constructed within a survey platform. Figure 5.5 displays common considerations for both approaches.

Figure 5.5

Decision Tree for Choosing Paper or Web-Based Survey Approach

Consider Using Paper Survey If:	Consider Using Web-Based Survey If:
Personal contact is needed in order to identify potential respondents. For example, we need to find them in a particular location doing a particular thing (at a park, at a school, voting).	Personal contact is not needed to identify potential respondents.
	We have a current email list that fulfills our sampling strategy.
Mail or personal contact will allow us to reach the population or fulfill our sampling strategy.	The potential respondents are receptive to email.
	The potential respondents have equal access to email (unless access is one of the variables in the study).
A mailed survey will convey a sense of urgency or value and encourage responses with a "please answer this" plea.	The potential respondents can access and manipulate the survey in electronic form.
Resources are available.	We are satisfied with a response rate that averages 10 percent or less.
Street addresses are available for a mailed survey.	We have limited resources.
	We have access to a survey platform.
The demographic will respond better to mail or in-person surveys, or will respond poorly to email.	
Higher response rate is important.	

CONCLUSION

This chapter explored surveys as a common method of data collection. Although all of us are routinely exposed to surveys, the information in this chapter illustrates that good surveys are not a matter of accident. Careful attention must be paid to composing and organizing questions and responses and to choosing the method of distributing the instrument.

As technology continues to evolve, surveys will be distributed through entirely new approaches. New platforms for surveys connected to social media continue to emerge, such as Survey Tool (connected to Facebook), Polldaddy, and Poll. We do not explore the array of Internet options for surveying various groups, but note that these new methods will certainly present advantages in terms of ease of use. It will be up to the researcher to determine whether these and other new approaches satisfy the requirements of a particular research design and method(s) of analysis.

Surveys lend themselves to analysis using qualitative methods as well as quantitative methods because they can contain a variety of question types. Open-ended questions can be analyzed for themes and patterns, and closed-ended questions can be coded and analyzed using quantitative approaches. The next chapter examines a wide range of qualitative and quantitative data analysis methods. Researchers should be familiar with these methods as they design questions and response options.

CHAPTER SUPPORT MATERIALS

Chapter Five Relevant Articles

Bradburn, Norman M., and William Mason. 1964. "The Effect of Question Order on Responses." *Journal of Marketing Research* 1:57–61.

Herzong, A. Regula, and Jerald G. Bachman. 1982. "Effects of Questionnaire Length on Response Quality." *Public Opinion Quarterly* 45:549–559.

Koren, Paul E., Neal DeChillo, and Barbara J. Friesen. 1992. "Measuring Empowerment in Families Whose Children Have Emotional Disabilities: A Brief Questionnaire." *Rehabilitation Psychology* 37:305–321.

Rogers, Theresa F. 1976. "Interviews by Telephone and in Person: Quality of Responses and Field Performance." *Public Opinion Quarterly* 40:51–65.

Torrieri, Nancy K. 2007. "America Is Changing, and So Is the Census: The American Community Survey." *American Statistician* 61:16–21.

Chapter Five Discussion Questions

1. From your perspective, are there any substantive differences between survey research and interviewing? If no, why not? If yes, what are they?

2. What types of information can you *not* collect from surveys? How does this diminish its utility as a tool for collecting data?

3. Of all of the forms of data collection discussed in this book, which types have the most error? The least? Where does survey research fall on this continuum?

4. Why are decreasing survey response rates seen as problematic? What other reasons can you think of, other than those given in this chapter, for decreasing response rates?

Chapter Five Practice Assignments

1. You are interested in finding out whether or not people voted in the last election, and why or why not. Things we know already that influence voter participation include whether or not the qualified voter has voted in the past, strength of partisanship, age, education, and income (though of course there are other things that influence voting). Put together a ten-question survey with a mix of open- and closed-ended questions. Then ask someone in the class to review your survey, and review someone else's survey—did he or she violate any of the principles of quality question writing? If so, how? What questions could be improved?

2. Using your library resources, access and read the following article:

> Koren, Paul E., Neal DeChillo, and Barbara J. Friesen. 1992. "Measuring Empowerment in Families Whose Children Have Emotional Disabilities: A Brief Questionnaire." *Rehabilitation Psychology* 37:305–321.

Answer the following questions: What is empowerment? What are the different dimensions of it? How is it measured in this study? What validity and reliability concerns did the authors address? What do they find about the instrument they created? Do you believe it? Why or why not?

3. Following up from practice assignments 1 and 2, suppose you now believe that a sense of political empowerment (also thought of as political efficacy) may influence voter turnout (it does). Also suppose that trust in government influences turnout. (For example, we know that high trust and high efficacy produce insider participation, whereas low trust and high efficacy produce outsider participation.) Now create a survey instrument to measure these three things: (a) type of participation, (b) efficacy/empowerment, and (c) trust in government.

4. Imagine you work for a polling company and need to determine what people think about who won the debate. Generate a question about who won. Generate a set of questions to be able to put that opinion into context, comprising questions about political party identification, strength of partisanship, education, gender, age, and income.

5. Read through a recent newspaper and find a reference to a survey. Then see if you can find the original survey research report. Provide the following information: (a) the citation for the newspaper article; (b) a summary of what the article states about the survey findings; (c) a link to the original research; (d) a summary of the original research findings; and (e) a discussion of whether there are any differences between what was reported in the paper and what the original findings state and, if so, what those differences are.

Chapter Five Linked Assignments

Throughout the text, we include a series of "linked assignments." These have been developed to walk the research methods student through the entirety of the research process by developing a research project that includes each phase of both applied and basic research.

Note: If your design includes primary data collection from surveys, you will complete this linked assignment.

You should begin this linked assignment by identifying the major concepts that you are planning to study and turning these into preliminary research questions. Then determine how you will field the surveys—written on the Web, written on paper, or verbally. Then design a draft questionnaire, including all of the components described in this chapter. Next, pilot the process for data collection and the instrument/questionnaire with a few people. After the pilot is completed, write up what you did and what the results were. Then modify the processes and instruments as needed. Finally, collect the data.

Chapter Five Link to Online Assignments

Read the following article about elections administration and the states' responses to federal implementation of voluntary voting system guidelines and adoption of different voting technologies:

Hale, Kathleen, and Mitchell Brown. 2013. "Adopting, Adapting, and Opting Out: State Response to Federal Voting System Guidelines." *Publius: The Journal of Federalism* 43:428–451.

1. Imagine that you are conducting an extension of this research and want to send out a survey to elections administrators in every election district around the country. Develop a survey instrument that could be used to gauge the type of equipment used in each district, the problems that administrators have been having with the equipment, and what they would like out of future equipment. Include in the materials you turn in your plan for how to conduct the survey (paper, Internet, phone) and the process you would follow to field your survey instrument.

2. Consider the same survey and how the content would change if you wanted to obtain the views of a stakeholder group, such as a nonprofit advocacy group for voters with disabilities, or actual/potential voters who have disabilities. Develop a survey instrument and your plan to conduct the survey, and compare it to your survey of election administrators.

Analyzing Data and Communicating About Them: What Do They Mean? How Can They Be Used?

Data Analysis

Afterwe have collected our **data**, whether they are in qualitative or quantitative form, we analyze them in order to provide an overview of the information we collected and to test the research expectations or hypotheses we have developed. An important component of all good analysis is to ensure that we establish causality to the greatest extent possible.

Remember from Chapter Two that good causal arguments meet four explicit conditions. For two variables X and Y, where X is believed to cause Y:

1. The two concepts must **co-vary**, meaning that there must be an observable, empirical relationship between the two.

2. Changes in X must precede changes in Y in time, which means that they demonstrate the proper **temporal order**.

3. There must be an identifiable **causal mechanism** that ties the two together (but this does not have to be observable—it can just be hypothetical).

4. The relationship between the two concepts cannot be **spurious**, meaning caused by a third unseen or unmeasured concept.

In qualitative data analysis, the best way to establish causality is to engage in a careful tracing of processes over time to determine how particular decisions and events lead to other decisions and events and eventually, step-by-step, proceed to generate the outcomes that we observe. For quantitative data, we have to engage in **multivariate analysis**. This means that we examine the simultaneous impact of multiple variables, and differentiate between our key **explanatory variables**, which are the concepts we believe to be theoretically the most important, and **control variables**, which are those that may also influence the outcome.

It is essential that we carefully follow analytical precepts to ensure that we have made a strong causal argument. However, the problem with empirical data analysis is that we can never fully establish causality in our studies. As a consequence, our findings are always contingent, and we must be careful in our writing and discussion about our research not to claim to have proven something.

CONTEXT AND DESCRIPTIVE ANALYSIS

Another limitation when we are studying particular cases or even when conducting large-sample quantitative analysis based on sampling is context. **Context** simply refers to the specific circumstances in which the events or phenomena of interest occur. Although we are interested in generalizability, and our data are increasingly generalizable with greater numbers of cases, it is nonetheless a fact that no situation can ever be replicated exactly—we cannot go back in time, nor can two bodies occupy one space. Thus truly understanding a phenomenon means understanding as much as possible about the context in which it occurs.

To understand context, we use archival information, interviews, and sometimes observation to provide information about the history of an issue or a group of people, the economy, the government, the major concerns of those people, any crises that may have occurred, resources available, and challenges. We look at both actors and institutions and the details of the environment in which phenomena occur to better understand how and why issues arise and why they are important. We also look for factors or dimensions of that environment that may be unique to that situation and thus limit our ability to generalize.

Sometimes we use context in our analysis for tracing processes. A key concept here is that of path dependence. **Path dependence** is a sequence of events in which a decision to undertake a particular action leads to additional similar actions. The natural consequence is that actors (individuals, communities, organizations) proceed down a particular "path," because staying on that course becomes increasingly cost-effective with every step, and leaving the course (or path) will impose additional costs. The longer one continues to pursue a particular path or course of action, that path becomes less and less flexible because the costs of starting over are so high. People who study path dependence note that in the long run, "staying the course" can itself be inefficient.

The classic example of path dependence is the QWERTY touch-typing keyboard, which was developed because early typewriters used keys that would jam when letters that are frequently typed together were situated next to each other. The QWERTY keyboard arranged letters to minimize these jams, thus increasing how quickly one could type. We still use the QWERTY keyboard because it is cheaper for manufacturers to maintain the older design and because typists are taught to touch-type with this particular arrangement in mind, in turn passing this information on to students learning to type. However, there is no longer a real logic to this arrangement, and several other arrangements of keys have emerged that increase the rate at which we can type. (For more information, see Arthur 1989 or David 1985.)

When path-dependent processes are in place, it is difficult for researchers to tease out cause from effect, particularly in politics, because of **recursive enactment**, or the process by which maintaining the path is self-reinforcing (for a clear and concise discussion, see Institute for Community Peace 2014). Our understanding of history and our beliefs and ideology are confirmed, while disconfirming information is ignored or denied. The most difficult aspect of the path-dependent nature of knowledge production is how to deal with, or combat, these potentially destructive processes. The most practical solution for the researcher is to engage in the activities associated with minimizing bias, which include reflection about personal biases and systematic review of subject feedback.

QUALITATIVE ANALYSIS

The basic philosophy behind **qualitative analysis** is that the whole is greater than the sum of its parts. Thick description (including multiple sources) about few cases is preferred over thin understanding of a few variables over multiple cases. The hope is that the use of qualitative techniques will produce **grounded theory**, or theory developed out of understanding the empirical world.

The central goal of qualitative data analysis is to draw out patterns, themes, and trends that reflect the original data as closely as possible, in a process called **pattern matching**. Qualitative analysis depends largely on systematic review of written or spoken words. A single field study easily generates hundreds of pages of documents, interview and observation notes, pictures, and other data; ethnographic studies run into the thousands of pages. Taken as a whole, these data are the most comprehensive guide to the phenomena we have investigated. In order to understand the whole, we have to systematically interrogate the conceptual elements of what we have seen and heard and the relationships of these elements to one another. In order to do this, we have to first identify and categorize the conceptual elements that exist in the words we have collected.

We do this in one of two ways: (1) categorizing materials and coding them for themes or (2) reviewing materials for patterns in narratives, processes, or activities. We then take our analysis and summarize our findings by developing data displays that capture our results and by developing a fuller narrative with examples to explicate those data displays. When we code qualitative data, we use all of the information we have collected.

Coding is an iterative process of review and reflection. We review the data and reflect on the results in at least three stages. Each stage requires considerable time and attention to detail. In the first review stage, we make a list of all possible themes that emerge from the data. We then reflect on the themes to determine whether there is overlap or similarity and whether we can (or should) collapse categories or expand them. We conclude this stage with a list of themes and patterns. At this stage, we also prepare working definitions of the concepts that we believe have emerged.

In the second stage, we review the data a second time, keeping in mind the themes and patterns generated in the first stage. In the second stage, we make note of the frequency with which these themes appear and identify patterns in further detail. It is often useful to create draft graphics at this stage. These often appear in the form of preliminary lists, and sketches of conceptual relationships. Once again, we note additional themes if necessary, and determine whether some of the initial themes ought to be merged, divided, or arranged differently. We reflect again as before, and make necessary adjustments.

The third stage of review involves selecting data to use in the data displays and in thick description. In this round of review, we look for examples and quotes that illustrate the themes and patterns we have identified. It is entirely likely that we will reach this stage of the coding process and prepare draft data displays, then return to reexamine the coding strategy and the decisions we made.

In creating data displays, we generate a form of shorthand in order to communicate to other people the context and complex phenomena that we study. We write a narrative that captures the thick description around these displays. The displays can take different forms:

- Tables of data
- Listing of themes

- Illustrative statements
- Summaries of common phrases/themes
- Themes by groupings to identify trends

In writing up our analysis, we must clearly communicate our processes and assumptions. We also will have more confidence in our results if we have employed **triangulation**, which refers to the use of multiple approaches that include data sources, analysis techniques, researchers, or theories. The effect is that we arrive at a similar set of conclusions or explanations by multiple means, which gives us greater confidence in the findings. Finally, we can enhance the reliability of our findings if we have more than one researcher analyzing the material and both researchers produce identical results; this is called **inter-coder** or **inter-rater reliability**. If reliability is a concern, consideration should be given in advance to plan for data collection by multiple researchers who will code the data together.

As an example of the coding process, in the national program evaluation, some of the questions we asked focused on identifying factors that influenced the success of faith- and community-based organizations providing domestic violence victim services, and whether the strengths and struggles of faith-based organizations were different from those of secular nonprofit organizations. We conducted an eight-case comparative case study with four faith-based and four community-based organizations, including site visits, document reviews, interviews, and focus groups. To answer these questions, we engaged in a three-step coding of all the data collection materials, including the notes from observations in the site visits and from the interviews. From these, we developed the following list of emergent themes:

1. Community partners are a key to success.
2. Institutional and systemic factors may mitigate or enhance success.
3. Race and ethnicity issues may mitigate or enhance success.
4. Faith in God was seen to enhance success by representatives of both types of organizations.

In the case of the statewide needs assessment, from our site visits we observed differences in the facilities that were open to all as compared to those that charged a fee. We reviewed our interview notes and site visit notes to explore this further. One theme that emerged was related to the partnerships that site

Figure 6.1
Qualitative Data Display Illustration: Discussion of Partners in Statewide Needs Assessment

	Fee-for-Service Center A	Fee-for-Service Center B	Fee-for-Service Center C	Open-Access Community Center D	Open-Access Community Center E	Open-Access Community Center F
Volunteers		Mentioned 1–2 times	Mentioned 1–2 times	Mentioned 5+ times	Mentioned 3–4 times	
Business Partners	Mentioned 3–4 times	Mentioned 1–2 times	Mentioned 5+ times	Mentioned 3–4 times	Mentioned 3–4 times	Mentioned 1–2 times
Government			Mentioned 1–2 times	Mentioned 5+ times	Mentioned 1–2 times	Mentioned 1–2 times
Foundations		Mentioned 1–2 times		Mentioned 1–2 times	Mentioned 1–2 times	Mentioned 1–2 times
Nonprofits	Mentioned 1–2 times			Mentioned 1–2 times	Mentioned 3–4 times	Mentioned 3–4 times
Faith Community	Mentioned 1–2 times		Mentioned 1–2 times	Mentioned 5+ times		Mentioned 5+ times
Other	Mentioned 3–4 times	Mentioned 1–2 times	Mentioned 3–4 times		Mentioned 3–4 times	Mentioned 1–2 times

directors mentioned to us. Figure 6.1 illustrates the data display that we created to depict the relationship between number of partners and whether the site was open to all. These types of displays present information in a powerful form. Here, the data display tells the story for us: open-access community centers mention more and different partners and mention partners more frequently. Such visual displays often spark additional discussion; for example, it is easy to imagine recommendations for program designs that could be made as a result of studying this particular display.

QUANTITATIVE ANALYSIS

The point of **quantitative analysis** is to determine whether and what kind of relationships exist among variables. When we use quantitative data from a sample, we attempt to infer parameters of an unknown population from the known sample. The first step in this process is to reduce the qualities of social phenomena to numbers by coding these qualities. Once we have data in numeric form in a dataset, we then choose the most appropriate statistical test or tests, analyze the data, and interpret meaning from our results.

We begin with **univariate** statistics (also known as **descriptive statistics**) to understand the distributive properties of a single variable. We then identify our dependent variable (denoted with the capital letter Y), which is the variable that we are trying to understand, and analyze Y in conjunction with an independent variable (denoted with the capital letter X), which is the variable thought to cause changes in Y. We use **bivariate statistics** to determine the effect of changes in the independent variable (X) on the variable of interest, the dependent variable (Y). Most important, we then analyze the simultaneous effect of multiple independent variables on the dependent variable in multivariate analysis, in order to control for the effects of spurious relationships.

In the sections that follow, we discuss coding, univariate or descriptive statistics, statistical significance, bivariate statistics, and multivariate statistics. We provide basic instructions for conducting univariate analysis, as these mathematical tools represent simple skills that all practitioners and students need to have. We then discuss statistical significance from a practical perspective, with a focus on what statistical significance is and why researchers care. We also provide a shorthand guide for reading the (often) dense data analysis tables that are commonly found in academic articles and government reports. For the bivariate and multivariate analyses, we provide a general guide to understanding the particular conditions under which statistical tests should be used and why.

Coding

The process of coding quantitative data means assigning a number to each level of measurement in each of the variables. For example, if we collect data on gender, we could assign a 1 to males and a 2 to females. We also create a **codebook**, or a record that includes the shorthand names we give our variables, the questions that produced them, and the corresponding possible categories for each variable. We focus in this part of the chapter on coding data that we collect ourselves. A later example illustrates the application of coding and creation of a codebook for secondary data. Quantitative coding is similar to qualitative coding in that both are iterative, as are all parts of the research process. However, the mechanics of quantitative coding are approached differently, as we describe here.

The first step in coding comes after we have finalized our data collection instruments. We assign each substantive element of our instruments (or variable) a shorthand variable name. We then assign numeric values for the variables that are closed-ended. From this, we begin to create a codebook, which is a listing of each variable name used in our database, the question behind that variable, and the rules to follow for entering the numeric values into the database.

For open-ended items, data are coded after they have been collected. Similar to the qualitative coding process, we read through all of the responses to each open-ended question and compile a list of categories that match the responses. We review the responses a second time by comparing them to the list of categories. In this review, we combine, expand, and/or rearrange categories as needed; it may also be necessary to rename categories or create new ones. Finally, we arrange the categories by topic and then assign them numeric values that serve as codes. The convention that we follow in numbering is to group by decades (groups of ten) using two-digit numbers and a new decade for each major code category; subcategories within each decade are reflected by a change at the unit level.

For example, imagine that we asked a class of one hundred students an open-ended question about the best part of the class. We might get answers that would include things like "the stories the professor told," "the extra study sessions," "the teacher was nice and helpful when I went to her office to ask questions," "the videos were good," "nothing," and so on. We might then come up with the following major categories: A/V equipment, extra help, professor, teaching assistant, none,

Figure 6.2
Illustration of Coding for Quantitative Analysis

Code	Course Substance	Code	Course Delivery	Code	Course Personality
01	Good/important topics	10	Good use of A/V	20	Engaged instructor
02	Quality examples	11	Interesting lectures	21	Knowledgeable instructor
03	Challenging material	12	Helpful overheads	22	Helpful instructor
04	New/different material	13		23	Helpful graduate teaching assistant

and so on. We next refine these categories, arrange them by topic, and assign numbers. For example, we could have major topic categories about the substance of the course, the delivery of the course, and the personalities involved in the course. In the example in Figure 6.2, these topics have been arranged into three groups according to concept; each concept is coded with numbers that begin with the same numeral. Here, we see the major topic categories of substance of the course (beginning with the decade labeled 0), delivery of the course (beginning with 1), and the personalities in the course (beginning with 2). Subcategories within each decade are reflected with changes at the unit level (01, 02, 03; 10, 11, 12; and so on).

As we enter data in the database, it is critical to always and exactly follow particular coding rules. When we have more than one coder, all people must be trained in the exact same manner as to how to interpret these rules. In addition, it is important to go back after data have been collected and to **clean** those data. Cleaning data means reviewing the data and correcting any substantive and typographical errors in entry or classification. In a typical cleaning, an independent individual (someone other than those who coded and entered the data) randomly selects cases and reviews the coding in the database to ensure that all of the data have been classified and entered correctly.

Levels of Measurement

We care about the level of measurement of variables because the way that data are measured determines the types of statistical tests that can be performed as well as those that cannot be used. Our coded variables can have one of four levels of measurement: nominal, ordinal, interval, and ratio.

Nominal variables are characterized by discrete categories that are not ordered or ranked. For example, gender is a nominal variable typically comprising two categories, male and female. Other examples of nominal variables include race, party identification, and so on.

Ordinal variables possess discrete categories that are ordered or ranked with respect to each other. Any variable that uses an ordered scale (typically 1–5 or 1–7) that ranges from worst to best (or vice versa) is an ordinal variable, as are variables that consist of a list of items ranked by preference.

Interval variables possess discrete categories, order, and also a fixed distance between categories, or a consistent form of measurement between the categories. Examples of interval variables include temperature, age, and intelligence test results (IQ).

Ratio variables consist of discrete categories ordered with fixed distance between categories, and a fixed 0. Examples of this type of variable include time, weight, length, areas, and the like.

Commonly we collapse interval and ratio variables into one category, frequently referred to as **scale variables**.

Descriptive Statistics

One of the first steps in univariate analysis is to create a frequency distribution. The frequency distribution displays the different categories of a variable and the number (and, in some cases, percentage) of cases that are observed in each category. For example, in the election administration case study, we could examine the relative number of states that participated fully in the federal program to certify voting equipment versus the other options. Table 6.1 illustrates the resulting frequency distribution of this categorical variable.

Take note of a few standard features on this table. The number of units of observation are included in the lower left. We differentiate between the population size (using N) and the sample size (using n). This study examines states as well as the District of Columbia, which generates a total of 51 units of analysis. These units represent the population (there are no other states that could be added to this group); thus the designation is N. The percentage of observations that fall into each category are listed next to the category, accompanied by the raw figure in parentheses. These percentages are calculated simply by

Table 6.1
Frequency Distribution Example: State Requirements for Certification of Election Equipment

State Requirements for Certification	Percentage (Number of States)
Requires federal certification	31.4 (16)
Requires testing by federally accredited lab	19.6 (10)
Requires testing to federal standards	25.5 (13)
Does not mention federal requirements	23.5 (12)

$N = 51$
Source: Adapted from data presented in Hale and Brown (2013).

dividing the number of observations from each category by the total sample or population size. For example, the first category we present is "Requires federal certification." To calculate this figure, we divide the number of cases that fall into this category (16) by the number of states (51) to obtain 31.4 percent. We can also present the same information as a bar chart, which is shown in Figure 6.3.

With typical computer software, it is also possible to generate other forms of display; the table and bar chart are the most common approaches used in academic presentations, journal articles, and books.

Measures of Central Tendency   Another key dimension of every variable is the **measure of central tendency**, which is a measure of the most common value of the variable. We commonly think of this most common value as the "average" value. We can measure central tendency or average in several ways. Which average we use will depend on the level of measurement of the variable.

For nominal data, we look for the **mode**, or the category with the most observations in it. For example, we may have collected output data from a program that provides training on enhancing "soft skills" for unemployed people seeking work. Our output data include a count of how many people attend each class, as well as descriptions of each of those people, including gender and race/ethnicity. We see from the data that 75 separate people attended these courses, including 37 women and 38 men. The modal category for gender is males. Among these 75 people, 28 indicated that they are white, 11 nonwhite Hispanic/Latino,

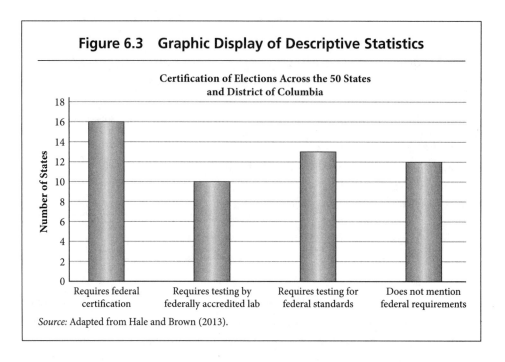

Figure 6.3   Graphic Display of Descriptive Statistics

Certification of Elections Across the 50 States
and District of Columbia

Source: Adapted from Hale and Brown (2013).

31 African American, 5 Asian/Pacific Islander, 5 American Indian, and 4 Other, which sum to more than 75 given multiple selections by respondents. The modal category for race and ethnicity in this case is African American. If there were equal numbers of whites and African Americans (for example, 30 in each category), the variable would be referred to as **bimodal**, meaning that it has two modes.

The second measure of central tendency is the **median**, which is simply the value of the middle case in the distribution. We use the median if we have ordinal data. We also use the median if we have scale data with **extreme outliers**, meaning data that are significantly out of the range of most of the other data and therefore distort the measure of central tendency when determined by calculation through other available methods. For example, when finding or reporting the average value for income and housing prices, the convention is to use the median, as these variables often have large outliers.

We calculate the median in one of two ways. If there are only a few data points, we arrange them in order from lowest to highest and take the middle value. For example, we can examine a set of observations that contains the following values:

4, 7, 8, 2, 1, 1, 6, 5, 9

We arrange these from lowest to highest to find the middle observation, or the median:

1, 1, 2, 4, 5, 6, 7, 8, 9

In this case the median is 5. If we have an even number of cases, we add the middle two values and divide by 2. To illustrate using the example above, we remove the first observation to create a set with an even number of observations:

7, 8, 2, 1, 1, 6, 5, 9

We arrange these from lowest to highest to find the middle observation, or the median:

1, 1, 2, 5, 6, 7, 8, 9

In this case, our sample size is eight, so we take the middle two observations, here 4 and 5, add them and divide by 2 to arrive at the median:

$$(4 + 5)/2 = 9/2 = 4.5$$

In this case, the median is 4.5.

If there are too many observations to arrange them sequentially by hand, we use computer software (for example, Excel or SPSS) to identify the observation at the 50th percentile, which is also the median value. To illustrate using the example here, we could survey each of the seventy-five students in the soft skills employment training class about how useful the class was. This survey included a question about how useful the information was, and the survey allowed for a response on a 7-point Likert scale where $1 =$ not at all useful and $7 =$ extremely useful. Typical statistical software will generate percentile values; here, the value at 50 percent is 6, meaning that the median is 6. This also indicates that a majority of students found the course to be very useful.

The third measure of central tendency is used for interval and ratio data (or scale data) without extreme outliers; this is the **mean**, or what is most typically referred to as the average. The mean is the sum of the observations divided by the total number of observations, and is denoted with μ for the population and $\bar{X}$ for the sample. The formula for calculating a mean is:

$$\bar{X} = \sum_{i=1}^{n} X \frac{1}{n}$$

In the mean equation, $\sum$ is referred to as the summation operator. $\sum X$ indicates that we add up the values for all of the observations for some variable X; $i = 1$ indicates that we start adding at the first observation; n over the summation operator indicates that we stop adding at the last observation, and the n in the denominator indicates that we divide the sum by the sample size.

For example, if we continue with the data shown earlier:

$$4, 7, 8, 2, 1, 1, 6, 5, 9$$

1. We add them together: $4 + 7 + 8 + 2 + 1 + 1 + 6 + 5 + 9 = 43$

2. Then we determine the value of n (count up the number of observations)

3. Then we divide the sum by n, or $43/9 = 4.78$

In the example of the soft skills class, imagine that we also had participants take a test at the start of the class measuring their awareness of the competencies associated with soft skills training, including fifty questions about (1) time management; (2) professionalism (things like proper dress, work ethic, attitude, and giving and accepting constructive criticism); (3) communication skills (including workplace-appropriate language, answering the phone, email etiquette); and (4) conflict resolution. We could score the test to determine how many of the questions the participants answered correctly and then calculate the percentage of questions answered correctly by dividing the number of correct answers by the total number of questions. To calculate the mean, or average, of correct answers of course participants prior to taking the soft skills class, we would sum these scores (which add to 4,885) and divide by the number of people who went through the training program, or 75. The mean score from our pretest is 65.

Measures of Dispersion   Measures of central tendency give us information about the most typical values of our observations; however, this information is not particularly useful without also understanding the distribution (or spread) of the data across the range of values. Thus the next step we consider in univariate analysis is **measures of dispersion**, or how our data are distributed.

If we have nominal data, we use the variation ratio (v), where

$$v = 1 - (n \text{ of modal category})/n$$

For example, in the election administration analysis, we constructed a dataset with $N = 51$ states and a variable with four categories. Across those states, 16 required federal certification, 10 required testing by a federally accredited lab, 13 required testing to federal standards, and 12 did not mention federal requirements. Here, the modal category is states that require federal certification, with 16 data points. We calculate the variation ratio as

$$v = 1 - (16/51) = 1 - .314 = .686$$

If all the cases fall into the modal category, then the v score is 0. The logic of this process is that the closer the mode approaches 0, the less variation occurs, and the more representative the mode is of all cases in the distribution. In this example, the largest category is that of states which require federal certification; however, this does not suggest that most or even half of the states are included in that same group.

With ordinal and scale data, the first measurement that we examine is the **range**, sometimes denoted with a capital R. The range is the absolute value (denoted with $|X|$) of the distance between the largest and smallest observations, and essentially tells us how much dispersion (spread, or room) there is around the mean. When the range is tight around the mean, this indicates that the calculated average gives us a lot of information about the variable. To calculate the range, we take the absolute value of this distance. Continuing with the data we've been using:

$$4, 7, 8, 2, 1, 1, 6, 5, 9$$

the range is $|9 - 1| = 8$.

The next step is to calculate the **standard deviation** from the **variance**. We do this because it tells us how typical our mean is for the data we have. The smaller the spread (or the tighter the range), the more representative the mean becomes. We denote the standard deviation and variance as:

σ^2 population variance

σ population standard deviation

s^2 sample variance

s sample standard deviation

The formula for standard deviation is:

$$s = \sqrt{\frac{\sum (X_i - \bar{X})^2}{n - 1}}$$

The steps are simple. First we calculate the variance, sometimes denoted as s^2, and then take the square root of that for the standard deviation. To calculate the variance, we determine the distance of each observation from the mean, square it and then add the values together, then divide by the sample size minus 1. When calculating this by hand, it is easiest to put together a calculation matrix such as the illustration in Table 6.2.

$$s^2 = (.64 + 4.84 + 10.24 + 7.84 + 14.44 + 14.44 + 1.44 + .04$$
$$+ 17.64)/8 = 71.56/8 = 8.945$$
$$s = 2.99$$

To review, our measures of central tendency and dispersion depend on the level of measurement of the variables. Table 6.3 displays the measures of central tendency and dispersion associated with each level of measurement.

Statistical Significance

Remember that the idea behind inferential statistics is that we are inferring information about a population from sample data. It is possible that we see a mathematical relationship in the sample data that would not be present in the population, and thus we distinguish between relationships that are **statistically significant** and those that are not. Statistical significance means that the

Table 6.2
Illustration of Calculation Matrix

X	Values	$(X_i - \bar{X})$	$(X_i - \bar{X})^2$
X_1	4	−.8	.64
X_2	7	2.2	4.84
X_3	8	3.2	10.24
X_4	2	−2.8	7.84
X_5	1	−3.8	14.44
X_6	1	−3.8	14.44
X_7	6	1.2	1.44
X_8	5	.2	.04
X_9	9	4.2	17.64

Table 6.3
Measures of Central Tendency and Dispersion
by Level of Measurement

Level of Measurement of Variable	Measure of Central Tendency	Measure of Dispersion
Nominal	Mode	Variation ratio (v)
Ordinal	Median	Mean absolute deviation
Interval/Ratio	Mean	Variance, standard deviation, coefficient of variation

relationships are strong enough that we believe that we can make an inference from the sample to the population. Note that the techniques we use to statistically analyze our data only apply if we have a random sample. If we have a biased sample, we cannot assume that the relationships we observe from the sample will be present in the population.

To determine statistical significance, we examine the strength of the relationship between the variables. This is dependent in part on sample size. Thus a common shorthand for understanding what makes a good sample size is that the larger the sample size, the stronger the relationship and our ability to make inferences.

If a relationship is statistically significant, we have confidence that what we see in the sample will also be true for the population. We express our confidence in terms of **levels of significance** or **confidence levels**; these are also understood as levels of certainty about whether what is true for the sample is also true for the population. We choose the confidence levels for analysis; typical choices that researchers make are to set the confidence levels at 99 percent, 95 percent, or, at the lowest, 90 percent. So when we say that a relationship we observe is statistically significant at 99 percent confidence, we are saying that if we took 100 repeated samples from the population, we would find the same relationship 99 times out of 100.

We start by identifying a specific hypothesis of no relationship between the two variables, referred to as the **null hypothesis**. We may choose to specify an **alternative hypothesis**, which can come in the form of a statement that there is a relationship between two variables, and we may also specify that one variable will be larger than another, called a **directional hypothesis**. We then calculate the test statistic to determine whether the relationship is significant or not.

Through our statistical analysis, we determine whether the relationship we are seeing in the sample is mathematically strong enough for us to believe that it also exists in the population—this is also sometimes referred to as the **probability**. If it is significant, we can draw conclusions about the relationships we see in the sample. If it is not significant, we conclude that there is no discernible relationship between the independent and the dependent variable.

When looking at computer output or a data table in a journal article, we want to differentiate the variables that are significant from the ones that are not. As a shorthand, we look at two things. For output from statistical analyses, we look at something called a p-value or significance level. In articles and data tables, we usually look for the coefficients associated with variables that are starred or in italics or bold. A **coefficient** is the estimated effect that an independent variable has on the dependent variable. The p-values, or probabilities we look for are

.10 (the weakest level of significance that is typically acceptable)

.05

.01

.001 (the strongest level of significance)

If the p-value associated with our coefficient for each variable is lower than one of these levels, we state that there is statistical significance. The smaller the p-value, the greater certainty we have about the relationship. Alternatively, we can also look for t- or z-scores on computer output. These scores are critical values associated with significance levels. The score that is used depends on the sample size of the data. When a sample has fewer than 120 observations, we use t-scores (also known as "student's t"). If the sample size exceeds 120, we use z-scores. The values associated with t-scores for significance vary depending on how many observations are in the data. In contrast, z-scores are actually standardized scores with a mean of 0 and a standard deviation of 1; this standardization facilitates comparison across variables. The scores are fixed values that are equated with specific p-values. Larger z-score values indicate higher levels of significance, but the specific values vary based on sample size. Tables that present z-score values in relationship to probabilities can be found in many excellent reference sources, and we refer readers to those for further information if needed.

A final note in our general discussion of statistical significance: when we analyze relationships between variables, the default assumption is that we do not have information about the direction of the relationship (positive or negative). This default assumption is reflected in what is known as a two-tailed test, which does not provide information about direction but sets a higher threshold for confirming statistical significance in comparison to tests that do. In contrast, it is possible to use statistical tests that are based on our suppositions about the direction of the relationships we are examining. In these cases, we use so-called one-tailed tests. One-tailed tests of statistical significance provide information about direction, but at the expense of accuracy. This means that we are setting a lower threshold for determining a statistically significant relationship, thus increasing the chances that we will make a Type I error.

Bivariate Statistics

After we have described a single variable, the next step is to look at whether two theoretically related variables have a statistically significant relationship between them. The type of test we use to determine this depends on the level of measurement of the variables. A shorthand reference tool for determining the most appropriate test is illustrated in Table 6.4, which lists bivariate tests by combinations of dependent and independent variables at different levels of measurement.

Table 6.4
Bivariate Tests by Level of Measurement

Level of Measurement of Dependent Variable	Level of Measurement of Independent Variable	Most Appropriate Test
Nominal	Nominal	Chi-square with extensions
Ordinal	Ordinal	Chi-square with extensions
Scale	Scale	Pairwise correlation
Scale	Nominal, 2 categories	t-test
Scale	Nominal, more than 2 categories	ANOVA
Scale	Ordinal	Pairwise correlation

Cross-Tabulation   In the situation in which two variables are nominal or ordinal, we want to know if the relationship between them is more than random. To do this, we calculate a **chi-square statistic**. As a first step, we produce a cross-tabulation, which is a tabular display of rows and columns where each row and column represents one category of one variable, and the display indicates the distribution of the observations among the cells. The purpose of the cross-tabulation (or crosstab) is to display the overlap between the categories of the two variables. The chi-square statistic is a mathematical representation of this overlap and follows something called a chi-squared distribution. The chi-square statistics are reported as standard tables and organized according to **degrees of freedom** or how much information is available to estimate parameters given how many parameters are being estimated, which are defined as

$$\text{d.f.} = (\#\text{ of rows} - 1)(\#\text{ of columns} - 1)$$

If the computed chi-square statistic is larger than the **critical value** from the chi-squared table, then there is a relationship between the variables, and the null hypothesis is rejected. Symbolically:

$$H_0: \pi_{ij} = \pi_i \pi_j$$

$$\chi^2 = \sum\sum \frac{(0 - E)^2}{E}, \text{ where}$$

$\sum\sum$ = sum over the entire table; O = observed values; and E = expected values.

After we have determined that there is a statistically significant relationship between the two variables, we want to know the strength of that relationship. To determine that, we perform something called a **nonparametric test**, or a test that is conducted when there are no assumptions made about the distribution of the population data. There are a variety of these depending on (1) whether variables are nominal or ordinal and (2) if nominal, how many categories are used to constitute the variables.

Frequently used nominal-level tests consist of:

Phi (ϕ). The most direct measure of association, or strength of relationship between two variables, for nominal data is the phi coefficient; ϕ is bounded between 0 and 1. When ϕ is equal to 0, that means there is no mathematical relationship between the two variables. If the two variables are perfectly related, then $\phi = 1$. However, there is one limitation to this measure: we can only use ϕ for 2×2 tables, meaning that each variable only has two possible answer categories.

Cramer's V. We can use the Cramer's V statistic for nominal data with any number of rows and columns. The measure it gives us is bounded by 0 and 1. If V is close to 1, this means that by knowing the values of one variable, we can guess closely what the values of the other variables are likely to be. Otherwise put, the relationship between the variables is strong. A Cramer's V value of 0 means that the variables are not related.

Lambda (λ). This bivariate test, lambda, is not based on a chi-square distribution, but can be used to look at the relationship between two nominal variables. Lambda is an **asymmetric measure**, meaning that the test requires that we identify which variable is dependent and which variable is independent in advance of the calculation.

This means that we have to hypothesize which variable influences the other. Lambda is based on the logic of making a proportional reduction of error under the situation in which we presume that we do not know the values of one of the two variables; here, we presume we know nothing about the values of the dependent variable. We examine the information from the modal category of the independent variable (about which we do have information), and from that make guesses about the values of the observations of the dependent variable. We then reverse the process and compare the errors made in the second step with those in the first step.

Frequently used ordinal-level tests consist of:

Gamma (γ). Gamma is based on comparing pairs of variable categories and seeing whether a case has the same rank on each. The values range from -1 to 1; a value of 0 means that there is no association between the variable categories. This allows us to examine the direction of relationships.

Kendall's tau (τ). This also ranges from -1 to 1, where 0 means no relationship. The test has several variations. In the tau-b test, the cross-tabulation table has to be square, meaning there are the same number of categories for the dependent and independent variables, but with the tau-c test it does not.

Sommer's d. With Sommer's d, it does not matter what the size of the table is. This measure is also asymmetric, so we have to identify the dependent and independent variables in advance of calculating the statistic. This measure is also bounded by −1 and 1 and is interpreted in the same way as the other ordinal bivariate tests.

In the example of the soft skills class, we might be interested in whether or not there is a relationship between gender and being employed three months after the end of the course. These are both nominal variables (with participants coded as either male or female, and employed or not employed). Our cross-tabulation of the dataset is shown in Table 6.5.

We then calculate a chi-square statistic to determine whether there is a systematic relationship between gender and employment status after the course ended, using a significance test of 95 percent confidence (or a *p*-value less than .05). From the computer-generated output, we see that the chi-square value is 0.122, with a *p*-value of .727. Because this *p*-value is greater than .05, we state that there is not a statistically significant relationship between gender and employment status. If the relationship were statistically significant, we would want to understand the strength of that relationship by looking at the results of one of the nonparametric tests for nominal-level data. Here, the Cramer's *V* value associated with the chi-square statistic in our example is 0.041, which is very close to 0; this reaffirms our knowledge that there is no relationship between the two variables.

t-tests   We conduct what are referred to as **difference of means** and **difference of proportions** tests when we are interested in the effect of some nominal variable with only two categories on an interval or ratio dependent variable. To calculate a difference of means, we compute:

$$\mu_1 - \mu_2 = \left(\bar{X}_1 - \bar{X}_2\right) \pm z_{crit}\left(\sqrt{\frac{s_1^2}{n_1} + \frac{s_2^2}{n_2}}\right)$$

Table 6.5
Illustration of Bivariate Crosstab Table for Soft Skills Class

	Employment		
Gender	No	Yes	Total
Male	20	16	36
Female	18	17	35
Total	38	33	71

To calculate a difference of proportions, we compute:

$$\pi_1 - \pi_2 = (p_1 - p_2) \pm z_{crit} \left(\sqrt{\frac{p_1(1-p_1)}{n_1} + \frac{p_2(1-p_2)}{n_2}} \right)$$

where p = sample proportions

For example, in the soft skills class, if we wanted to know whether there was a difference between men and women and the percentage of classes they attended, we would conduct this test. The null hypothesis (which we test) is that there is no difference in attendance between the groups; if the mathematical analysis shows a statistically significant difference, we reject the null hypothesis and conclude that we can infer from our sample data to the population that there is in fact a difference between genders in terms of class attendance. The computer-generated output indicated that the value of the statistic related to this (the t-test) is -1.179, with a p-value of .242. This is higher than .05, the critical value for a 90 percent two-tailed test, so we do not reject the null hypothesis, meaning that there is no statistically significant difference between males and females in how many classes were attended.

ANOVA   We conduct an **analysis of variance (ANOVA)** when we are interested in understanding the effects of a nominal independent variable with more than two categories on an interval or ratio dependent variable. The ANOVA is much like the t-test, but in this case our independent variable has more than two categories. We calculate ANOVA by establishing the overall mean (also known as the grand mean), the means for each group, and the deviations of the individual and group means. We use these to calculate how much variance in the dependent variable is explained by group membership; the more variance explained by group membership, the higher the related statistic, called an F-test. Each F-test has related statistical significance.

For example, we may want to determine whether people of different racial and ethnic backgrounds perform at different levels on the pretest. In this case, we would test the null hypothesis that white, black, Asian/Pacific Islanders, American Indians, and Hispanic/Latinos perform at the same level. If the results of the test show that there is a difference, we reject the null hypothesis and conclude that people of different racial and ethnic backgrounds perform at different levels. If the results of the test show that there is no difference, we do not reject the null hypothesis. When we run the test using statistical software, the F-test associated with ANOVA is .08, with a related p-value of .998. Using a 95 percent level of confidence and related alpha level of .05, we do not reject the null hypothesis.

Correlation Coefficient   Correlation is a measure of association between two scale variables; the **correlation coefficient** presents this relationship as a numerical value. This statistic is also known as Pearson's r, pairwise correlation, rho, or the Pearson product-moment correlation coefficient. It is denoted as

ρ for the population

r for the sample

The correlation coefficient is bounded by -1 and 1, and a value of 0 indicates that there is no relationship between the two variables, or independence.

Correlation is specifically a measure of linearity of association and is either positive or negative, depending on the direction of the relationship between the variables. If X increases by one unit and Y always increases by exactly k units, then $\rho = 1$; if X decreases by one unit and Y always increases by exactly k units, then $\rho = -1$; if there is no mathematical relationship between two variables X and Y, $\rho = 0$. The values between 0 and 1 indicate positive correlation; the values between 0 and -1 indicate negative correlation. Correlation values (even those close to 1 or -1) only indicate a mathematical relationship; correlation between two variables is only one of four required conditions to establish causality and alone is not sufficient to establish causality.

As an example, we may want to understand whether or not there is a relationship between the percentage of soft skills classes attended by program participants and their performance on the posttest. Our null hypothesis is that there is no relationship between these two variables. When we generate the correlation coefficient for these variables from our dataset through a computer program, we find a correlation coefficient value of .392, and a related p-value or significance level of .001. If we set our criteria for rejecting the null hypothesis at 99 percent confidence, meaning that our related alpha level is .01, and compare the two, we find that the significance level of the test statistic is lower than our alpha level and consequently reject the null hypothesis of no relationship. Note that in our example, $r = .392$, which is positive. We would interpret this to mean that as the number of classes attended by program participants increases, so does their knowledge about soft skills (measured by the posttest score). We do not have sufficient evidence, however, to make a causal claim about the relationship between attending these classes and knowledge of soft skills. Here, we have met three of the conditions required for making a causal claim: (1) correlation (positive and statistically significant); (2) time order (attending the classes happens before taking the posttest); and (3) logical causal or theoretical mechanism (it makes sense that the more information about soft skills that participants are exposed to, the more knowledge they will have about these skills). However, we have not yet met the fourth condition: nonspuriousness. This is why we turn to multivariate analysis.

Multivariate Statistics

Bivariate analysis is only the start of our examination of the determinants of variance in our dependent variable. As the soft skills example illustrates, one of the greatest limitations of bivariate analysis is our inability to establish a causal relationship between two variables because we cannot attend to the last condition of causality, nonspuriousness. These analyses are further limited because they cannot give us information about the magnitude of relationships that may exist. To address these limitations, we engage in multivariate analysis in which we examine the effects of multiple variables on one dependent variable at a time. The process we use is **multivariate analysis**, in which we examine variance in our dependent variable given the presence of changes in the key explanatory variable and other control variables.

There are a variety of methods available for conducting multivariate analysis. The key to determining the most appropriate method is the level of measurement of the dependent variable. As a shorthand, we use the scheme presented in Table 6.6. The table presents the most appropriate multivariate test for scale variables, nominal variables with two and with more than two categories, and ordinal variables.

Ordinary Least Squares Regression The simplest place to begin a discussion of multivariate analysis is with what is referred to as **ordinary least squares regression (OLS)**, the technique used when the dependent variable is either an interval or ratio variable. Conceptually, the OLS technique minimizes the sum of squared differences from a line we would draw between the independent and dependent variable on a two-dimensional graph, which generates what

Table 6.6
Multivariate Tests Based on Dependent Variable Measurement

Level of Measurement of the Dependent Variable	Most Appropriate Multivariate Analysis
Scale	Ordinary least squares regression
Nominal with 2 categories	Logistic regression
Nominal with > 2 categories	Multinomial logistic regression
Ordinal	Ordered logistic regression

is referred to as the best linear fit when predicting the value of the dependent variable.

OLS generates two critical pieces of information for each variable in an estimated model. First, it derives a probability for the estimated coefficient (or b), allowing us to determine whether or not the strength of the mathematical relationship in the sample data is strong enough to infer that it also exists in the population. Second, the estimated coefficient provides information about the effect of each variable on the dependent variable *ceteris paribus* (all else equal), meaning the effect when each of the other variables is held constant at 0. Thus we read the estimated coefficient for each independent variable as "a 1 unit increase in X will, on average, result in an increase of b units in Y."

OLS tells us about the relationships between a single dependent variable and independent variables that take the form:

$$\text{Population: } Y = \alpha + \beta X + \varepsilon$$
$$\text{Sample: } Y = \hat{\alpha} + \hat{\beta} X + \hat{\varepsilon}$$

OR

$$Y = a + bX + e, \text{ where}$$

Y is the dependent variable, or the variable for which we are trying to explain variance by the combination of independent variables in our model.

a is the constant, or intercept of the line, and is the value of Y if all of the independent variables in the model are 0. The value of a is found as follows:

$$a = \bar{Y} + b\bar{X}$$

X represents the independent variables; when we have more than one independent variable, we denote each variable with a new numbered subscript. The level of measurement of the independent variables does not have to be consistent. However, in order to use OLS, nominal variables must be transformed into **dummy variables** (variables constructed to have only two categories and used with one category omitted).

b values are called the slope coefficients or partial slope coefficients in the multivariate models. They indicate by how many units the dependent variable will increase if the independent variable increases by one unit.

$$b = \frac{\sum (X_i - \bar{X})(Y_i - \bar{Y})}{\sum (X_i - \bar{X})^2}$$

We calculate the standard error (SE) of *b*, which we need in order to calculate the statistical significance, as follows:

$$b = \frac{\hat{\sigma}}{\sqrt{\sum (X_i - \bar{X})^2}}$$

From this information, we can make inferences about *b*, and we can construct confidence intervals around *b*, where

$\beta = b \pm t/z\ SE$ with $n - 2$ degrees of freedom

And we calculate the *p*-value of *b*

$t = b/SE$

e is the error term. Computer-generated output does not provide a specific error term; however, conceptually the error is the unsystematic variance in the dependent variable. The key here is "unsystematic"—if there is a systematic element in the error term, we cannot have confidence in the actual effects of the independent variables in the model.

Another important element that comes from regression analysis is a measure of goodness of fit, noted as r^2, or *r*-square. This measures the amount of variance in the dependent variable explained by the combination of independent variables in the model. The r-square value is bounded by 0 and 1 where a statistic close to 0 means that the model explains very little about the variance in the dependent variable. In the case of a multivariate model (more than one independent variable), we use an adjusted r^2 measure, which accounts for overlap in explained variance among the independent variables. Another measure of goodness of fit which captures that model as a whole is the F-test. We can also calculate the F statistic to determine whether we can infer from the overall model to the population the way that we do with each variable, where

$$F = \frac{r^2 (N-2)}{1 - r^2}$$

Models that explain very little are termed **misspecified** or **underspecified**, meaning that we believe that the model does not include the correct concepts or enough concepts, respectively.

Going back to our soft skills example, we now want to revisit our understanding of the effects of having attended the soft skills class on performance on the posttest. We believe that other things might influence performance, such as educational level (the more education a participant has, the better either his or her study or test-taking skills may be) and possibly even length of unemployment (as a proxy for a decline in soft skills that the participant may have experienced after leaving the workforce). The results of the multivariate regression analysis are shown in Table 6.7.

Parsing out the components of this table, we pay careful attention to the following. First, though 75 people were enrolled across the four courses, only 69 are included in the final regression analysis (indicated on the table with n). This difference exists because complete data are not available for 6 participants. These participants either did not provide complete demographic information or did not complete both the pre- and posttest. When information about any unit of analysis is missing from the dataset, the associated observations are dropped completely from the multivariate analysis. Second, two of the three variables are significant at 95 percent confidence—percentage of classes attended and participant's educational attainment. Both of these also have a positive relationship with the posttest.

The way we interpret the marginal effect of each of these variables, meaning the effect that each variable has as compared with the others, is that a 1 percent increase in class attendance translates into a .194 increase in posttest performance. Because there were ten classes, for each extra class attended, the

Table 6.7
Relationship Between Soft Skills Course Participant Background and Course Attendance to Posttest Performance

		Results from Regression Analysis	
Variable	Variable Description	B	Significance/ p-value
Percentage of classes attended	Scale variable with possible responses: 0–100% of 10 possible classes	.194 (.055)	.001
Participant's educational attainment	Ordinal variable with possible responses 0–8, with 0 as no education and 8 as a graduate degree	2.807 (.832)	.001
Participant's length of unemployment	Scale variable measure in months unemployed	−.216 (.160)	.181
Constant		60.922 (5.272)	.000

$r^2 = .255$
$n = 69$
Note: Standard errors are in parentheses () next to their associated coefficients.

final grade on the posttest will go up by about 2 points, meaning that going from zero to ten classes would increase the posttest score by almost 20 points. Educational attainment is measured on an 8-point ordinal scale, and each level increase is related to a 2.8-point increase in the posttest score, meaning that zero to eight changes in educational level would be related to about 22 points change, meaning that the marginal impact of prior education is slightly greater than attending classes alone. Third, we interpret the constant as what the average score on the posttest is if all of the explanatory variables are set at 0. Thus a person who attended no classes, has no educational attainment, and has not been unemployed for any length of time would score approximately 61 percent on the posttest. Fourth, the r-square value is .255, meaning that the variables included in our model explain approximately 26 percent of the variance in the posttest scores among program participants.

OLS is based on several assumptions that are taken up in many excellent books, but four of these assumptions are critical to understand (see, for example, Gujarati 1998). First, we need to have a random sample; without meeting this condition, we may introduce systematic bias into our findings and consequently make inferences about the population from the sample that are untrue. Second, the relationship between the variables must be linear; nonlinear mathematical relationships between the dependent and independent variables are not revealed by this method. Third, the dependent variable has to be measured at the scale, interval, or ratio level. Fourth, we cannot have strong collinearity among our independent variables.

Strong **collinearity** (also termed **multicollinearity**) occurs when there is significant overlap between independent variables; this overlap means that there is also overlap in the way that the independent variables associate with the dependent variable. The result is that it is less likely that we can attribute significance to one variable or another, essentially rendering meaningless the value of multivariate analysis. An example of this overlap is found in the concepts of educational attainment and income; higher levels of one are strongly associated with higher levels of the other. If both concepts are included in the same model, it is difficult to attribute an effect to one concept or the other.

When the correlations between two or more variables are high enough, the values of the coefficients are affected, and they become inaccurate in two ways: (1) estimated coefficients that should be significant may not be, and vice versa; and, in extreme cases, (2) the signs of the coefficients may change. For example, imagine we decide that pretest score on the soft skills test will be a good predictor of posttest score (which it is) and we add that variable into the model we estimated earlier. The problem with adding this variable to the mix is that it is highly collinear with other variables in the analysis and alters the estimated coefficients in such a way that we can no longer be sure of our findings.

Strong collinearity among independent variables is common and is often fueled in part by the use of dummy variables. A dummy variable takes the values 0 and 1 (something is one thing or the other, yes or no). For example, say we are interested in the effects of race on posttest performance in the soft skills program. If we create a series of dummy variables around a concept (white versus nonwhite, black versus nonblack, and so on), we have to eliminate one variable from our analysis; if we do not, we have in essence included every possible explanation for variance and introduced perfect collinearity among the variables.

There are myriad ways to detect and address multicollinearity. This is also true for other violations of the key regression assumptions. We recommend generating a correlation matrix as an automatic step in every multivariate analysis. We also strongly recommend that time and attention be devoted to conceptualizing relationships between variables and their operationalization; if concepts overlap in our common understanding of the world around us (as with education and income), it is likely that the measures we use will overlap as well. If we understand this at the outset, we will be prompted to look for the best and most specific measures of our concepts of interest so that our findings can represent the environment as closely as possible.

Regression with a Dummy Dependent Variable When our dependent variable is a dummy variable (0, 1), the data can be analyzed using either a **linear probability model (LPM)** or logistic regression (also referred to as logit). An LPM approach simply uses the OLS model with a dummy dependent variable, but this only works if all variables in the model are dummy variables. If this is not the case, we use **logistic regression**, the results of which are based on maximum likelihood estimation (as opposed to OLS, which is based on minimizing the squared distance of errors).

In short, logistic regression produces a measure of the likelihood that the results observed in our sample would actually occur in the population, and then develops confidence intervals around each of the estimates. The written model will look familiar; however, the interpretation of the coefficients is not the same—they are known as **odds ratios**.

$$\hat{Y} = \hat{\alpha} + \hat{\beta}_1 X_1 + \hat{\beta}_2 X_x = \hat{\varepsilon}$$

Because their interpretation is not immediately intuitive, we can simply "translate" them into predicted probabilities using the following formula:

$$\Pr(Y=1) = \frac{1}{1 + e^{-z}}, \text{ where}$$

$$z = \hat{\alpha} + \hat{\beta}_1 X_1 + \hat{\beta}_2 X_x + \hat{\varepsilon}$$

The value of z ranges from $-\infty$ to ∞, while the probability ranges from 0 to 1. By translating the logistic regression results into probabilities, we can make a prediction that a certain result will occur given different types of circumstantial assumptions.

Consider again our case of the soft skills training course. We may have data on whether or not participants received jobs. Our dependent variable may be coded as 1 if the participant gained employment and 0 if the participant did not. We might then model these possibilities with three variables: how many classes participants attended, length of unemployment, and gender. In this case, we find that length of unemployment is not significant, nor is gender, but the percentage of classes attended is a positive and significant predictor, which increases the probability of gaining employment after the course ends.

Regression with a Nominal Dependent Variable with More Than Two Categories When we have a nominal dependent variable with more than two categories, we utilize an analysis called multinomial logistic regression. This analysis yields a series of outputs in which each category of the dependent variable is set against all of the other categories combined as the method of examining the effects of the independent variables on the dependent variable. We generate predicted probabilities for the different possible effects of the range of the independent variables on the dependent variable, in a similar manner as for logistic regression.

Regression with an Ordinal Dependent Variable When we have an ordinal dependent variable, we use an approach called ordered logistic regression. A basic principle behind this approach is that the effect of the independent variables is the same across each level of the dependent variable. When an ordinal dependent variable has many categories, some analysts simply use OLS regression techniques because the interpretation of the coefficients is so much more straightforward.

Codebooks

Earlier in this chapter, we discussed coding for primary data, or data that we collect ourselves. Coding is also commonly used for secondary data, as illustrated in Figure 6.4. This illustration presents a portion of the codebook for the election administration and technology research project. All of the data in this portion of the codebook were published before our study began.

Most of the data sources are standard sources of secondary data, such as the U.S. Census Bureau, PEW Center on the States, the National Conference of State Legislatures, and state websites. Several of the sources are published scholarly works, including journal articles and books. It is typical to use secondary data to introduce demographics, political conditions, levels of need or demand, and institutional relationships into an analysis of public service issues.

Although the codebook is not presented in a decision-style format, it does illustrate at least two aspects of decision making that apply to our analyses. When we use secondary data, the data are arranged in fixed arrays that we are not usually able to alter or manipulate. These arrays limit our analyses, and also shape the way we think about particular concepts. Another aspect of decision making involves the selection of particular measures when operationalizing concepts. Here, political influence is represented by the political party of the governor; clearly, there are other measures of political influence. The decision to use this variable was grounded in the applied experience of election administrators; another alternative would have been to use political party measures that reflected legislative power. In the end, we chose a measure linked to the governor because in some states (about one-third), the state chief election officer is appointed either by the governor or by a group over which the governor has appointing authority. We balance this choice with the variable that measures whether the state chief election officer is selected by popular vote. Our selection of variables and measures is not necessarily correct or incorrect; it is up to us as researchers to justify our choice.

CASE APPLICATIONS OF QUALITATIVE AND QUANTITATIVE ANALYSIS

All of the studies highlighted throughout this text used either qualitative or quantitative analysis. When both forms of analysis are employed together, this is referred to as **mixed methods**. Typically we use mixed methods because we want to understand the characteristics of a phenomenon (so we use descriptive or univariate statistics to describe each of the variables), the relationships present in the phenomenon (so we use bivariate and multivariate analysis), and why these relationships exists (so we use either a combination of multivariate analysis with a well-developed theory and/or we include qualitative analysis). Tables 6.8 and 6.9 illustrate the qualitative analyses and quantitative analyses used in the case studies, respectively.

In the statewide needs assessment, for example, we needed to understand what resources were in existence, so we deployed a survey that would identify

Figure 6.4
Codebook Example for Election Administration and Technology Project

Variable	Variable—Full Name	Variable Description	Variable Coding
Region	Region of Country	Region of country based on U.S. Census Regions and Divisions	1 = Pacific (WA, OR, CA, AK, HI) 2 = Mountain (MT, ID, WY, NV, UT, CO, AZ, NM) 3 = West North Central (ND, SD, MN, IA, NE, KS, MO) 4 = East North Central (WI, MI, IL, IN, OH) 5 = Northeast (PA, NY, NJ, CT, RI, MA, VT, NH, ME) 6 = West South Central (TX, OK, AR, LA) 7 = East South Central (MS, AL, TN, KY) 8 = South Atlantic (WV, DE, MD, DC, VA, NC, SC, GA, FL)
IGRPlan	Intergovernmental Relationships in State HAVA Plan	Proportion of local officials on state HAVA planning committee Alvarez and Hall 2005	Ordered ranges 1 = 10–15% 2 = 15.1–20% 3 = 20.1–25% 4 = 25.1–30% 5 = 30.1–35% 6 = 35.1–40% 7 = 40.1–45% 8 = 45.1–50% 9 = 50.1–55% 10 = 55.1–60%
IGRVoteList	Intergovernmental Relationships in State Voter List Maintenance	Locus of intergovernmental responsibility for maintaining statewide voter registration system required by HAVA Alvarez and Hall 2005	1 = state responsibility 2 = shared state and local responsibility 3 = local responsibility

CEOPopElect	Chief Election Official–Popular Election	Is state chief election official elected by popular vote? State websites	1 = Yes 0 = No
PCGov	Party Control–Governor	Which party holds the governor's office? (from http://www.ncsl.org/?tabid=21321, accessed 12/2/11)	1 = Republican 2 = Democrat 3 = Other
PolCulture	Political Culture	State political culture Elazar 1966	1 = Traditional 2 = Moralistic 3 = Individualistic
DemoRaceB	Demographics–Race Black	Percentage of African Americans in state, 2010 (from http://quickfacts.census.gov /qfd/index.html, accessed 12/2/11)	Percentage
DemoRaceW	Demographics–Race White	Percentage of Whites in state, 2010 (from http://quickfacts.census.gov/qfd /index.html, accessed 12/2/11)	Percentage
DemoGSP	Demographics–GSP	Gross state product	Dollars in 1,000s
DemoIncome	Demographics–Income	Median household income, 2009 (from http://quickfacts.census.gov/qfd/index .html, accessed 12/2/11)	Median
GPPInfoPer	Government Performance Project–Information Performance	Government Performance Project Information Performance Grades for the states PEW Center on the States, 2008 (http://www.pewcenteronthestates .org/uploadedFiles/Information%20 Performance.pdf, accessed 1/23/12)	Index score 0 = 100

Table 6.8
Case Comparison of Use of Qualitative Analysis

	Community Garden	Statewide Needs Assessment	Election Administration and Technology	National Program Evaluation	Criminal Justice Policy Reform
What Was the Approach?	SWOT Community meetings Interviews Focus groups	Coding and pattern matching for facility site visits Coding, pattern matching, and descriptive statistics for interviews	Coded for major themes and pattern matching across level of election administrator	Coding and pattern matching for site visits Coding, pattern matching, and descriptive statistics for interviews	Coding and pattern matching for interviews, open-ended survey questions; case studies; and archival document analysis
Why Was This Approach Selected?	Needed to understand community resources and needs	Needed to determine differences across facility types and types of individuals	Needed to determine whether there were common experiences and views	Needed to determine differences and similarities across types of organizations	Needed to define and operationalize concepts Needed to understand relationships
What Were the Strengths and Weaknesses of This Approach?	(+) Results were important to the community (–) There was limited participation of certain groups	(+) For the facilities, this was a simple but elegant approach to analysis (–) For the individuals, number of responses (60+) made the coding time consuming	(+) Results illuminated quantitative findings (–) Small *n* of interviews meant we couldn't pick up differences across state type	(+) Results were used to establish validity of survey instrument (+) Results helped us understand surprising survey results	(+) Results were used to triangulate quantitative findings and establish context (–) The process was time intensive

Table 6.9

Case Comparison of Use of Quantitative Analysis

	Community Garden	Statewide Needs Assessment	Election Administration and Technology	National Program Evaluation	Criminal Justice Policy Reform
What Was the Approach?	—	Descriptive and bivariate statistics	Descriptive, bivariate, and multivariate analysis	Descriptive and bivariate statistics	Descriptive, bivariate, and multivariate analysis
Specific Bivariate and Multivariate Tests	—	Chi-square Pairwise correlation	OLS, logistic and ordered logistic regression	t-tests, chi-square, pairwise correlation, ANOVA	OLS Time series
Why Was This Approach Selected?	—	Needed to understand whether there were patterns in activities and needs by region, wealth, population density, and type of organization	Attempted to understand state compliance choice while controlling for multiple possible causal factors	Needed to understand differences in capacity across organization types and over time	Needed to understand differences across the states over time
What Were the Strengths and Weaknesses of This Approach?	—	(+) We were able to establish simple relationships (−) We could not control for spuriousness	(+) We were able to control for multiple causal factors simultaneously (−) Use of proxy variables	(+) We were able to determine differences by type of organization and over time (−) We could not control for spuriousness	(+) We were able to control for multiple causal factors simultaneously (−) Use of proxy variables

resources from organizations, and described the findings using descriptive statistics. We also wanted to know what needs were present across the state, what types of women had these needs, and why the needs existed to begin with. To answer these questions, we engaged in in-depth interviews of women who were receiving services, coded those interviews, conducted bivariate statistical analyses to look at the relationship between demographic characteristics of the women and their needs, and then engaged in qualitative analysis to better understand why we were seeing the relationships that the interviews uncovered.

Although we did not set out to develop a theory of change in the statewide needs assessment, one began to evolve as we continued our analysis. Figure 6.5 illustrates the concepts that emerged from our review of current resources, needs, and program designs around the state. The policies and programs section of this illustration contain the best practices that we observed through our research.

This theory of change model can be the basis for developing policy recommendations to achieve the outcomes that seem likely given the intervention strategies that we saw in action. We did not proceed with multivariate analysis in our study; the theory of change model suggests relationships that might bear fruit if examined more closely using multivariate methods. We could design a new study with those variables and multivariate analysis in mind (see Chapter Seven for a discussion of next steps).

Contrast this to the election administration and technology case, in which we were interested in identifying causal relationships across the states and understanding which variables were actually related to state decisions as well as which were more important. In this case, we needed to use multivariate analysis. We operationalized our dependent variable as the state response to federal voting equipment testing guidelines (voluntary voting system guidelines, or VVSG), and coded state options based on state laws. The options were to adopt the federal standards, test in a federally accredited laboratory, adapt federal standards to meet state preferences, or opt out altogether. This variable can be thought of as either a nominal variable with four categories or potentially an ordinal variable. We therefore ran a series of analyses using both multinomial logit and ordinal logit. The results, in conjunction with the information gleaned from the key informant interviews, led us to conclude that in fact what we had were discrete categories with no order.

Figure 6.5
Proposed Theory of Change Model Developed from Statewide Needs Assessment Case

Current Resources	Needs	Suggested Policies and Programs	Potential Outcomes
Over 3,000 organizations in 67 counties across the state, providing:	**Transportation**	**Low-Resource Areas**	**Short term**

• Transportation (26.8%)	• Flexible and dependable driver
	  • Shopping
	  • Appointments
	  • Church
	  • Socializing
	• Maintenance of personal vehicle
		• Develop programs that
		  • Leverage existing resources
		  • Leverage in-kind resources
		  • Include passionate staff
		  • Attract volunteers
		• Develop policies that
		  • Include funding streams to encourage collaboration and mixed-use enterprises
		  • Focus on partnerships with transportation
		  • Provide funding for small, qualified, and dedicated staff
			• Increase interest in population needs
			• Develop plans to increase programs
			• Enhance partnerships and collaborations

	Housing Related		**Medium term**
• Homemaker services (25.9%) • Housing (11.7%)	• Affordable housing • Maintenance of personal home • Cleaning	**High-Resource Areas**	• Provide new and enhanced services to target population • Increase community awareness to target population and needs

	Food	• Develop programs that
		  • Leverage local fundraising expertise and partnerships with business
		  • Are attached to the strong tax base
		  • Include means-tested fee-for-service
		• Develop a government-sponsored RFP in areas without a program for planning
		  • Require local financial and leadership support
		  • Require government technical assistance
			Long term

• Food stamps (0.4%) • Nutritional/meal services (28.2%)	• Affordability • Shopping • Preparation		• Enhanced quality of life for target population • Enhanced cross-generational community engagement
	Medical Care		
• Medical care (28.5%) • Wellness (28.2%) • Mental health (3.4%) • Alzheimer support (1.5%) • Health insurance counseling (0.4%) • Prescription expense assistance (0.4%)	• Affordability • Prescription drugs • Interpretation and advocacy		
• Leisure/recreation (28.2%) • Education (28.3%)	**Entertainment**		

This latter finding is quite significant conceptually. Ordered categories would suggest a continuum of possible state responses to voluntary federal initiatives, ranging from no involvement with the federal program to complete adoption of all federal certification and testing program protocols. The lack of order suggests a different arrangement entirely. Instead, we found three discrete options including complete adoption, complete opting out, and adaptation to state conditions. This difference may serve as the basis for additional research about state-federal relationships. As with the statewide needs assessment, the end of our analysis provided a new basis for exploring additional questions; analysis in both cases illustrates the connections between the end of one research study and the seeds of ideas for future work.

In the case of the national program evaluation, we were first interested in comparisons between the grant-funded and nonfunded organizations, and then in comparisons across these organizations over time, including before the groups were funded by the federal government, at six months of funding, and at one year of funding. In this study, we described what we found using univariate analysis and compared across groups using *t*-tests and other bivariate analysis techniques. We also utilized the qualitative findings to help us build a context for our conclusions. During the second round of analysis, we found from the surveys a precipitous drop among the funded organizations in their evaluation capacity, so we utilized the qualitative portion of the study to determine why this had happened. We concluded that our pilot testing of the survey instrument had been flawed—in piloting, we had relied on a group of organization leaders who had more formal training in evaluation and measurement than the population did, and thus what we were measuring was not a drop in capacity but actually learning on the part of participants. That is, when they first completed the capacity survey, they had incorrectly answered the evaluation questions because they did not understand the full meaning of the technical terms that were used. In the time between the first and second round of the survey, they were exposed to this material and changed their responses in the second wave of the survey. Finally, we used the results from the qualitative portion of the study to validate the self-administered capacity survey instrument.

DECISION TREE

We end this chapter with a more global reflection on the issue of data analysis. The options for analyzing data are extensive and can be combined in any number of ways. It can be overwhelming to be faced with the array of possibilities. In Figure 6.6, we outline a systematic approach to data analysis. This approach allows the researcher to segment each aspect of a research project, whether the project is large or small.

The decision tree in Figure 6.6 serves many purposes in the applied research process. It is helpful to use this decision tree prior to beginning analysis, to distinguish between data that will be used for qualitative versus quantitative analysis. This particular decision tree also outlines the relationships between variables that may be measured with different forms of data. It is also useful to employ this decision tree during the research design phase when operationalizing variables and identifying levels of measurement. The decision tree also outlines links to the decision trees in previous chapters that reflect earlier stages of the research process.

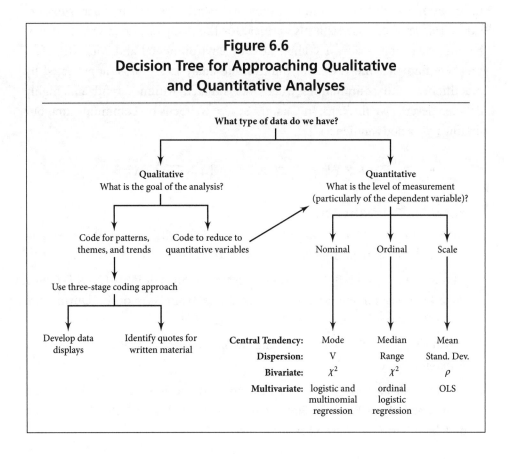

Figure 6.6
Decision Tree for Approaching Qualitative and Quantitative Analyses

CONCLUSION

In this chapter, we outlined the basic structure for analyzing the data we collect. The approaches that we discussed range from basic description to sophisticated multivariate tools. Every research project calls for a unique blend of description and analysis, and it is not possible to develop a standard approach. What is useful is to understand the range of tools that are available and to select the tools that best fit our research project constraints.

We offer the following comments with respect to analysis for the applied research audience, including community partners, public administrators, and nonprofit leaders. In our experience, consumers of the results of applied research projects are very interested in the descriptive aspect of data analysis, including descriptive statistics, the use of qualitative data, and a discussion of context, including historical development of the idea under consideration. In applied research, the audience is often interested in capturing and synthesizing this basic information to establish common ground as a starting point for further discussions. This level of analysis is also critical for the study of public service issues, because causation is always complicated by environmental and contextual factors. We find that the results of multivariate analysis are most appreciated by practitioners and communities when well situated within careful and highly detailed descriptive findings. In Chapter Seven, we focus on communicating our findings to various audiences.

CHAPTER SUPPORT MATERIALS

Chapter Six Relevant Articles

Arthur, Brian. 1989. "Competing Technologies, Increasing Returns, and Lock-in by Historical Events." *Economic Journal* 99:116–131.

Chung, Yiyoon, Julia B. Isaacs, and Timothy M. Smeeding. 2013. "Advancing Poverty Measurement and Policy: Evidence from Wisconsin During the Great Recession." *Social Service Review* 87:525–555.

David, Paul. 1985. "Clio and the Economics of QWERTY." *American Economic Review* 75:332–337.

Fording, Richard C., Sanford F. Schram, and Joe Soss. 2013. "Do Welfare Sanctions Help or Hurt the Poor? Estimating the Causal Effect of Sanctioning on Client Earnings." *Social Service Review* 87:641–676.

Ribar, David C., and Lauren A. Haldeman. 2013. "Changes in Meal Participation, Attendance, and Test Scores Associated with the Availability of Universal Free School Breakfasts." *Social Service Review* 87:354–385.

Chapter Six Discussion Questions

1. Why do we not use the range with nominal data?

2. What are the limitations of bivariate analyses generally? Which of the conditions of causality do these types of analysis violate? Given that, why do we bother with bivariate analysis?

3. In what ways could descriptive statistics be useful for nonprofit organizations? Bivariate analysis? Multivariate analysis?

4. What would happen if the unit of observation for two different variables in an analysis you are trying to conduct is not the same?

5. If your data collection efforts have low validity and reliability, what impact would this have on your quantitative data analysis calculations? On the conclusions you draw from the study?

6. What are the possible limitations of qualitative data analysis? What value does this approach add, and particularly for applied research?

Chapter Six Practice Assignments

1. Imagine you have surveyed seven random people about their income, gender, and the number of years they spent in school, and obtained the following information. For each of these variables, (a) determine the level of measurement; (b) identify the best measure of central tendency and calculate it; and (c) identify the best measure of dispersion and calculate it.

Observation	Gross Income	Gender	Years in School
x_1	$20,000	F	14
x_2	$35,000	M	16
x_3	$65,000	F	19
x_4	$12,000	M	9
x_5	$104,000	M	20
x_6	$45,000	F	18
x_7	$35,000	F	13

2. Calculate the mode, mean, median, variance, standard deviation, and range for each of the following two sets:

a. **3, 6, 2, 5, 4**

b. **1, 3, 1, 1, 5**

3. Imagine that you are interested in the effects of employee training programs on promotion over a several-year period. You collect data on the number of training hours an employee has and whether and how often he or she has been promoted over a five-year period. What is the level of measurement of these variables? What univariate and bivariate analyses would you conduct? Why? If you were going to collect demographic data to use as controls for understanding promotion in a multivariate analysis, which would you pick? Why? What would the level of measurement be for these variables?

4. You are conducting research for the nonprofit organization you work for, looking at all of the grant applications the organization has submitted, and you are trying to determine why some get funded and some do not. You find that your organization has submitted 120 applications over the past ten years. The variables on which you collect data to help you make this determination include the year the application was submitted, the amount of the grant, who wrote the grant, and the topic of the grant application. For each variable (dependent and independent), list what the level of measurement would be. Discuss what type of descriptive, bivariate, and multivariate analyses you would conduct and why.

5. Go to Figure 6.4 (Codebook Example for Election Administration and Technology Project). For each variable in the codebook, identify the level of measurement. Next, give a justification for your answer.

Chapter Six Linked Assignments

Throughout the text, we include a series of "linked assignments." These have been developed to walk the research methods student through the entirety of the research process by developing a research project that includes each phase of both applied and basic research.

In this linked assignment, you will analyze the data you collected in the linked assignment from either Chapter Four or Chapter Five. First, determine whether quantitative or qualitative analysis is the best approach to analyze the type of data you have. Explain which approach you take and why. Second, analyze the data. If you have qualitative data, use each of the three approaches (coding, patterns, and trends) and some form of data display to summarize your information. If you have quantitative data, develop a codebook, develop a database, perform descriptive analysis, and either perform bivariate analysis or discuss what tests could be used and why. Third, interpret your findings in light of your research question.

Chapter Six Link to Online Assignments

Two assignments follow. The first focuses on quantitative analysis, the second on qualitative analysis.

Project A   Using the soft skills class database (either in Excel or SPSS format) and the soft skills class codebook shown in Table 6.10, answer the following questions.

1. What is the level of measurement for each of the variables in the database?

2. For each variable, (a) solve for the mean, median, and mode; (b) articulate which is the most appropriate measure of central tendency and why; and (c) identify the appropriate measure of dispersion and solve for it.

3. Imagine you are trying to understand whether there is a relationship between each of the demographic variables and whether or not the program participant had a job six months after completing the soft skills class. For each demographic variable, (a) identify the most appropriate bivariate test to use, and discuss why; (b) calculate the test statistic; and (c) put the findings into words.

4. Now imagine you are trying to understand whether there is a relationship between each of the demographic variables and the average number of hours participants work after completing the soft skills class. For each demographic variable, (a) identify the most appropriate bivariate test to use, and discuss why; (b) calculate the test statistic; and (c) put the findings into words.

5. Continue the analysis in point 4 by creating a multivariate analysis that includes (a) any theoretically important or statistically significant demographic variables and (b) the percentage of classes attended and the posttest score. What do you conclude about the utility of the soft skills class for enhancing employability?

Table 6.10
Codebook for Soft Skills Class

Variable Name	Variable Description	Variable Coding
Participant#	Unique identifier for participants—random assignment	Scale variable
Gender	Participant's gender	1 = female
		0 = male
REWhite	Participant's race/ethnicity–white (multiple selections possible)	1 = White
		0 = other
REAfricanAmer	Participant's race/ethnicity–African American (multiple selections possible)	1 = African American
		0 = other
REAsianPI	Participant's race/ethnicity–Asian/Pacific Islander (multiple selections possible)	1 = Asian/Pacific Islander
		0 = other
REAmericanInd	Participant's race/ethnicity–American Indian (multiple selections possible)	1 = American Indian
		0 = other
REHispLatino	Participant's race/ethnicity–Hispanic/Latino (multiple selections possible)	1 = Hispanic/Latino
		0 = other
REOther	Participant's race/ethnicity–Other (multiple selections possible)	1 = Other
		0 = other
#Child<12	Number of participant's living children under the age of 12	Count
#Child12–18	Number of participant's living children ages 12–18	Count

Variable	Description	Codes
Education	Participant's level of educational attainment	1 = Some high school 2 = GED/equivalent 3 = High school diploma 4 = Some college 5 = Two-year/associate's degree 6 = BA/BS degree 7 = Some graduate/professional 8 = Graduate/professional degree
UnempLength	Length of participant's unemployment—measured monthly	Count
ClassesAttend	Percentage of soft skills training classes attended by participant (of 10 possible)	Percentage
PretestScore	Percentage of correct answers on the soft skills pretest (of 50 possible) taken at registration before course began	Percentage
PosttestScore	Percentage of correct answers on the soft skills posttest (of 50 possible) taken on the last day of classes	Percentage
Job3mos	Did participant have paid, regular employment 3 months after completing the soft skills course?	1 = yes 0 = no
Job6mos	Did participant have paid, regular employment 6 months after completing the soft skills course?	1 = yes 0 = no
Avehrs	For employed former participants, on average, how many hours of paid, regular work from employment do they complete in a given week?	Count
Course	In which course did participant enroll?	1 = Jan-Mar 2 = Apr-June 3 = July-Sept 4 = Oct-Dec

Project B Use primary data from the national program evaluation collected for one of the case study sites (Mountain Advocates) to answer this question: "What are the biggest barriers to running a domestic violence program in a rural area?"

1. Develop a list of major themes and show the stages of your work.

2. Develop a data display.

3. Write an "answer" to the question for this case using the themes, data display, and illustrative quotes.

4. Discuss whether other "answers" are possible given your approach to developing themes.

chapter SEVEN

Writing and Presentations

Writing and making research presentations for public administration and nonprofit organizations takes many different forms depending on the audience for the materials. In applied research, we write reports for others when we have examined their organizational or issue area needs, called **needs assessments**, or when we have examined their work processes or the efficacy of their efforts, called generically **funder reports**. We write to compete for the opportunity to study something and respond to a **request for proposals (RFP)** with a grant application. We also write for stakeholders in the form of **annual reports** that summarize what an organization has done and accomplished in a given year, **Form 990s**, and **public relations releases** in which we briefly highlight an issue or activity important to an organization. We also may choose to write about our studies for an academic audience through **journal articles** or **university press books** in which we enter into a community of discourse about theories, methods, and findings. Finally, students may be interested in writing **applied dissertations** in which, guided by academic advisers, they tackle real-world problems in pursuit of a PhD.

Each of these forms of writing has a different purpose and audience, and consequently the documents have different formats. We begin by addressing common considerations for all forms of writing, including general tips for writing. We offer hints and approaches for developing a productive writing process, for sharing information and obtaining constructive criticism, and for enhancing the readability and appeal of writing about applied research and generally. In the sections that follow this general discussion, we investigate the purpose, audience, and proper format for various types of writing, and the steps we take in the writing process.

GENERAL TIPS FOR WRITING

Effective writing is a critical component of the research process—without it we cannot expect to communicate our findings to others, and **communicability** is one of the basic principles of a quality research process (discussed in Chapter One). However, it is also the step in the research process with which many researchers struggle the most. These struggles result from several factors, including lack of planning, lack of familiarity with the process, and concerns about having others review our work.

It is critical to keep in mind that the writing process is **iterative**. We never construct a perfect, or even an adequate, written product the first time. Effective writing requires planning, implementation, and multiple rounds of review and revision. In the sections that follow, we provide some suggestions for creating an approach to writing that helps us address this component of the research process in a reasoned and objective way and address any self-consciousness we have.

A Productive Writing Process

We begin the writing process by establishing the type of product we are developing and the timeline for submission. We work backwards from any firm **deadlines** to develop a realistic timeline that includes time to develop and refine an outline, write a first draft of the full document, and then proceed through a minimum of three rounds of revisions. Whatever the actual amount of time in terms of workdays that we have to develop our written product, a general rule of thumb is to allot 5 percent of our writing time for planning and outlining, 50 percent of our writing time for writing the first draft, and 15 percent of our writing time for each subsequent round of revisions. It is important to note that this timeline does not account for other steps in the research process, such as developing literature reviews, creating a research design, and collecting and analyzing data; the time needed for these other aspects of the research process must be added in to arrive at the overall timeline for a finished product. Although each stage of writing is important, writing the first full draft is probably the most important stage because writing follows a path-dependent process: once that first draft is complete, we have invested so much time and thought into its construction that it is difficult to start over from scratch.

Studies have been conducted looking at the set of conditions that produce the most productive writers (see in particular Gray 2005). These studies share some common suggestions. First, productive writers make time to write steadily each day instead of engaging in writing marathons immediately before a deadline. Second, productive writers focus on one writing project at a time. Third, productive writers regularly share their drafts with other people.

In developing outlines, we start by following the general format of the type of writing in which we are engaged. Some professors encourage their students to first determine "what your contribution to knowledge is going to be and organize the paper accordingly" (Wolfinger 1993, 87). Another rule of thumb is to consider the iterative nature of the research process and that most of us learn a great deal through the act of reducing the research process to writing. What this means, we think, is that most writing will benefit from a thorough revision of the first draft. It is common that a first draft is highly descriptive and that the act of writing analyses and conclusions will spark new ideas about how to organize the work.

Feedback and (Constructive) Criticism

Reviewing and editing our writing is sometimes a painful process. We suggest subjecting most types of work to three major levels of review. First, we **self-edit** our work for readability and flow and then make changes. Second, we ask a close colleague to read and edit our work for comprehensiveness and appropriateness and make additional changes. Third, we reach out to a known senior colleague who is a **content expert** to read and comment on our work to ensure that we have carefully crafted our argument and conclusions.

The first type of review is often the easiest. We do not have to ask other people for their time, nor do we have to deal with their critiques or possible criticism. A first step in this process that helps most people is to slowly read their work aloud—often when we edit quietly "in our head" we miss critical errors, whereas reading aloud allows us the opportunity to catch less obvious errors. Some suggest using a checklist of critical elements alongside this review to ensure that we have covered all of the necessary components of the research (see, for example, the checklist for student papers and theses in Baglione 2008).

The second type of review is essentially an open **peer review** of our material. As we engage in the research process, we are entering into one of a variety of communities of discourse; this community of discourse can be internal to organizations or external to other organizations, public administrators, nonprofit leaders, policymakers, or academics. We want to ensure that our work meets the needs and standards of that community, and who better to help us do this than our peers. Oftentimes students and professionals alike are reticent about asking anyone else other than a teacher or supervisor to review written work, for fear of criticism. However, the overall quality of our written products improves when we routinely ask others to review our work and in turn review theirs. Two common points that people need to keep in mind while engaging in this type of review are that (1) no writing is perfect in the first draft, the second, and frequently even the final draft; and (2) criticisms of our writing are not personal criticisms. In addition, stakeholders may also be involved in reviewing our writing. The applied research arena always includes stakeholders who are interested in the written products that emerge from a project, and who may be also engaged in writing alongside us in the research process.

The third major round of review that is useful, if time permits, is review with senior colleagues who have some (and perhaps substantial) content expertise. For this type of review, we focus on higher-level concerns: Have we framed the problem and its importance properly? Are there other conclusions we may draw from the analysis? Do we fully understand the implications of our findings? This type of review in particular is critical to effectively entering and engaging into a community of discourse. Related, Mintrom (2003) advises a give-and-take style of review when working with collaborative partners. Initial reviews are directed at outlines in the early stages and then proceed to "draft" final reports, until agreement is reached on style as well as substance. Funders in particular may want this type of final review before a document is completed, particularly if the document will move directly into the public domain when the study is finished.

Gray (2005) suggests an additional round of review with a group that is referred to as "capital-E experts". Capital-E experts are the best-known scholars in the entire discipline or the most important people in the field who work in our area (2005, 56). According to this line of advice, having these people review our work is essentially political: we are entering into our community of discourse one-on-one to ensure that the top scholars and decision makers are aware of our work. Although this is an intriguing idea, we do not encourage this step in the review process as it is quite time consuming.

Readability and Appeal

In addition to the structure and substance of our written work, we have to be mindful of its **readability** and appeal. Oftentimes writing about research findings can seem repetitive and—quite frankly—somewhat boring. There are several ways to improve this. Although most writing for research will never win a Pulitzer Prize for Literature, there is no reason that applied research products must be dry or painful to read.

First, although the different forms of writing with which we engage are formulaic to a degree, this does not mean that we have to be plodding in our writing, describing step by painful step what we did and found. These elements must be included in our work products, but they do not have to be written in a strict chronological order. For example, in our review of the literature and development of an empirical theory, we are best served by writing that synthesizes major concepts. When we write about our methods, we need not delve into excruciating detail about decision making or an exacting recitation of each step of analysis. Rather, we provide an overview of our approach and justify it, highlighting analyses that include the important findings (positive or negative) in tables, figures, and other data displays that we support with narrative that summarizes those findings.

Second, our research involves the real world, and the topics are interesting. The places we go are fascinating, the organizations we study are complex and nuanced, and the people who are part of our investigations are multifaceted and intriguing. During the data collection process, we are best served if we keep extensive notes about all the details and nuances of the settings and of the people from whom we are collecting information. These details are interesting to our readers and make our writing real and appealing; we should always find ways to weave this information throughout our writing. Although many studies ensure confidentiality or anonymity to people and organizations, we can create composite people—archetypes—that illustrate our findings in a way that brings them to life and conveys authentic importance to readers.

For example, in the criminal justice policy study discussed in this book, the final product appeared in the form of a book; the main chapters were introduced with vignettes that illustrated the unique stages of innovation that were discovered in the research. These vignettes contained composite characters who were representative of public administrators and nonprofit leaders from all over the country whose interviews and case studies informed the study. The names were fictional, and the confidentiality of the interview subjects was preserved. The vignettes took the reader on a journey similar to that of the pioneering administrators whose work inspired the research. The overall effect was to knit together complex concepts through a story of innovation that unfolded through several "characters" across the main chapters of the book. The vignettes were short and appeared only at the beginning and end of each main chapter; the remainder of the writing was standard academic prose. However, this addition allowed practitioners to draw comparisons between their own work and that of the characters; because they were able to relate to the story, they were also able to identify skills and knowledge that they could use in their work.

A book-length project provides considerable space for developing a story, yet the technique can be used in most of the other forms of writing that we discuss in this chapter. An introductory paragraph that describes a problem or condition in human terms can be a very effective component of needs assessments, funding reports, annual reports, grant applications, and even academic articles. Because we focus on applied research, the connection to practice is essential in our written work, and stories about the conditions and problems we study can be powerful communication tools.

A Note About Style

Tables are common to most reports and presentations in applied research. Style guidelines and requirements are diverse and vary widely across academic disciplines. Similarly, government agencies and nonprofit organizations typically maintain their own written style requirements, which are not similar to academic styles. Regardless of the audience, neat, clean, crisp tables create a professional look for reports and presentations. We offer the following comments about our most common approach.

Using the guidelines that the *Chicago Manual of Style* provides, we follow several criteria for creating data tables for publications and presentations. First, we use the table tool available in our word processing software of choice to create the table, as opposed to cutting and pasting the results from any statistical or data analysis software we use, even if that software puts the results into a table as well. Second, we use roman font in the table, but do not use bold and italics. Third, we use Arabic as opposed to Roman numerals, and all tables are presented in numerical order in the narrative. Appendices are ordered in alphabetical order, and if there is more than one table within an appendix, we start at 1 for each appendix. Fourth, we use brief titles for each table, and if details are needed to explain the purpose or content of the table, we include those in a note at the bottom of the table instead of including that information in the title. Fifth, we have a heading for each column that identifies (briefly) the information and measurement of that column. These headings can have more than one level if necessary. Sixth, we do not use vertical lines in the tables, but we do use three mandatory horizontal lines. One line is at the top of the table under the table title and above the column headings. A second line is between the column headings and the data provided in the table. The third line is at the bottom of the table. We may also use horizontal lines to enhance the readability of the data presented in the table and when we are showing sums for the columns. Lines are easily generated through the standard toolbar for Word documents. Seventh, the first column is sometimes referred to as a "stub column" and is used to denote layers in the data presented. If we use this column, we include brief titles or descriptions for the layers, but we can use colons and indention to identify the different layers. The data within each of these rows should conform to the placement of the identifiers in the stub column. Eighth, if we have missing data within the table, we use three centered ellipses (. . .) in the blank cell, or we leave those cells blank. Ninth, we avoid the use of symbols within the body of the table. Finally, all footnotes end with a period, even if they are sentence fragments. Explanatory notes about the overall table are not numbered, but footnotes are. Table 7.1 illustrates the standard look of a table created for an applied research report.

Table 7.1
Illustration of Table Format and Style

Table Number

(Brief) Descriptive Title of the Table

Stub Column	Column 2 Title %	Column 3 Title Average	Column 4 Title $
Row 1 description	65	18	4,500
Row 2 description	70	. . .	800
Row 3 description	90	45	
Row 4 description	55	30	1,800

Note: The purpose of this table is to demonstrate proper table format according to the *Chicago Manual of Style*.

TYPES OF WRITING

We now turn to investigate various types of writing that are common to the applied research process. Each has its own characteristics and applications. The utility of these forms of writing is limited only by the researcher's imagination. Frequently, a project will utilize combinations of different forms of writing to reach different audiences.

Needs Assessments and Asset Mapping

One of the most basic but also important aspects of applied research is identifying the needs and assets of a given organization, geographic community, or community of interest. A needs assessment or **asset map** is often a precursor to developing a theory of change and logic model (discussed in Chapter Two). Frequently what happens when we engage in this type of work is that an organization or community is experiencing some kind of distress, and key stakeholders inside or outside the organization (or both) have determined that a change needs to be made. Before that happens, researchers will engage in a systematic examination of the strengths and weaknesses of the organization or community. The purpose of this type of writing is to identify and describe these elements and the evidence that exists for each in such a way that leaders of the effort for reform can draw conclusions about what types of changes need to be made. Sometimes the researchers are also asked to provide preliminary recommendations for changes or interventions.

A common process for beginning this type of writing is a **SWOT analysis**, which examines the internal and external environments of an organization or community. The internal environment is studied for its strengths and weaknesses. Elements vary according to the particular study, but typically include financial resources, operating practices, staffing levels, and similar characteristics. The external environment is studied for the threats and opportunities that may affect the organization or community. Again, particular elements vary, but they reflect the political, institutional, and sociodemographic environment. The product that results is typically reduced to a 2×2 matrix, as illustrated in Figure 7.1. The SWOT analysis itself is a form of mixed-methods analysis that is commonly used in practical settings (see Emerson, Menkus, and Van Ness 2010 for extensive discussion of the method).

The type of written product that accompanies this work is a report of varying length depending on the magnitude of the issue area. Length ranges typically

Figure 7.1
SWOT Analysis Display for the Community Garden Case

	Strengths	Weaknesses
Internal	**City** • Community spirit/pride • Land availability • Stakeholder interests **The Sustainability Idea** • Right idea at the right time • Easy project to market	**Financial Resource Instability** • Funding continuity using grants **Human Resource Instability** • Seasonal nature of student support • Initial citizen interest • Leadership
External	**Support** • Funding opportunities • Access to farm equipment/supplies **Civic Engagement** • Community interaction • Entertainment • Educational programs **Individuals** • Healthy living • Skills development	**Unknown Public Commitment** • Factions • Uncertain community-wide interest • Interest of some limited to specific sites **Environmental Limitations** • Weather • Security • Land ownership
	Opportunities	**Threats**

from thirty pages to more than three hundred. Needs assessments typically consist of the following components:

1. *Executive summary.* Summarizes in one to two pages the charge, data collection, major findings, and recommendations.

2. *Introduction.* Sets forth the charge to the researchers and establishes the history and context of the issue, organization, or community. Sometimes a literature summary will be found in this section, or it may be found in a stand-alone section that follows immediately after the introduction.

3. *Methods.* Details the types of data that were collected, when, from what sources, and how they were analyzed.

4. *Findings: needs.* Describes in detail the needs and causes of the problem or issue. This may be divided among multiple sections.

5. *Findings: assets.* Describes in detail the strengths and opportunities. This may be divided among multiple sections.

6. *Conclusions and recommendations.* Begins with a brief overview or summary of the project and findings. The researcher(s) then present conclusions and make recommendations about possible approaches for change or improvement.

Grant Applications

When we write grant applications, it is in the hope of obtaining resources for our work from an outside funding source. Oftentimes this process begins by locating a request for proposals (RFP) from the funder, which lays out the purpose of the grant program, specific activities and deadlines if they are required, the amount or range of amounts possible for awards, and application requirements and deadlines.

Sometimes the funder will only allow invited grant proposals; in this case, what it requests is a **letter of intent (LOI)** in lieu of a full grant proposal. LOIs usually ask for brief descriptions of the organization(s), the project for which funding is sought, and how much the project will cost and how funds will be used. The funder reads all of the LOIs and determines which most closely align with the goals of the funding program and then specifically invites those organizations to follow up with a full proposal.

Requirements for full grant proposals vary widely depending on the funding body and the amount of the grant. Government RFPs are usually significantly longer and more burdensome than those issued by private funders. Proposals for government grant projects must follow the requirements for documentation, page length, and so on exactly, or the proposal will immediately be deemed as unresponsive and will not be considered, no matter how wonderful the idea is. Deadlines are critical for responses to government RFPs; proposals that are late even by a single minute will not be reviewed or considered.

RFPs for research projects vary in their specificity. More frequently than not, these RFPs are general calls for research questions and designs around a particular topic of concern to the funding agency. Sometimes these RFPs seek proposals for evaluations of other grant programs. If the program is already under way, the RFP description of the program may be specific. If the program and its evaluation are being considered simultaneously by the funder, the RFP may be vague. In the latter case, the goal of the grant writer is to develop the best possible design based on the information provided. In such cases, an important caveat for the grant writer is that he or she is likely to be required to alter the design once the programmatic decisions about the program are finalized; these alterations can occur after the funding award has been made, and can be significant.

Generally speaking, grant proposals for research projects are focused around presenting several key components. These include an explanation of responsive research questions, the best design to answer those questions (in this context, a design that is scientifically rigorous but also realistic given time and financial resource constraints), and presentation of the credentials and skills of the research team as they relate to the research project. In addition, the proposal includes a realistic timeline for completion of the work, which details each of the steps in the process, including both administrative and research functions. Typically we develop a **Gantt chart** to display this timeline, which presents on one page the major categories of work activities as rows and the time units as columns (these can be weeks, months, quarters, or years, depending on the length of the project); we identify tasks in the corresponding cells. An example of a Gantt chart used in the statewide needs assessment is displayed in Figure 7.2.

Responses also include a budget that outlines expectations of costs, broken out by budget category (personnel, travel, equipment, and so on). The budget is always more than a simple list of expenses. A **budget narrative** accompanies the financial information; the budget narrative explains for each budget item why the cost is necessary and what assumptions were made to arrive at the cost estimate. An illustration of a budget and budget narrative appears later in this section.

When preparing a grant budget, it is also important to take note of funder requirements regarding allowable and unallowable expenditures and the process for making changes to the budget as the research proceeds. It is also critical that researchers consider how any budget shortfalls will be met. Budget shortfalls can occur for a couple of reasons, and both are quite common. Expenses can easily expand if research conditions change. Funders can also decide to cut back on particular budget items even after the project is under way. We suggest that researchers examine their own institutional requirements for obtaining funding support in advance of submitting a grant proposal so that they are prepared if funds run short and so that they satisfy any additional requirements of the institution.

To offer an example of the grant proposal process, we illustrate a plan to seek funding to replicate the statewide needs assessment that was conducted in a

Figure 7.2
Gantt Chart Example for Statewide Needs Assessment

	Administration and Report Development	Approach 1: Organizations	Approach 2: Individuals
September 2010	Write and submit IRB application	Create and pilot interview protocol	Create and pilot survey instrument Generate list of organizations
October 2010	Conduct literature review and obtain secondary source data	Identify and contact people for interviews	Send out survey Send out 1st follow-up
November 2010	Complete literature review and obtaining of secondary source data	Start interviews	Send out 2nd follow-up
December 2010	Develop interim report for Alabama Women's Commission	Continue interviews	Contact and interview organizations that have not responded to survey
January 2011		Data analysis	Contact and interview organizations that have not responded to survey Data analysis
February 2011	Develop final report for Alabama Women's Commission	Finalize data analysis	Finalize data analysis
March 2011	Give final presentation to Alabama Women's Commission		

single state. This plan is not complex, but does have many moving parts. The plan is based on our experiences with the single-state study, which we term a pilot study for the purposes of our plan. We illustrate the implementation of the plan through two documents; one is a planning document, and the other is a budget.

Figure 7.3 illustrates the work plan for the replication study. Simply stated, we plan to survey twenty-two states and to conduct case studies based on site

Figure 7.3
Planning Process Example for National Replication
of the Statewide Assessment

Month	Project Administration	Survey	Case Studies
August	Solicit state lists	Revise instrument Apply for IRB	
September	Finalize details on grant funding for case studies	Develop email database	
October	Train RA on survey process	Send out survey	Select case study states and sites
November	Train RA on case study process	Send out reminder 1	Apply for IRB Set up site visits
December		Send out reminder 2	Site-visit states 1–2
January	Write semiannual funder report	Clean data	Site-visit states 3–4
February	Rewrite report introduction	Data analysis	Site-visit states 5–6
March	Rewrite report literature review	Write up findings	Site-visit states 7–8
April	Rewrite report methodology		Data coding and entry
May			Data analysis
June	Submit final funder report		Write up findings
July	Revise work for publication		

visits and interviews in eight of those. Our work plan is divided into three distinct areas to reflect administrative tasks and two separate timelines and tasks related to the two methods of data collection (survey and case study). Note that the administrative timeline includes time for training student assistants and revising written work. The methodological timelines include the basic steps that apply to each method (discussed elsewhere in this text). The three timelines are integrated generally toward the common goals of developing findings, communicating these to the funder, and producing other material for publication.

The timeline is a planning document as well as an outline of a process. The timeline itself must be revised many times during the execution of the study, because as written it is not integrated with any other responsibilities that the researchers or graduate students might have. It also does not consider delays or challenges that occur regularly in the research process; for example, an IRB submission might require revision, or site visits might have to be rescheduled. For those reasons, in our experience it is useful to construct a draft timeline at the outset of an idea for a project and to revisit it regularly. It is also prudent to build in extra time for the unexpected. The planning document is useful for research and writing beyond grant proposals. In the case of a grant proposal, it is critical to assess the funder's deadlines and work backwards to determine the feasibility of submitting a proposal.

The budget and budget narrative are illustrated in Figure 7.4. The budget lists the resources that we need in order to design and execute the study, in addition to the resources that are available to us as researchers (here, in our work as university professors). In general terms, we ask for two graduate students to work with us, time off from teaching one course over twelve months, and money to travel to conduct site visits and interviews.

The illustration presents a few common features of the typical budget submitted with a grant proposal. One is the level of detail required. Imagine how different this budget would appear if it were reduced to a request for $76,675, or a request for $67,500 plus indirect expenses, or a list of expenses. Embedded in that detail are assumptions about the number of individuals who will work on the project, and the support that they need in order to do so. Related, in order to prepare a budget, we must already be quite knowledgeable about what we intend to do. This budget accompanies other elements of the grant proposal, including the research design. Another common feature is the use of notes as a way to

Figure 7.4
Budget Summary and Budget Narrative

Line	Budget Item	Amount	Description
1	Graduate research assistant support	$27,000	Twelve months of standard stipend of $1,000 per month for two graduate students, plus benefit charge of 35%
2	Travel	$30,500	Eight trips to eight different states at 6 days/5 nights and two travelers per trip
3	Faculty support	$10,000	Two course releases at $5,000 per course and one course per faculty PI on the project
4	Miscellaneous	$1,000	Copying, long-distance charges for conference calls
5	Subtotal of direct expenses	$67,500	
6	Indirect expenses @ 15% of direct	$8,175	
7	Total	$76,675	

The following budget reflects support needed for replication of a survey in 22 states that satisfy particular criteria in terms of available information about organizations, and for site visits and personal interviews in each of 8 states in that group. We expect to interview 5–10 individuals at each of four locations in each state.

Notes:

Line 1. Graduate student stipend does not include tuition remission; 35% is the amount approved for internal allocation of the cost of health care effective January 1, 2014.

Line 2. Assumptions include $500 airfare per person per trip; $900 in ground transportation costs per trip, including car rental, taxi, and parking fees; $204 meals per person per trip at $34 per day (the state rate); and $150 hotel per night per person. Individuals traveling may include faculty or students or a combination of the two.

Line 3. $5,000 is the standard cost for hiring an adjunct for one course for one semester.

Line 6. This rate is the maximum allowable by this funder. It does not reflect $13,000 in graduate research assistant tuition for two assistants for 12 months.

streamline the initial presentation of information yet also provide the necessary details in a succinct fashion.

Each institution and funding source maintains its own cost accounting system and reporting format; this illustration does not adhere to any particular form or set of requirements. For each project, we have to revisit guidelines and policies. Depending on the organization, assumptions about costs are treated as hard-and-fast amounts or as best estimates; again, it is important that we are knowledgeable in these areas. In some cases, funds awarded for one purpose may be shifted to another purpose or may be lost entirely if not spent exactly as proposed. For each project, we should also check to make sure that we are aware of expenses that are not permitted either by the funder or by our organization, and ensure that we have not included those expenses in our grant proposal.

Funder Reports

There are several types of funder reports that can be written as part of the sponsored research process. Typically, funders require regular reporting from their grantees about their progress. Through these progress reports, funders learn how their funds are being used and to what effect. Many funders prescribe specific guidelines for grantees to follow, including specific questions they would like grantees to answer. These progress reports can be as frequent as quarterly or as far apart as once a year. Although there is variance by funder in what specifically is required in these reports, generally they are five to ten pages in length and consist of the following sections:

1. Summary of activities to date

2. Summary of findings to date

3. Plans for next steps

4. A budget or budget narrative of expenses to date

It is commonplace for grantees to want to write these progress reports with a focus only on the positive, sidestepping any difficulties or problems with their funded research, in the belief that by showing themselves in the best possible light, they increase their possibilities for future funded research. On the basis of our experience as both grantees and grantors, we provide different advice. Of course we should always highlight our good work, but we should also identify the challenges we encounter. These challenges are many and real and are actually part and parcel of the problem(s) that funders seek to address through their grants. When we acknowledge and pay attention to struggles, particularly when we can discuss how to overcome them, we enter into honest dialogue with funders that has the potential to help them understand better how to structure their own programs and that perhaps may alter their expectations.

Substantive reports to funders about research findings take a different form. These are typically lengthy, ranging anywhere from thirty to three hundred pages, and are written at the end of the data collection and analysis process. In some ways, substantive reports to funders read a bit like an expansive research paper. Typically these types of funder reports consist of the following sections:

1. *Executive summary.* In one to two pages, we set forth the research question(s), briefly discuss the data that were used, and highlight findings and conclusions.

2. *Introduction.* This section provides an overview of the research question and its importance, the background as to why the sponsored project was funded, the context and history of the issue being studied, and an overview highlighting each of the sections in the rest of the report.

3. *Literature review/empirical theory.* Depending on the purpose of the sponsored research, there may or may not be a formal literature review/ empirical theory section. In cases where there is not, the relevant literature is typically discussed in the introductory section.

4. *Methods.* This section describes in detail the research design employed, why it was the most appropriate, how and from where data were collected, and how data are analyzed.

5. *Findings.* This is a detailed description of the findings, typically written around summary data tables. Depending on the research questions and methods with which data were collected, findings can be presented in one section only or in multiple sections.

6. *Conclusions.* This section begins with a summary of the purpose and findings and then discusses the findings within the broader context of the phenomenon and draws conclusions for the funder. These conclusions often take the form of policy, process, or research recommendations.

Sometimes funders also want condensed versions of research reports that move beyond the executive summary and take the form essentially of a policy memo or briefing. In these cases, writing should be focused on briefly condensing what is often complicated information into a pithy format that presents the issue, causes, interventions, and potential solutions. This particular form of writing is often difficult for academics, who are typically trained to believe that detail is very important for understanding the recommendations; however, the skill of translating complicated information into a brief (one- to two-page) overview can be very useful.

Stakeholder Documents

We may also need to write what are sometimes referred to as **stakeholder documents**, including annual reports, Form 990s, responses to public information requests, and public relations or media releases. Each of these serve a different purpose and have a different form.

Annual Reports   Annual reports are a summary of organizational efforts and their results, and serve several functions for organizations. They can be used for internal purposes as a way to assess the effectiveness of strategies and tactics and for future planning by organization boards and executives. Externally they can be used for direct fundraising, as promotional material, and as supporting evidence and documentation for grant applications. These documents usually consist of the following components:

1. An executive summary in the form of a one- to two-page overview of the entire document
2. The mission and a brief history of the organization, including founders and key milestones
3. A description of organizational capacity, including the board of directors, key staff, and individual and institutional funding support
4. A description of extant organizational goals, strategies, tactics, and programs along with annual accomplishments for each
5. Either an analysis or a description of outputs from activities and programs
6. A discussion of lessons learned
7. Plans for the coming year
8. A budget summary

The program and budget information contained in the annual report can serve as the basis for other common types of writing found in nonprofit organizations and public agencies.

Form 990s   Also known as an annual information return, Form 990 is required annually for nonprofit organizations, some charitable trusts, and other political groups, and is filed with the Internal Revenue Service (IRS). These reports must be made available to the public upon request. It is rapidly becoming the norm to post this report on an organization website as well. Form 990 requires annual information on organization mission, volunteers, accomplishments in furtherance of mission (for example, charitable activities, courses, assistance to people in need, collective bargaining, member meetings, recreational activities), and activities unrelated to mission. Information about income, expenses, compensation, and governance and management structure are also required. Explicit instructions for 990s are found on the IRS website (www.irs.gov). The purpose of the form is to provide the general public with information about the activities of the organization and how donor funds are being used. Program descriptions and descriptions of annual accomplishments are brief and similar to those found in the annual reports of many nonprofit organizations.

Public Relations Releases   Public relations releases, or public information statements (often called press releases), are brief statements that summarize an activity or finding from an organization and are meant to gain positive attention for the organization. Usually these are sent to local media outlets in the hope that they will generate interest and a subsequent story by a news outlet. These releases need to be pithy (direct, not wordy, and informative), and usually consist of the following components:

1. An attention-grabbing title
2. A paragraph describing the organization
3. One to three paragraphs describing the activity, event, or outcome of interest and its importance; if announcing an event, where and when it will occur must be made clear
4. If applicable, a discussion of how this information can be used by the intended audience
5. Contact details for more information

In the current work environment, these releases are sent to news sources via email. If staff time permits, the release is also followed up with a phone call. Organizations may want to provide a condensed version in social media format for followers of their organization.

Journal Articles

As noted in previous chapters, academic journal articles have an important place in the research world because they are seen as the best possible information currently available on a given topic by virtue of the double-blind peer-review process. We write these articles in order to enter a community of discourse about the area of our research and to discuss the findings from our work.

With the exception of some journal articles that involve in-depth, qualitative data and process tracing, most of these articles follow a common format, consisting of the following:

1. An abstract summarizing the purpose of the research and major findings (one paragraph or about 250 words)

2. An introduction that describes the research questions and their importance and provides an overview of the rest of the article, including the findings (1–2 pages)

3. A discussion of the empirical theory that is tested, imbued throughout with citations and culminating in testable hypotheses (5–7 pages)

4. An overview of the methodology and data analysis approach that describes what was done and justifies why it is appropriate (3–5 pages)

5. A full explanation of the findings, typically arranged around summary data tables (7–10 pages)

6. A conclusion section that begins by summarizing the entire article in one or two paragraphs and then discusses the implications of the findings for our understanding of the field and possible future research questions (2–5 pages)

7. Back matter, including the bibliographic listing of works cited and any necessary appendices

Most journals have maximum lengths for submission of around thirty pages in total (counted as double-spaced Times New Roman 12-point font or its equivalent).

The process of getting an article accepted and printed in a peer-reviewed journal is long. After the manuscript has been submitted, the journal editor will review it to determine its appropriateness to the journal. It is possible for the article to be returned to the author without review. Most journals operate under policies that allow the editors to reject submissions if they do not feel that the work is a good fit for the journal audience; **desk rejection** means that the material will not proceed to any stage of peer review. If the topic of the piece is appropriate for the journal, the editor will send it to several scholars in the field for review. Most editors ask for reviews to be returned in four to eight weeks so that the journal can make a decision; sometimes this process can take upwards of ten to twelve months. Typically, articles are rejected at this point; top journals have acceptance rates well below 20 percent (meaning that rejection rates are in excess of 80 percent). Sometimes editors will issue a **revise and resubmit** letter to the author, indicating that the journal is interested in publishing the article if revisions are made. The smart author makes these revisions as soon as possible and resubmits the manuscript. The revised manuscript then goes through a second round of reviews, usually by the same reviewers, and a decision is made at that point whether or not to publish it. If the manuscript is accepted, it then proceeds through copyediting and formatting checks before it appears in print. The publication production timeline is quite lengthy, and journals typically hold a backlog of accepted articles; after acceptance, an article may not appear in print for a year or more.

The revision process is challenging and requires special attention as a form of writing related to applied research. In the revision process, the author receives three or four responses to the article, including comments from two or three peer reviewers and the editor. The editor summarizes the sense of the reviews and notes the comments that he or she feels are most critical. These comments range from relatively straightforward requests for additional citations to more complex requests for reorganization of the material and clarification of the theoretical approach, data sources, and/or methods. Sometimes editorial review indicates that there is disagreement about the appropriateness of particular data or methods, and the comments call on the author to justify the approach that has been taken. The prudent author approaches revisions in a systematic manner that acknowledges the value of peer review and the broader discussion in the discipline about his or her research. We suggest that the author begin by composing a list of each of the comments made by the editor and each of the reviewers. The list then serves as a checklist for proceeding with the revision. The author must decide whether and how to deal with the requests and comments, which may be in conflict. The letter from the editor serves as the guide for interpreting which comments are most important. When the revision is complete, the author prepares a letter of explanation for the revision and transmits this to the journal editor with the revised submission. The letter of transmittal explains in detail the revisions that were made in response to requests from reviewers, and also explains why any requested revisions were not made, if that is the case. The letter of transmittal also explains any additional changes that the author made.

Because of changes in technology, new electronic-only journals have become quite popular. These are more cost effective, as there are no printing and mailing costs. We recommend caution and due diligence before submitting a manuscript to one of these outlets. Some e-journals are of high quality; however, many others are considered to be of low quality or even of no quality at all. Several attempts to judge the quality of these journals have been made. As a basic guideline, we look at the rejection rate (higher is better, as a signal of exclusivity), the journal's ties to well-known associations and sections in the field, and the credentials of the members of the journal's editorial board, which should comprise well-known scholars in the specific discipline and at reputable institutions. New journals can—and do—satisfy these criteria; it is also important to note that an established track record is considered to be an indicator of quality. In addition, others suggest examining the quality of the content, journal history, standards of acceptance, audience, regularity of publication, maintenance and usability of the website, and external recognition (Lopez-Ornelas, Cordero-Arroyo, and Backhoff-Escudero 2005). As a rule of thumb, the best outlets are the well-known and respected ones.

Applied Dissertations

Applied dissertations are more common for students in public administration and policy programs than for those in political science programs, but are present in both. These types of dissertations are exciting to conduct and more interesting to read than many basic dissertations, but are also quite difficult to do well. Although this book is not a guide to writing a dissertation, we have included a section on writing the applied dissertation, as so little attention has been paid to it in other texts.

Applied dissertations have the same elements found in any dissertation: a testable (and, one hopes, interesting) research question, a testable empirical theory with corresponding hypotheses, a research design, sections on findings, and a conclusion that discusses implications for the field as well as other research questions that the findings generate. What differentiates applied types of dissertations from basic dissertations is the necessity of conducting primary field research, and typically the use of mixed methods. This type of research, as should be clear from reading Chapter Four, is time intensive and potentially resource intensive as well. Thus careful planning and the ability to spend several years on data collection, analysis, and writing are prerequisites for the successful completion of the applied dissertation.

One potential benefit of the applied dissertation is that there are more avenues open for applying for external funding when conducting applied rather than basic research in these fields. For example, consider a dissertation about the effects of income inequality in America. This topic can be approached using secondary data from the U.S. Census Bureau and other sources; it can also be approached by analyzing original data gathered from individuals and organizations and by analyzing organizational and/or community efforts to address specific problems through particular programs or initiatives. Problem-solving research is attractive to funders seeking social and/or political change. In our example of poverty or income inequality, it is relatively easy to imagine drafting a grant proposal for travel funding to conduct data collection in a sample of communities as part of an applied dissertation. It is challenging to imagine an attractive grant proposal in this arena that did *not* propose to collect original data from individuals and organizations.

PRESENTATIONS

Beyond writing, we use applied research in myriad other ways. Sometimes we are asked to present our findings to stakeholders, including the target audience of our work or funders, and we present these materials to academic audiences as well. As a general rule of thumb, the presentations we make are targeted to the interests of the audience and the typical format and norms that are familiar to the audience. This means that we need to always be aware of any jargon we use and to define and interpret it as appropriate for our different audiences. To a general audience, we pitch our writing and discussion at about the eighth-grade reading and learning level. The level that we target should increase as appropriate, depending on the degree to which our audience is more specialized or professionalized.

Presentations take various forms, ranging from oral presentations delivered in front of a group to a poster presentation that is seen and read by individuals on their own initiative. Each approach has strengths and weaknesses. People learn and take in information in different ways. Some people are auditory learners, meaning that they are most likely to receive information by hearing it and translating it. Others are visual learners who see information and understand it. Still others are tactile and experiential learners, meaning that they need to touch or experience information in order to understand it. All of these people may be in any presentation audience, so we need to develop presentations of material that reach as many people as possible.

To respond to the multiple learning styles of an audience, it is common to combine an oral presentation with either written material projected on a screen (for example, a PowerPoint presentation) or handouts rather than delivering an oral presentation alone. PowerPoint presentations should highlight main talking points rather than provide the talking points word for word. They are useful when they help the audience engage. In applied research, pictures from the data collection phase provide interesting points of departure for the researcher and may also prompt audience questions and discussion. Charts and graphs are also useful; it is essential to carefully label these kinds of visual aids so that the visual material does not raise unnecessary questions that detract from the credibility of the presentation. Handouts are useful when very complicated information needs to be presented; one negative aspect is that the audience members may become distracted in reading the handouts and fail to listen to the presenter.

If the presentation is being made in the form of a **poster**, the typical arrangement is a gallery-style display in which the audience mills around a room or conference space looking at different presentations. The audience members will linger at some posters and ignore others. In some cases, authors remain with their posters to answer questions. Regardless, in this venue we are best served by using large fonts for the title, author's name, research question, and main findings. Detail is minimal. These presentations are also enhanced with pictures, graphs, and tables. Professional poster design services are available; we suggest a careful review of the style and format options to make sure that the presentation meets the needs of the audience.

Figure 7.5, available online, shows a picture of a poster that we used in multiple presentations to practitioners about the statewide needs assessment. This poster format is one that we designed ourselves. It is worth noting that this visual presentation contains some material that was also included in our final report. Specifically, the county-level maps and pictures of facilities were part of our analysis. What was new for this poster is the table that explains and compares best-practice facility models. This information was part of our original analysis and was included in our final report in narrative form (written), but we did not display it in graphic form. We geared this information to the poster because we felt that it best represented the type of information most interesting to the various audiences who had the opportunity to view it. These audiences were primarily midlevel state and local public administrators responsible for public service programs for older individuals. (You can view and download this sample poster at www.wiley.com/college/brownhale.)

This type of addition illustrates two important aspects of the applied research process. One is the value of graphic displays. It is worth investing a bit of time thinking about how to present information in poster form, whether or not such a display is required as part of the research process. The exercise of distilling information and creatively communicating important points can enhance a written report as well. The process of creating a graphic display helps clarify and organize key points; the resulting display may also be a useful addition to a written report (either in the body of the report or as an attachment). The poster also illustrates the continuously reflexive and iterative nature of the research process. It was not immediately obvious to us how to illustrate the best-practice information that we had gathered; our approach became apparent only after reflection and further discussion about the report with stakeholders, including funders, who wanted very specific ideas about how to proceed in developing new program ideas.

To accompany poster presentations, researchers may also provide a handout that presents essentially an executive summary for those who are interested. This is particularly helpful if there is nuanced information that accompanies a poster presentation or if the researchers want to propose recommendations. If the presenter remains with the poster, he or she should also be prepared with a short explanation of the project; many people refer to this as an "elevator speech," a description that can be given in the thirty to sixty seconds that one might discuss it with a stranger during an elevator ride. The point is to engage audience interest enough that they want to find out more information about the project.

Presenting Material to Stakeholders

Stakeholders of applied research vary widely, from the people who are the topic of our work, to service providers, policymakers, and funders. We think about presenting information from an applied research project differently depending on the stakeholder audience. The content outline of the presentation is essentially the same—we discuss the purpose of the research, the type of data we collected, and major findings—but how we interpret those results will differ. This difference has to do with addressing the reasons that particular stakeholders are interested in our work. Both external and internal stakeholders can be interested in the same topics. We tend to think about the external environment when we present to providers, policymakers, and funders; we tend to think about the internal or organizational environment when we focus on future planning and program development.

For example, if we conducted a statewide assessment of the need for and the availability of summer programs for indigent youth, we would frame our discussion differently depending on the audience. For service providers, we might focus on the range of services and on evidence of which types seem to work best. This kind of information focuses on program design and implementation issues, and may also dovetail with discussions of future planning. For policymakers, we might discuss the needs we found and offer suggestions for how government initiatives might be structured to encourage more programming; we could also discuss the role that nonprofit organizations play in this service area and consider support for those organizations. For funders, we might focus on areas that present either very great need or very specific need and provide an overview of the range of programs and the cost of each that might address those needs.

An example of a community presentation is available online as Figure 7.6. The figure is the PowerPoint portion of the presentation made in the case of the community garden/sustainability study. Several aspects are notable. One is that we used the basic format of a SWOT analysis as the framework, but adapted it to the audience. Second, the presentation included considerable information about why we were making the presentation. Although many people in the audience were part of various stakeholder groups we had interviewed, we knew that the audience would include people who were new to this study and who were not familiar with the background discussions that had taken place over several months. (You can view and download this sample PowerPoint presentation at www.wiley.com/college/brownhale.)

It is also worth noting that virtually any of the written documents that have been discussed in this chapter and throughout the book could serve as the basis of a report to stakeholders. We are not generating different information to provide to stakeholders (or community members or policymakers)—we are using the information that we have gathered throughout the research process and making it interesting and germane to these audiences. For example, a table or chart presenting descriptive statistics or a budget or a research project timeline might each find its way into a report or presentation to stakeholders. Thus reports and presentations delivered to stakeholders are not separate from the research process, but rather are integrated throughout the process.

Academic Presentations

For those of us in academic settings who engage in applied research, we must present the results of our work to both stakeholders and other academics. Academic audiences require a different type of presentation than stakeholder audiences. In these cases, we either present our studies at a conference or are invited to give a talk to a department or other university audience.

The conference panel presentation format typically allows a twelve- to fifteen-minute oral presentation for each of three or four papers; each is typically accompanied by a PowerPoint presentation. These presentations follow the format typical of a journal article in which we briefly touch on the research question and its importance, our hypotheses, our data collection and analysis techniques, our major findings, and our conclusions. In the fields of public administration, public policy, and political science, it is not typical to read research papers aloud; instead we conversationally present our material organized around main questions, ideas, and findings. It is common in this approach that several people are giving papers on similar topics and that each is allotted the same amount of time. One or two academics are designated as discussants for the panel and are assigned to tie the different papers together, provide feedback on each paper specifically, and discuss major implications for the discipline.

Invited research presentations typically follow the same format as the conference panel presentation, with two important differences. First, the presenter is usually the only speaker on the agenda. There is more time allotted for the presentation (typically about thirty minutes), and the presenter is expected to delve into the material more deeply. Second, the invited research presentation does not have a designated discussant. The idea behind this presentation format is that everyone in the audience will participate by making observations about the work, asking follow-up questions, and providing suggestions for different ways to approach the topic in future stages of the research project.

An increasingly common practice in the academic realm is to present the same paper at multiple conferences in the discipline or at conferences in different disciplines. In some cases, the title and content of the paper remain the same; in others, the paper is continually improved and the title changed to reflect the evolution of findings (see Dometrius 2008; Sigelman 2008). There is no agreement about the acceptability of this practice in the discipline. Further, conventions vary across the disciplines as a whole; in some conference settings, papers are accepted for presentation only when they are also accepted for publication. In the usual academic conference settings likely to be visited by users of this book, papers are presented in various states of readiness for publication, so revision of a conference paper is very much the norm. Put another way, conferences are seen as the first place to test out new research. As a general rule of thumb, we believe that conference paper presentations should advance research development; therefore, significant revisions of the material should occur with each conference iteration.

The use of PowerPoint is also a common feature of academic presentations and of many presentations regardless of audience or venue. Visual aids can be quite powerful and can enhance the spoken presentation. Too often, however, PowerPoints do little more than visually represent the speaker's text. As with other visual displays (posters, for example), it takes time and careful attention to do more than reprint tables and construct bulleted lists of concepts and citations. Yet the visual display of our information is a rich medium. There are many excellent texts and articles on the presentation of visual information, and we do not treat that subject in detail in this book, except to provide several illustrations from our work. We refer readers to the wide-ranging and beautiful work of Edward Tufte (1983, 1990). We also suggest that PowerPoint users in particular consider moving beyond the teleprompter in their use of presentation slides (see Salmond and Smith 2011). Too often, we follow time-honored traditions without considering how the visual nature of the presentation can be enhanced. Ultimately, the additional communication that we achieve is worth the extra effort, as we hope to connect our work to communities of practice as well as academics. New electronic formats such as Presi may hold promise for certain kinds of presentations; however, we offer the same cautions as with PowerPoint.

CASE ILLUSTRATIONS OF WRITING AND PRESENTATION

The case studies used in this text employed a variety of techniques discussed in this chapter, as summarized in Table 7.2. For most of the cases, an array of written products was generated, and myriad presentations were made to various audiences. This suggests that we need to have multiple writing and presentation skills to adapt to the interests and learning styles of the varying audiences that we engage in applied research, even for the same project. More broadly, it also suggests that we can bring "standard" research to practitioners and community members by developing any number of different types of presentations.

DECISION TREE

The range of possibilities for presentation formats is too vast for us to do more than address the basic dimensions in this book. That said, there are common considerations that, if addressed, will substantially improve the overall quality of any presentation of applied research. Too often, particularly in academic settings that are common to many who may use this book, we follow a pattern or convention rather than think about how to effectively communicate in an engaging manner.

Decisions About Making Presentations

The questions posed in Figure 7.7 serve as a starting point for considering obvious logistical items, the nature and expectations of the audience, and the purpose of a research presentation. Our observations are intended as a jumping-off point for further investigation rather than as a prescription. As with the other aspects of applied research, the decisions are ultimately those of the researchers.

Good presentations are not the result of good logistics; however, poor logistics can sink even a good presentation. Common logistics issues include time allocation and use and availability of audiovisual equipment. Presenters may also need to consider disability accommodations for audience members; public venues should address these concerns automatically. Experience suggests that it is always wise to investigate operating conditions well in advance, although that is not always possible. Presenters will want to pay close attention to any particular requirements for format, time, or technical support.

Understanding the audience is essential. We suggest several questions to guide the researcher's thinking here. A key consideration is the level of detail

Table 7.2
Case Comparison of Types of Writing and Presentations

	Community Garden	Statewide Aging Assessment	Election Administration and Technology	National Program Evaluation	Criminal Justice Policy Reform
Types of Writing	SWOT analysis Grant funding summary Site descriptions Administrative documents for meetings	Interim funder reports Final funder report Needs assessment	Academic journal article	Interim funder reports Final funder report Academic journal article Practitioner book chapter	University press book
Types of Presentations	Stakeholder presentations Community meetings (SWOT, grant funding summary, site descriptions, slides)	Academic presentation (oral with slides) Funder presentation (oral with 2-page handout) Stakeholder presentation (oral with 2-page handout) Practitioner presentation (poster)	Academic presentation (oral with slides)	Academic presentation (oral with slides) Practitioner presentation (oral with slides)	Academic presentation (oral with slides) Practitioner national conference (oral) Community book talk (oral) University book talk (oral)

Figure 7.7
Decision Tree for Approaching a Presentation

Questions to Ask When Designing a Presentation

What are the logistical considerations?

 What is the size of the audience?

 How much time is available?

 Has a format been specified?

 Will time be available for questions? If so, has a question format been specified?

 What are the audiovisual requirements or options?

 What technical support is available?

 Are accommodations required that you must address?

Who is the audience?

 Academics

 Practitioners with technical expertise

 Policymakers, including elected officials

 Lay audience

What level of detail does the audience expect?

How can you summarize complex issues or concepts?

What challenges do you expect?

 To concepts

 To definitions

 To details

 To relationships

 To conclusions

What is the purpose of the presentation?

 Convey findings

 Build relationships

 Build consensus

 Generate conversation about new ideas

 Make recommendations

 Persuade

that the audience expects. There may be overlap in some areas; however, the academic, technical, policymaker, and lay audiences each suggest different levels of detail. Related, it is important to consider in advance the ways in which complex issues can be summarized. It is also critical to consider how summaries can be created without losing essential information and meaning.

Advance consideration of the challenges that might be expected is also worthwhile. Challenges can come in many forms, and Figure 7.7 lists a few major categories of challenges that we have encountered in our work. Anticipating issues and concerns serves two purposes. One is that it makes it easy to prepare responses to use if the situation arises. Another is that this exercise can hone the presentation itself. When we anticipate possible opposing views or commonsense questions, we are more likely to address those in our presentations in some way, making it more likely that our message will be conveyed accurately. The expected number of audience members and level of expected formality also provide clues about responding to questions and whether the presentation will include free-ranging discussion or none at all.

Of course the purpose of the presentation is also important, and Figure 7.7 lists several common options. One presentation may serve multiple purposes; our list is intended to foster thought about the issue and to suggest several purposes that may occur more or less simultaneously, although one goal may be most important. We also note that applied research presentations by nature engage a cross-section of different audiences, each with a different set of expectations about the information we are presenting. Thus a presentation that is designed to accomplish one purpose may transform into an entirely different presentation depending on the audience; a question posed by an elected official, for example, can turn an informational presentation into a policymaking discussion. The rich nature of applied research and its natural intersection with the communities around us suggest that no presentation is entirely routine and that each research presentation will serve as the platform for further discussion. In this way, the applied research cycle begins again as new questions are asked and new projects are designed to investigate possible answers.

CONCLUSION

When we began thinking about writing this book, our purpose was twofold. First, we wanted to find a way to engage and instruct our students in applied research, relating to them its importance, how engaging it can be, and how nuanced and complex the decision-making process for best carrying out this research can be. Second, we hoped to provide a blueprint for practitioners, be they current practitioners trying to enhance programs while simultaneously jogging their memory about how to go about this, or future practitioners, those in school right now making crucial decisions about their future career paths. Our ultimate goal was to provide a comprehensive, readable, and practical guide to conducting applied research.

For both groups, we also hoped to demystify the research process and make it accessible to those who want to understand how to study public service. The process as a whole is complex, but the individual components are relatively straightforward to understand and use. We have found that successful research requires a comfortable relationship with ambiguity and uncertainty, as well as a strong adherence to the right tools and the proper orderly process. We have also learned that successful research is about confidence in the face of an overwhelming number of choices regarding what to study, when, where, why, and how. We hoped that this book would provide experiences that build confidence for readers, as well as skills. There is much to be gained from small projects, and there is much to be learned from traveling down the wrong road before finding the right one.

We also hoped that readers would take away an in-depth understanding of how organic, connected, and unending the research process should be. We form ideas and research questions from our experiences, our readings, and, most important, from the experiences and works of others. We turn these into theories and hypotheses, or stories and guesses that are intricately tied to the lived experiences and work of thousands of others. We construct research designs and data collection plans, making trade-offs between the elegance of the rules of high-quality research and the gritty reality of problems, situations, and possible solutions. We collect those data, often engaging with wonderful, complex, and complicated people and their problems, all the while knowing that we will end with an incomplete and flawed picture, but we nonetheless strive to reflect reality to the best of our ability. We then analyze these data and draw conclusions about them, often with the hopes of making a real difference, while fighting the fear of doing harm. We then try to communicate all of this to others, the best of us able to provide the information fluidly and to engage others in a complicated discourse.

We engage in this process with critical principles in mind. The purpose of applied research is to better the conditions of those around us. The process is inherently messy and iterative, and projects are never truly finished. We must always strive to develop, implement, and deliver the most rigorous research possible, but at the same time, we have to live and engage in an imperfect world full of constraints on resources and on availability and access to the best possible information. We try to be as objective as possible while knowing that true objectivity is impossible. The research process is an unfolding of reality in a dynamic and complex environment, and as researchers we engage in a reciprocal process with the community and people in it. We have a responsibility to take our work and our research partners seriously and to treat them with respect.

Within this context, we are mindful that public service organizations are continually scrutinized and challenged to deliver more for less, and to achieve policy goals that may be ill-defined or simply unattainable. We live in a world of measurement; the universal call for accountability suggests that wise public administrators and nonprofit leaders and others engaged in public service enterprises will continue to look for new ways to measure performance. The applied researcher must deftly strive to strike a balance between these pressures and the best possible research product. We hope that those who engage this text find it useful and that students learn to love and appreciate the research process as much as we do. After all, as Kurt Vonnegut reminds us in *Cat's Cradle*, "New knowledge is the most valuable commodity on earth."

CHAPTER SUPPORT MATERIALS

Chapter Seven Relevant Articles

Baglione, Lisa. 2008. "Doing Good and Doing Well: Teaching Research-Paper Writing by Unpacking the Paper." *PS: Political Science and Politics* 41:595–602.

Gray, Tara. 1999. "Publish, Don't Perish: 12 Steps to Help Scholars Flourish." *Journal of Staff, Program, and Organizational Development* 16:135–142.

Mintrom, Michael. 2003. *People Skills for Policy Analysts*. Washington, DC: Georgetown University Press.

Salmond, Rob, and David T. Smith. 2011. "Cheating Death-by-PowerPoint: Effective Use of Visual Aids at Professional Conferences." *PS: Political Science and Politics* 44:589–596.

Wolfinger, Raymond E. 1993. "Tips for Writing Papers." *PS: Political Science and Politics* 26:87–88.

Chapter Seven Discussion Questions

1. Consider the writing you have done in the past. What processes and steps did you follow that led to a successful product? When you have produced suboptimal written products, what process or steps did you follow in those cases? What is different between them?

2. Reflect on the last time someone provided criticism of your writing. How did you react? What could you do to make your reaction more positive?

3. Thinking about the different forms of writing described in this chapter, identify the common elements among all (or almost all) of them. What differentiates each type of writing from the others?

4. What purpose do Gantt charts and budget narratives serve in grant proposals? Imagine that you are a funder of a grant program. What would you look for in a Gantt chart and in a budget narrative when determining which proposals to fund? Why?

5. Think about past presentations that you have seen. What separated the good ones from the bad ones? What engaged you and kept you interested in the material? How could you emulate that?

Chapter Seven Practice Assignments

1. For any written product, three levels of review are recommended: self, peer, and senior colleague. Imagine you are engaging in this process in the coming months. Identify and discuss the following: (a) what process you would follow for a self-review; (b) whom you would ask for a peer review, and why he or she would be most appropriate; and (c) whom you would ask for a senior colleague review and why that person would be most appropriate.

2. Search the Internet for an example of each of the types of writing described in this chapter. Provide a full citation for each piece (one per type of writing), including the appropriate hyperlink.

3. Imagine it is August 15 and you are in your first class of the semester. The majority of your grade will be based on a research paper due no later than

December 1. From looking at the instructions, you expect that developing your research question, conducting the literature review, and developing a design will take you four weeks, and that completing the data collection and analysis will take another four weeks. Develop a timeline for turning in your final paper by December 1 that allows you to engage in all of the steps in the writing process described in this chapter.

4. Find an annual report for a nonprofit organization that you are interested in, and read it. Select one of the activities described in the report and imagine that you are working for the organization and that the activity has not yet taken place. Write a public relations release for the activity utilizing the descriptions of the components of a public relations release in this chapter.

5. Find a journal article about a subject that you are interested in. Imagine that you had written it and were going to make a presentation about the material. Develop a PowerPoint presentation for this article.

Chapter Seven Linked Assignments

Throughout the text, we include a series of "linked assignments." These have been developed to walk the research methods student through the entirety of the research process by developing a research project that includes each phase of both applied and basic research.

The last of the linked assignments is perhaps the hardest. You will need to pull together each of the steps in the research process in one of three forms: a research paper (using journal article format), a research poster, or an oral presentation accompanied by a PowerPoint or slide presentation. Regardless of the format, the materials should consist of the following:

1. The research question and a brief discussion of why it is interesting

2. An empirical theory developed out of the relevant literature

3. Hypotheses or research expectations

4. A discussion of the research design

5. An overview of the findings

6. Conclusions about the topic from the findings, and suggestions for additional ways to examine and/or further develop the research question

Chapter Seven Online Assignments

Using the Internet, locate a website for a grantmaking foundation and the GAO.

Part A. Identify a current RFP for each. Prepare a plan for how to write the grant proposals.

Part B. Identify a report prepared by each. Write a critique of each of the reports, taking the perspective of a particular stakeholder. From the perspective of this stakeholder, what do you find helpful about the information and the way it is presented? What suggestions do you have for improvement? What criticisms do you have, if any?

GLOSSARY

Academia   Referring to higher education- and/or university-based work

Agreement bias   Psychological condition in which respondents want to appear positive (agreeable) and not negative (disagreeable) in general, regardless of how they actually feel about the idea, proposal, or decision that is the subject of the question

Alternative hypothesis   As opposed to the null hypothesis, a statement of expectation of finding a relationship between two variables

Ambiguity   Confusing or unclear phrasing in surveys

Analysis of variance (ANOVA)   Statistical test measuring how variance in a variable is explained by three or more groupings with the variable

Annotated bibliography   Summary of sources used in a research project, usually containing bibliographic information; research question, theory, and hypotheses; description of data; summary of findings; and notes about how each source can be used by the researcher

Annual report   Summary and analysis of what an organization has done and accomplished in a given year, including budgeting and financial matters

Anonymous   Response option in which researchers neither know nor report on the identity of study participants

Applied dissertation   A research project undertaken in partial fulfillment of the requirements for a PhD and that tackles real-world problems; guided by academic advisers

Applied research   Research that focuses on understanding or trying to solve practical problems, as opposed to basic research, which focuses on furthering our understanding of theoretical relationships, whether empirical or normative

Archival documents   Historical documents and records of past actions, including records of government offices, nonprofit organizations, newspapers and other forms of media

Argumentativeness   Wording of questions in surveys that subtly convinces respondents that a particular perspective is correct

Asset mapping   Identification and articulation of strengths and opportunities available in a given community or to address a particular problem

Asymmetric measure   In statistics, test requiring the identification of the dependent and independent variables prior to performing the calculation

Attrition   Process by which some study subjects drop out of the study over time

Availability sampling   Selecting population units for study based on their availability or ease

Basic research   Research that advances knowledge and looks for relationships between theoretical constructs and their related variables; compared to applied research

Before-and-after design   Experimental design that includes a pretest and a posttest

Behavioral coding   In pilot-testing survey instruments and processes, observing respondents to watch for questions that take longer to answer or that appear more difficult or confusing

Benchmarks   Empirical measures used to capture the results of a policy intervention or progress toward a goal

Beneficence   A principle of ethical research in which research designs are constructed to maximize positive outcomes for humanity while minimizing harm to study participants

Best case sampling   Practice of selecting population units for study as cases because the units exemplify the phenomena

Bias   Error introduced into a study

Bimodal   Having two modes, or two nominal categories with the same values that are larger than the values of the other categories

Bivariate statistics   The analysis of the mathematical relationship between two variables and the joint probability of inferring these relationships from a sample to a population

Budget narrative   Written description of a numerical budget item that clarifies the entry and explains the underlying calculations and assumptions

Case study   Approach to data collection using an in-depth examination of an event, geographic area, or public problem

Causal argument   Theory or hypothesis that establishes a cause-and-effect relationship between two variables that meets four criteria: correlation, temporal order, logical causal mechanism, and nonspuriousness

Causal mechanism   The actual influence that one variable has on another

Census   The population

Central limit theorem (CLT)   Theory which holds that, for any simple random sample, the sample mean will fluctuate around the population mean, and as sample size increases, test statistics will more accurately reflect the true population parameters; see *normal approximation rule*

Challenges   In logic models, the problem or issues to be addressed

Chi-square statistic   Bivariate analysis of two nominal or ordinal variables to determine the strength of the mathematical relationship between them and the joint probability of inferring those relationships from the sample to the population

Cleaning   The process of reviewing data to ensure proper coding and proper data entry

Closed-ended questions   Survey questions that contain a fixed list of possible response categories

Clusters   Groups in which each population element exists in one and only one group at a time

Codebook   A document that describes every variable in a database, including the variable name, meaning, source of data, and coding

Coding   Reducing a qualitative descriptor of a phenomenon to a numeric value

Coefficient   Test statistic; the estimated effect that an independent variable has on the dependent variable

Cognitive interview   In pilot testing survey instruments and processes, an interview with respondents about how they understood the questions and response categories, whether any were confusing, or whether anything should be added or amended

Collinearity   The strength of the mathematical relationship between two variables

Communicability   Clear and understandable relay of information from a study to other researchers and/or the broader public

Communicable   A characteristic of high-quality research which holds that research should clearly articulate and communicate all parts of the research process to others

Comparative case study research   Approach to nonexperimental research design in which multiple cases are selected and studied to compare and contrast conditions and outcomes

Comparison cases   Population units selected for study as cases based on differences in either the key outcome variable, key explanatory variable, or context, used to help improve the credibility of findings

Comprehensive community change initiative (CCCI)   Coalitions or collaboratives formed across sectors and focused on making broad-based improvements in distressed communities

Concept   A word or phrase that is used to represent an idea or phenomenon; a precursor to the development of variables

Confidence levels   Levels of certainty about whether what is true for sample data will be true for population data in testing statistical significance

Confidentiality   Response option in which researchers know but do not report the identity of study participants

Construct   A single measure of a concept, where the concept can be measured in multiple ways

Construct validity   The condition that results when the concepts under study are operationalized accurately

Contamination   Outside forces other than an intervention or key explanatory variables that affect a research study

Content analysis   Approach to data collection based on the systematic analysis of recorded materials for common themes using the application of a strict set of rules

Content expert   A known senior scholar who may be asked to read or comment on work to ensure that it is carefully crafted

Context   The environment, including history, in which a particular phenomenon occurs

Context effect   Phenomenon in which the order of statements and questions together affect the answers given

Contrasting cases   Population units selected for study as cases in order to contrast the variance in either the dependent variable or the explanatory variable of interest

Control group   In experimental and quasi-experimental research, refers to the group that does not receive treatment

Control variables   Variables included in a causal model to control for nonspuriousness

Convenience case selection   Population units selected for study as cases based on accessibility

Correlation coefficient   Measure of bivariate association between two scale variables

Co-vary   When two variables demonstrate a mathematical relationship between them

Critical cases   Population units selected for study as cases because they are so important or well known that they must be included in order for others to accept the conclusions

Critical value   In hypothesis testing, used for comparison to determine whether or not a calculated test statistic is significant

Data   Information gathered to understand a particular issue or phenomenon

Deadline   The date that a project or manuscript is due

Deductive theories   Reasoned explanations from laws or rules to specific outcomes

Degree of control   Extent to which nonexperimental factors influence an experiment

Degrees of freedom   In statistics, how much information is available to estimate parameters

Demographics   The characteristics of people or geographic areas, including aspects that can change and aspects that do not

Dependent variable   Denoted as Y; the phenomenon that is the object of explanation

Descriptive statistics   Mathematical description of a single variable, including central tendency and dispersion

Desk rejection   Editorial rejection of a manuscript before peer review, typically because the material does not meet either the standards or substantive focus of the journal

Difference of means   A measure of the magnitude of differences between the measure of central tendency of two variables, or between the central tendency of groups within one variable—for example, gender as a subcategory of another variable

Difference of proportions   A measure of the magnitude of differences between the proportions of two variables, or between the proportions of groups within one variable—for example, race as a subcategory of another variable

Direct observation   A form of data collection that involves watching and documenting actions, events, or processes

Directional hypothesis   As opposed to the null hypothesis, a statement of expectation of finding a positive or negative relationship between two variables

Disproportionate random sampling   The process of selecting population units for study by oversampling a particular stratum to more accurately make inferences about the population parameters from the sample

Double-barreled questions   Survey questions that have two or more parts but only allow for one answer

Double-blind peer-reviewed journals   Journals in which articles have gone through a process in which author identifying information is removed for review by content experts, and content expert identifying information is removed when changes are suggested by the editor to the author before publication; the purpose is to enhance the quality of published research

Dummy variables   Variables consisting of only two categories

Elite interviewing   Collecting interview data from people who hold top positions of influence, often elected officials

Emotional bias   Triggered in a respondent by provocative or negative associations with research questions or response categories

Empirical analysis   The study of extant evidence

Empirical theory   An explanation of an event or phenomenon based on a combination of observations, findings from other research, and logic

Endogenous change   Process in which study subjects change during the life of an experiment without reference to exposure to a treatment

Error   The difference between our sample characteristics and the population characteristics; unexplained variance

Estimated parameters   Descriptions of a population inferred from sample data

Ethical issues   Concerns in research about the research's beneficence, respect for subjects, and justice

Ethnography   Approach to data collection in which researchers fully immerse themselves in a culture for an extended period of time to better understand that culture

Evaluation framework   Term for a theory of change used when part of a program evaluation

Exhaustive   Principle in building response categories for survey questions that requires that all possible responses a respondent may give should be included in the prepared set of possible question responses

Expected value   In repeated samples from a population, the average of the averages or the long-run average

Experimental contamination   Research error that occurs when a treatment is accidentally delivered to the control group members, or when control group members believe that they received the treatment and, as a consequence, behave differently than they would have otherwise

Experimental design   Approach to research in which the effects of an intervention are tested with an experimental group against a control group, with random assignment of subjects to each group

Experimental group   In experimental and quasi-experimental data collection, the group of subjects who are given a treatment

Explanatory variable   The primary or most important predictor of variance in a dependent variable

Exploratory research Research that contributes to the development of new theories based on observations of new or unexpected phenomena

External events Incidents that occur during the life of a study that have nothing to do with the study but nonetheless influence how subjects behave or answer questions

External validity Measure of whether a research design is able to establish transferability or generalizability

Extreme outliers Observations for a variable that are largely distant from almost all of the other observations

Factorial design A form of experimental design that includes one control group and multiple experimental groups

Falsifiability The guiding principle of the approach to science based on the idea that knowledge is built through the process of subjecting hypotheses to disproof, as opposed to trying to prove them to be true

Filter questions Questions that divide survey respondents into categories of those who have information about a topic and those who do not, allowing respondents with no information to skip ahead while prodding respondents with information about a given topic to provide that information

Focus group Research approach in which a small group of people is brought together for a moderated conversation

Form 990 Internal Revenue Service information return filed by most nonprofit organizations

Full attribution Response option in which researchers know and report the identity of study participants

Funded research Research conducted with the financial support of a sponsor

Funder reports Reports to financial sponsors of research, typically including a summary of activities by the date of the report, summary of findings by the date of the report, plans for next steps, and a budget or budget narrative of expenses to date

Gantt chart Graphical display laying out planned activities on a timeline

Generalizability Ability to extend research findings in one study of a specific case or cases to other similar instances

Grand theory Theory concerned with developing overarching links between phenomena that guide research questions

Grand tour question A broad question designed to be easy to answer, interesting to the subject, and not controversial or confrontational, which is used to begin an interview

Grounded theory Theory developed about a phenomenon based on in-depth empirical observation and analysis of one or more cases

Hawthorne effect Phenomenon that occurs when people change their behavior because they know they are being observed

History In experimental research, refers to events from a subject's past that can affect the experiment

Hypotheses Testable expectations from empirical theories

Independence   In statistics, refers to the condition when an event A does not change the outcome of another event B; that is, the two events are unrelated

Independent variable   Denoted as X; characteristic believed to explain change in the dependent variable

Index   Aggregation of answers to multiple questions about a single concept to form an overall measure of that concept

Inductive theories   Development of explanations based on empirical data

Inferential statistics   Mathematical calculations based on known sample data to describe unknown population data

Information literacy   Understanding and being able to access the different kinds of information needed to answer questions and solve problems

Informed consent   Participant permission given to engage in research based on (usually) full knowledge about the purpose and expectations of the research project in which he or she has been asked to participate

Inputs   Resources that can be used to address or solve a problem

Institutional Review Board (IRB)   Organization within a university that reviews research proposals for compliance with ethical requirements

Instruments   The tools used to collect data

Intercoder reliability   Consistent coding across different people applying codes

Internal validity   Measure of whether a research design is able to establish causal linkages

Inter-rater reliability   A mathematical measure of agreement among two or more coders (or raters) about the value assigned to a particular variable

Interval variables   Variables with both discrete categories and order

Intervention   The experimental condition, or an outside element introduced into an experiment in order to examine its effect on the outcome of interest

Intervention analysis   An approach to data analysis in which the researcher examines the effects of a specific policy or program intervention on changes in behavior over time, collecting data both before and after the intervention

Interview   Approach to data collection in which researchers identify respondents and ask them questions; typically used with experts or key informants

Interview protocol   The guideline that lays out all processes, introductions, questions, and steps to be taken in an interview process

Iterative process   The continual reviewing and refining of our work while we are working within each step and across the steps of the research process

Journal article   A description of research and findings, and a discussion of implications published in a (usually) peer-reviewed format

Justice   A principle of ethical research in which research designs are constructed to ensure that research does not exploit others

Key informants   People who are sources of the best possible information because of their particular backgrounds or experiences; may or may not be elites

Letter of intent (LOI) Precursor to a full funding proposal; increasingly required by funders as a screening step before an invitation to submit a full proposal is given

Levels of significance Thresholds set to determine whether an observed relationship from a sample can be inferred to the population based on the strength of the mathematical calculation

Likert scale An ordered scale, usually with five or more categories, and balance among positive and negative choices

Linear probability model (LPM) Multivariate model in which all variables are dummy (or two category nominal) variables

Literature The published work in a particular discipline

Logic model Pictorial description of a problem, available resources, the hypothesized solution to the problem, and hypothesized outcomes

Logistic regression Multivariate analysis conducted when there is a dummy (or two category nominal) dependent variable

Longitudinal studies A form of survey research in which the same units (people, organizations) are studied over time

Mean The mathematical average or measure of central tendency taken with a scale (interval or ratio) variable; computed by summing all of the observations and dividing by the sample size

Measure of central tendency The calculation of the average value of a variable

Measure of dispersion Mathematical descriptor of the range of values a variable takes; appropriate measures vary depending on the level of measurement

Median A measure of central tendency for ordinal or scale variables with extreme outliers; the value at the 50th percentile

Method of agreement Selection of population units for study as cases because they exhibit the same values of key explanatory variables although they differ otherwise

Method of difference Selection of population units for study as cases because they exhibit different values of key explanatory variables although they are similar otherwise

Middle-range theories Theories concerned with developing explanations for specific phenomena

Mixed methods Analytic approach combining both qualitative and quantitative data

Mode Measure of central tendency for nominal variables; the category with the most observations

Model Mathematical description of empirical phenomenon

Model misspecification Incorrect modeling, typically caused by the use of too many variables or by the choices made in measuring concepts

Model underspecification A form of incorrect modeling, typically caused by failing to correctly include key explanatory factors or controls

Multicollinearity Condition in multivariate analysis in which two or more independent variables are strongly mathematically related, rendering estimated coefficients unreliable

Multiple-posttest design   In experimental research, a design in which one pretest measure and multiple posttest measures are taken, allowing the researchers to determine how lasting or sustainable the impacts from the intervention may be

Multiple-pretest design   In experimental research, a design in which multiple pretest measures and one posttest measure are taken, allowing the researchers to control for learning from the pretest

Multivariate analysis   Simultaneous analysis of the effects of multiple independent variables on a single dependent variable

Mutually exclusive   Principle in building response categories which holds that categories should not overlap

Needs assessment   Systematic examination of a social or political condition, frequently used to inform program planning

Nominal variable   A variable described by only discrete categories

Nonequivalent control group design   Form of quasi-experimental research design in which there is a control and test group but other experimental conditions may be relaxed

Nonparametric test   Test of ranked or ordered variables

Nonrandom/nonprobability sample   A sample drawn in which elements are selected for a particular purpose, including convenience

Nonresponse error   Bias introduced into survey research when a low percentage of the sample actually complete and return a survey, particularly if there is a systematic or common element among those who respond and those who do not

Normal approximation rule   Theorem which holds that, for any simple random sample, the sample mean will fluctuate around the population mean, and as sample size increases, test statistics will more accurately reflect the true population parameters; see *central limit theorem*

Normative analysis   The study of how things ought to be; compared to empirical analysis

Null hypothesis   A statement conjecturing that either there will be no relationship among two variables or no differences between them

Odds ratio   Mathematical calculation of the odds, or probability, of an event occurring (dependent variable) given the presence of a given event of interest (independent variable)

Open-ended question   Type of survey question that does not propose any sort of response options and does not limit the information that respondents choose to provide

Operationalization   Defining each of the elements of the research question and the hypothesis in a specific way that allows it to be measured

Ordinal variables   Variables with both discrete categories and order

Ordinary least squares regression (OLS)   Multivariate analysis conducted when the dependent variable is measured on a scale

Outcomes   The results or consequences of activities or interventions

Outcroppings   Physical objects in a community that are meaningful to a group under study; typically indicate values and significant historic events

Output   Measure of the implementation of activities

Paradigm   In philosophy of science, the common ways of thinking about problems in a given period of scientific development

Parameters   Descriptions or characteristics of a population

Parsimonious   Explaining as much as possible about a phenomenon with as few variables as possible

Participant observer   A researcher who interacts with subject participants as a participant and as a collector of data simultaneously

Passive observer   A researcher who watches, listens, and takes notes but does not interact with the research subjects

Path dependence   Characterization of political or social phenomena in which once a choice has been made (setting a path) and the longer that process goes on, the harder it will be to stop it or stray from the course set by the original choice

Pattern matching   Approach to qualitative data analysis in which data are examined for trends and patterns that emerge

Peer review   Process used in academic publishing in which an editor serves as an intermediary between the author and experts in the field; the editor takes an author's submission, strips it of identifying information, and sends it to experts for review, comment, and suggestions about publication

Periodicity   In interval sampling, an error that arises when sampling units are arranged systematically by a substantive trait or characteristic

Pilot   A test of the processes and instruments to be used for data collection prior to the start of data collection to ensure that they work

Placebo effect   Phenomenon in which study subjects change their behavior according to the false belief that they are part of the test or treatment group even if they are enrolled in the control group

Popular press sources   The group of organized bodies that produce nontechnical transmittal of news and information to the general population

Population   All possible observations, subjects, or units

Poster   Form of academic conference presentation in which study information is reduced to key elements and placed on a large visual display for general review by conference attendees

Posttest   In experimental research, a measure taken of the dependent variable after the intervention

Pretest   In experimental research, a measure taken of the dependent variable before the intervention

Primary data   Original data collected by the research; as compared to secondary data

Probability   Mathematical examination of the (un)certainty of the occurrence of events

Probability sample   Sample drawn such that each case or element within a population has an equal chance of being drawn as part of the sample

Prompts   In interview research, follow-up questions that help guide the respondent to provide additional or more focused information

Proportionate random sampling   Selection of population units for study according to strata, based on the size of each stratum in the population

Protocol   Guideline that lays out all processes, introductions, and steps to be taken in a data collection effort

Proxy   A substitute measure of a concept used when direct or exact measurement is not possible

Psychometrics   The measurement of the validity and reliability of survey instruments

Public relations release   A brief summary used to increase media attention by highlighting an issue or activity; also known as a public information release or press release

Purposive sample   Intentional nonrandom selection of population units for study

Push polling   Approach seen in political campaigns in which a candidate may develop what appears to be a neutral public opinion "poll" that is really used to disparage the other candidate and/or bolster the candidate running the poll

Qualitative analysis   Systematic review of qualitative data for trends, patterns, and themes

Qualitative research   Research focused on observing complex political and social phenomena and then describing and analyzing those phenomena based on the observations in total; compared to quantitative research, which reduces these phenomena through a coding process to numeric representations of reality

Quality information   Information that is factually accurate, derived from a credible source through a public and transparent process, and produced using rigorous and standard techniques that adhere to appropriate ethical standards

Quantitative analysis   Mathematical explanation of relationships between and among events

Quantitative research   Research focused on reducing political and social phenomena to numbers by giving them numerical codes and then analyzing them with statistical techniques; compared to qualitative research, in which the same phenomena are analyzed in total

Quasi-experimental design   A research design that retains many of the components of an experiment but fails to qualify as a pure experiment on at least one element or criterion

Quota sampling   Selection of population units for study based on characteristics of the population critical for study and in proportion to those characteristics

Random assignment   In experimental and quasi-experimental research, the practice of assigning study participants so that each has the same probability of being placed into either the treatment or control group

Random sample   Sample drawn such that each case or element within a population has an equal chance of being drawn as part of the sample

Randomized comparative change design   Approach to experimental research utilizing both pretest and posttest measurements

Randomized comparative posttest design   Approach to experimental research taking only a posttest measurement

Range   The distance between the lowest and highest observed values of a variable

Ratio variables   Measurement that includes discrete categories, order among the categories, fixed distance between the categories, and a fixed zero

Reactivity   The concept that researchers may have an effect on the subjects of their research that would not exist if the researchers had not been there

Readability   Ease with which a research report can be read by the intended audience

Recursive enactment   Reinforcement of earlier choices, thus making changes and alterations difficult; see *path dependence*

Reflexivity   Concept that research and knowledge production happen in an iterative way, with each stage of the research process informing the next phase as well as additional iterations of past phases

Reliability   Condition in which repeated measurement yields the same result; indicative of stability and consistency

Replicate   To intentionally repeat a research process in order to check whether it is possible to obtain (nearly) the same results as were obtained in the original research

Request for proposals (RFP)   Invitation by funders for qualified applicants to submit a plan for a project to be considered for financial support

Research design   Overall approach to collection of data to answer a research question and/or to test hypotheses

Research instruments   The tools used to collect data

Research question   Question that guides a scientific inquiry

Researcher bias   Assumptions a researcher brings to the research process that may influence the outcomes of the research in a way that distorts reality

Respect for subjects   A principle of ethical research in which research designs are constructed to ensure that research protects a subject's autonomy and possible anonymity

Respondent validation   Process in which researchers provide their findings to participants for feedback

Response categories   Options from which a survey or interview respondent selects in order to answer a question

Response set bias   Occurs when the order of statements and questions together affect the answers given

Revise and resubmit   Communication from a journal editor to an author that the journal is interested in publishing a manuscript if certain changes can be made successfully

Sample   Observed information from a subset of a population used to infer parameters about the larger population

Sampling   The process of drawing a subset of population elements for study in order to make inferences about the larger population

Sampling frame   The set of sampling units out of which a sample is drawn for a study

Sampling interval   The quotient found by dividing the population size by the desired sample size

Sampling unit   A single member of the sample

Sampling with replacement   In random sampling, replacing each sampling unit back into the sampling frame after selection

Sampling without replacement   In random sampling, removing each sampling unit from the sampling frame and not returning the unit after selection

Scale   A set of responses ordered from lowest to highest that allows respondents to express their feelings about a topic

Scale variables   Includes interval and ratio variables

Scholarly sources   Published information in the form of scientific discussion and data analysis about a specialized topic that has undergone a blind peer-review process before publication

Secondary data   Using data that someone else has collected; as compared to primary data

Selection bias   An error in sampling in which differences in groups occur as a result of a flaw in the group selection process

Self-edit   To edit one's own work

Semistructured interview   Approach to data collection in which interviews are structured with a set of questions, but the interviewee is allowed to deviate from the questions if an interesting or unexpected topic emerges during questioning

Simple random sample (SRS)   Probability sampling approach in which each population unit has the same probability of being selected into the sample

Snowball sampling   Selection of known population units to participate in the study and to identify additional population units

Social desirability   An effect that occurs when respondents answer survey questions on the basis of social acceptability or social appropriateness, regardless of their true actions or beliefs

Sponsored research   See *funded research*

Spuriousness   Inaccurate attribution of a causal relationship between two variables X and Y in which both variables are caused by an unseen, unarticulated, or unmeasured third variable

Stakeholder documents   Documents critical to community organizations, usually including annual reports, Form 990s, responses to public information requests, and public relations or media releases

Standard deviation   Measure of dispersion in the distribution of data around the mean

Statistical significance   In inferential statistics, refers to the probabilistic establishment of a relationship between two or more variables due to more than just chance

Statistically significant   Describes the strength of a mathematical relationship such that it can be inferred from a sample to a population

Strata   Groupings based on components or characteristics of a population

Structured interviews   Approach to interviewing that utilizes predetermined questions and response categories

Subjective measures   Data gathered from the perspective of the respondent

Survey   Approach to data collection in oral or written form in which data are collected from individuals, usually about beliefs, opinions, characteristics, or behaviors that cannot be observed

SWOT analysis   An examination of the internal and external environment of an organization or community; stands for strengths, weaknesses, opportunities, and threats

Systematic observation   Principle of applied research which holds that evidence to support claims and hypotheses should come from multiple and structured observations, as opposed to anecdotes, suppositions, and beliefs

Temporal order   Condition of causality; the independent variable must occur before the dependent variable in time

Test statistics   Estimated population parameters from a sample

Testable   In reference to a research question, one for which empirical evidence can be collected and analyzed

Theory of change   A theoretical description of a problem; a program, intervention, or activity that is hypothesized to address the problem; the expected outcomes due to the intervention; and the causal linkages among these elements

Thick description   Reporting about phenomena by including extensive background and contextual information that will help explain observations and conclusions

Time series analysis   Approach to data collection and analysis in which observations of a phenomenon are taken over time, and data are examined to detect patterns and trends or to forecast future events

Trade and professional sources   Published material that focuses on issues of concern to the specific trade or profession and is written to be accessible to that audience

Treatment   In experimental and quasi-experimental research, the introduction of an outside element to examine its effect on a variable or outcome of interest

Triangulation   The process of collecting information on a single topic from a variety of sources using multiple methods in order to enhance believability of findings

Type I error   The error that occurs when the null hypothesis is falsely rejected based on sample statistics when in fact there is no population relationship

Type II error   The error that occurs when the null hypothesis is not rejected based on sample statistics when there is a relationship in the population among two variables of interest

Typical case   Population unit selected for study as a case because it represents or generally characterizes the phenomenon

Unit of observation   The level at which data are collected (individual, group, organization, city, county, state, and so on)

Univariate   Describing one variable

Univariate statistics   Mathematical description of one variable

University press books   Academic books that go through a blind review process and are considered to contain high-quality information

Unstructured interviews   Approach to data collection in which an interview begins with the researcher opening with a general topic and allowing the respondent to speak unrestrictedly about it

Validity   The condition in which the measurement approach accurately captures the phenomenon as intended

Variable   Measurable characteristic that represents a particular concept or aspect of a concept with two or more values

Variance   In statistics, the square of the standard deviation

Waves   Multiple iterations of a survey sent to the same respondents over time to capture change

Weighted index   Composite variable constructed by combining multiple survey questions and enhancing the impact of responses to certain questions by weighing these more heavily in the mathematical operations used to construct the variable

BIBLIOGRAPHY AND WORKS CITED

Alvarez, R. Michael, and Thad Hall. 2005. "Rational and Pluralistic Models of HAVA Implementation: The Cases of Georgia and California." *Publius: The Journal of Federalism* 35:559–577.

Arthur, Brian. 1989. "Competing Technologies, Increasing Returns, and Lock-in by Historical Events." *Economic Journal* 99:116–131.

Association of College and Research Libraries. 2000. *Information Literacy Competency Standards for Higher Education.* Chicago: American Library Association.

Auburn University Libraries. "Types of Periodicals." Accessed May 20, 2013. http://libguides.auburn.edu/types_of_periodicals.

Baglione, Lisa. 2008. "Doing Good and Doing Well: Teaching Research-Paper Writing by Unpacking the Paper." *PS: Political Science and Politics* 41:595–602.

Baker, Barbara, Kathleen Hale, and Giovanna Summerfield, eds. 2013. *Scholarship in Action: Communities, Leaders, and Citizens.* Champaign, IL: Common Ground Publishing/World University Forum.

Becker, Howard S. 1958. "Problems of Inference and Proof in Participant Observation." *American Sociological Review* 23:652–660.

Berman, Evan M., ed. 2007. *Encyclopedia of Public Administration and Public Policy.* 2d ed. (Jack Rabin, founding editor). Boca Raton, FL: CRC Press.

Berry, Frances Stokes, and William D. Berry. 1990. "State Lottery Adoptions as Policy Innovations: An Event History Analysis." *American Political Science Review* 84:395–415.

Bickman, Leonard, and Debra J. Rog, eds. 2009. *Sage Handbook of Applied Social Research Methods,* 2nd ed. Thousand Oaks, CA: Sage.

Bloom, Howard S., Carolyn J. Hill, and James A. Riccio. 2003. "Linking Program Implementation and Effectiveness: Lessons from a Pooled Sample of Welfare-to-Work Experiments." *Journal of Policy Analysis and Management* 22:451–575.

Boersema, David. 2008. *Philosophy of Science.* New York: Pearson Prentice-Hall.

Boser, Susan. 2007. "Power, Ethics, and the IRB: Dissonance over Human Participant Review of Participatory Research." *Qualitative Inquiry* 13:1060–1074.

303

Bradburn, Norman M., and William Mason. 1964. "The Effect of Question Order on Responses." *Journal of Marketing Research* 1:57–61.

Brians, Craig. 2010. "Review of the 'Information Literacy Instruction Handbook.'" *Journal of Political Science Education* 6:87–88.

Brown, Mitchell. 2008. "Improving Organizational Capacity Among Faith- and Community-Based Domestic Violence Service Providers." In *Innovations in Effective Compassion,* edited by Pamela Joshi, Stephanie Hawkins, and Jeffrey Novey, 39–60. Washington, DC: Department of Health and Human Services.

———. 2012. "Enhancing and Sustaining Organizational Capacity." *Public Administration Review* 72:506–515.

———. 2013. "Cross Integration of Community, Research, and the Classroom: Extensions of a National Evaluation." In *Scholarship in Action: Communities, Leaders, and Citizens,* edited by Barbara Baker, Kathleen Hale, and Giovanna Summerfield, 79–85. Champaign, IL: Common Ground Publishing/World University Forum.

Brown, Mitchell, and Kathleen Hale. 2011. *State-Wide Assessment of Alabama Women 65+: Organizations, Practices, and Participant Perspectives. Final Report to the Alabama Women's Commission.* Auburn, AL: Auburn University.

Camasso, Michael J., Radha Jagannathan, Carol Harvey, and Mark Killingsworth. 2002. "The Use of Client Surveys to Gauge the Threat of Contamination in Welfare Reform Experiments." *Journal of Policy Analysis and Management* 22:207–223.

Chung, Yiyoon, Julia B. Isaacs, and Timothy M. Smeeding. 2013. "Advancing Poverty Measurement and Policy: Evidence from Wisconsin During the Great Recession." *Social Service Review* 87:525–555.

David, Paul. 1985. "Clio and the Economics of QWERTY." *American Economic Review* 75:332–337.

Davis, James A. 1985. *The Logic of Causal Order.* Thousand Oaks, CA: Sage.

Dobyns, Henry F., Paul L. Doughty, and Harold Dwight Lasswell. 1971. *Peasants, Power, and Applied Social Change: Vicos as a Model.* Thousand Oaks, CA: Sage.

Doebbeling, Bradley N., Thomas E. Vaughn, Robert R. Woolson, Paul M. Peloso, Marcia M. Ward, Elena Letuchy, Bonnie J. BootsMiller, Toni Tripp-Reimer, and Laurence G. Branch. 2002. "Benchmarking Veterans Affairs Medical Centers in the Delivery of Preventive Health Services: Comparison of Methods." *Medical Care* 40:540–554.

Dometrius, Nelson C. 2008. "Academic Double-Dipping: Professional Profit or Loss?" *PS: Political Science and Politics* 41:289–292.

Dwyer, John J. M., and Susan Makin. 1997. "Using a Program Logic Model That Focused on Performance Measurement to Develop a Program." *Canadian Journal of Public Health* 88:421–425.

Elazar, Daniel J. 1966. *American Federalism: A View from the States.* New York: Crowell.

Ellis, Robert A., and Roger R. Moore. 2006. "Learning Through Benchmarking: Developing a Relational, Prospective Approach to Benchmarking ICT in Learning and Teaching." *Higher Education* 51:351–371.

Ellison, Julie, and Timothy Eatman. 2008. *Scholarship in Public: Knowledge Creation and Tenure Policy in the Engaged University.* Syracuse, NY: Imagining America.

Emerson, Sandra, Royce Menkus, and Kathy Van Ness. 2010. *The Public Administrator's Companion: A Practical Guide.* Washington, DC: CQ Press.

Fording, Richard C., Sanford F. Schram, and Joe Soss. 2013. "Do Welfare Sanctions Help or Hurt the Poor? Estimating the Causal Effect of Sanctioning on Client Earnings." *Social Service Review* 87:641–676.

Fowler, Floyd J., Jr., and Carol Cosenza. 2009. "Design and Evaluation of Survey Questions." In *Sage Handbook of Applied Social Research Methods,* 2nd ed., edited by Leonard Bickman and Debra J. Rog, 375–412. Thousand Oaks, CA: Sage.

Fulbright-Anderson, Karen, and Patricia Auspos. 2006. *Community Change: Theories, Practice, and Evidence.* Washington, DC: Aspen Institute.

Fulbright-Anderson, Karen, Anne C. Kubisch, and James P. Connell, eds. 1998. *Theory, Measurement and Analysis. New Approaches to Evaluating Community Initiatives,* vol. 2. Washington, DC: Aspen Institute.

Gerber, Alan S., and Donald P. Green. 2000. "The Effect of a Nonpartisan Get-Out-the-Vote Drive: An Experimental Study of Leafletting." *Journal of Politics* 62:846–857.

Gilliam, Franklin D., Jr., and Shanto Iyengar. 2000. "Prime Suspects: The Influence of Local Television News on the Viewing Public." *American Journal of Political Science* 44:560–573.

Gray, Tara. 1999. "Publish, Don't Perish: 12 Steps to Help Scholars Flourish." *Journal of Staff, Program, and Organizational Development* 16:135–142.

Gray, Tara. 2005. *Publish & Flourish: Become a Prolific Scholar.* Springfield, IL: Phillip Brothers Printers.

Gujarati, Damodar. 1998. *Basic Econometrics,* 3rd ed. New York: McGraw-Hill.

Hale, Kathleen. 2011. *How Information Matters: Networks and Public Policy Innovation.* Washington, DC: Georgetown University Press.

Hale, Kathleen, and Mitchell Brown. 2013. "Adopting, Adapting, and Opting Out: State Response to Federal Voting System Guidelines." *Publius: The Journal of Federalism* 43:428–451.

Hale, Kathleen, and Ryan Hankins. 2013. "Defining Best Practices: Engaging the Community Perspective of Success." In *Scholarship in Action: Communities, Leaders, and Citizens,* edited by Barbara Baker, Kathleen Hale, and Giovanna Summerfield, 86–94. Champaign, IL: Common Ground Publishing/World University Forum.

Hale, Kathleen, and Ramona McNeal. 2010. "Election Administration Reform and State Choice: Voter Identification Requirements and HAVA." *Policy Studies Journal* 38: 281–302.

Harding, Sandra J. 1991. *Whose Science? Whose Knowledge? Thinking from Women's Lives.* Ithaca, NY: Cornell University Press.

Harklau, Linda, and Rachel Norwood. 2005. "Negotiating Researcher Roles in Ethnographic Program Evaluation: A Postmodern Lens." *Anthropology & Education Quarterly* 36:278–288.

Hebert, Scott, and Andrea Anderson. 1998. "Applying the Theory of Change Approach to Two National, Multisite Comprehensive Community Initiatives." In *Theory, Measurement and Analysis. New Approaches to Evaluating Community Initiatives*, edited by Karen Fulbright-Anderson, Anne C. Kubisch, and James P. Connell, 2:123–148. Washington, DC: Aspen Institute.

Herzong, A. Regula, and Jerald G. Bachman. 1982. "Effects of Questionnaire Length on Response Quality." *Public Opinion Quarterly* 45:549–559.

Institute for Community Peace. 2014. "A New Model of Transforming Communities." Accessed April 30, 2014. www.instituteforcommunitypeace.org/ocp/pg=structuresand change.

Jones, Laurence F., and Edward C. Olson. 1996. *Political Science Research: A Handbook of Scope and Methods*. New York: Longman.

King, Gary, Robert O. Keohane, and Sidney Verba. 1994. *Designing Social Inquiry: Scientific Inference in Qualitative Research*. Princeton, NJ: Princeton University Press.

Klein, Andrew, Mitchell Brown, Mark Small, Rob Fischer, and Debby Tucker. 2009. "Evaluation of the Rural Domestic Violence and Child Victimization Grant Program Special Initiative: Faith-Based and Community Organization Pilot Program." NCJ 225722. Washington, DC: National Institute of Justice, U.S. Department of Justice. http://www.ncjrs.gov/pdffiles1/nij/grants/228192.pdf.

Koren, Paul E., Neal DeChillo, and Barbara J. Friesen. 1992. "Measuring Empowerment in Families Whose Children Have Emotional Disabilities: A Brief Questionnaire." *Rehabilitation Psychology* 37:305–321.

Kuhn, Thomas. 1970. *Structure of Scientific Revolutions,* 3rd ed. Chicago: University of Chicago Press.

Kumar, M. Jagadesh. 2013. "Making Your Research Paper Discoverable: Title Plays the Winning Trick." Tomorrow's Professor Mailing List, Msg. #1276. http://cgi.stanford .edu/~dept-ctl/cgi-bin/tomprof/posting.php?ID=1276.

Lee, Carole J. 2012. "A Kuhnian Critique of Psychometric Research on Peer Review." *Philosophy of Science* 27:859–870.

Leech, Beth L. 2002. "Interview Methods in Political Science." *PS: Political Science and Politics,* no. 4 (December): 663–688.

Lieberman, Robert C., and Greg M. Shaw. 2000. "Looking Inward, Looking Outward: The Politics of State Welfare Innovation Under Devolution." *Political Research Quarterly* 53:215–240.

Loeb, Susanna, Bruce Fuller, Sharon Lynn Kagan, and Bidemi Carrol. 2003. "How Welfare Reform Affects Young Children: Experimental Findings from Connecticut—A Research Note." *Journal of Policy Analysis and Management* 22:537–550.

Lopez-Ornelas, Maricela, Graciela Cordero-Arroyo, and Eduardo Backhoff-Escudero. 2005. "Measuring the Quality of Electronic Journals." *Electronic Journal of Information Systems Evaluation* 8:133–142.

Manheim, Jarol B., Richard C. Rich, Lars Willnat, and Craig Leonard Brians. 2007. *Empirical Political Analysis: Research Methods in Political Science,* 7th ed. New York: Longman.

Miles, Matthew B., and A. Michael Huberman. 1994. *Qualitative Data: An Expanded Sourcebook,* 2nd ed. Thousand Oaks, CA: Sage.

Mill, John Stuart. 1884. *A System of Logic, Ratiocinative and Inductive, Being a Connected View of the Principles of Evidence and the Methods of Scientific Investigation.* London: Longmans, Green and CO.

Miller, Daniel P., and Ronald B. Mincy. 2012. "Falling Further Behind? Child Support Arrears and Fathers' Labor Force Participation." *Social Science Review* 86:604–635.

Mintrom, Michael. 2003. *People Skills for Policy Analysts.* Washington, DC: Georgetown University Press.

Office of Violence Against Women. 2005. RFP for the Rural Domestic Violence and Child Victimization Enforcement Grant Program Special Initiative. Faith-based and Community Organization Pilot Program. Application #2005-93556-MA-IJ. National Institute of Justice. Washington, DC: U.S. Department of Justice.

Ospina, Sonia, and Jennifer Dodge. 2005. "It's About Time—Catching Up Method to Meaning: The Usefulness of Narrative Inquiry in Public Administration Research." *Public Administration Review* 62:143–157.

Perry, James L., and Kenneth L. Kraemer. 1986. "Research Methodology in the Public Administration Review 1975–1984." *Public Administration Review* 46:215–226.

Privitera, Gregory J. 2012. *Statistics for the Behavioral Sciences.* Thousand Oaks, CA: Sage.

Radin, Beryl A. 2006. *Challenging the Performance Movement: Accountability, Complexity, and Democratic Values.* Washington, DC: Georgetown University Press.

Ribar, David C., and Lauren A. Haldeman. 2013. "Changes in Meal Participation, Attendance, and Test Scores Associated with the Availability of Universal Free School Breakfasts." *Social Service Review* 87:354–385.

Riccucci, Norma. 2010. *Public Administration: Traditions of Inquiry and Philosophies of Knowledge.* Washington, DC: Georgetown University Press.

Rogers, Theresa F. 1976. "Interviews by Telephone and in Person: Quality of Responses and Field Performance." *Public Opinion Quarterly* 40:51–65.

Rubin, Herbert S., and Irene S. Rubin. 2004. *Qualitative Interviewing: The Art of Hearing Data,* 2nd ed. Thousand Oaks, CA: Sage.

Saldaña, Johnny. 2009. *The Coding Manual for Qualitative Researchers.* Thousand Oaks, CA: Sage.

Salmond, Rob, and David T. Smith. 2011. "Cheating Death-by-PowerPoint: Effective Use of Visual Aids at Professional Conferences." *PS: Political Science and Politics* 44:589–596.

Schutt, Russell K. 2006. *Investigating the Social World: The Process and Practice of Research,* 5th ed. Thousand Oaks, CA: Sage.

Sigelman, Lee. 2008. "Multiple Presentations of 'The Same' Paper: A Skeptical View." *PS: Political Science and Politics* 41:305–306.

Tolbert, Caroline J., and Ramona S. McNeal. 2003. "Unraveling the Effects of the Internet on Political Participation?" *Political Research Quarterly* 56:175–185

Torrieri, Nancy K. 2007. "America Is Changing, and So Is the Census: The American Community Survey." *American Statistician* 61:16–21.

Tufte, Edward R. 1983. *The Visual Display of Quantitative Information.* Cheshire, CT: Graphics Press.

———. 1990. *Envisioning Information.* Cheshire, CT: Graphics Press.

U.S. Department of Health and Human Services. 2009. *Code of Federal Regulations. Title 45. Public Welfare. Department of Health and Human Services. Part 46. Protection of Human Subjects.* Accessed May 10, 2013. http://www.hhs.gov/ohrp/humansubjects /guidance/45cfr46.html.

Van Evera, Stephen. 1997. *Guide to Methods for Students of Political Science.* Ithaca, NY: Cornell University Press.

Vonnegut, Kurt. 1963. *Cat's Cradle.* New York: Random House.

Wolcott, Harry F. 1994. *Transforming Qualitative Data: Description, Analysis, Interpretation.* Thousand Oaks, CA: Sage.

Wolfinger, Raymond E. 1993. "Tips for Writing Papers." *PS: Political Science and Politics* 26:87–88.

Wonnacott, Thomas H., and Ronald J. Wonnacott. 1995. *Introductory Statistics,* 5th ed. New York: Wiley.

Yin, Robert K. 1984. *Case Study Research: Design and Methods.* Thousand Oaks, CA: Sage.

INDEX

Page references followed by *fig* indicate an illustrated figure; followed by *t* indicate a table.

A

Abstract (journal), 64

Academic presentations: conference panel format for, 275; invited presentation format for, 275–276; PowerPoint presentation used in, 275–276; practice of presenting same paper at multiple conferences, 276

Academic publications. *See* Scholarly publications

Agreement bias, 182

Aid to Families with Dependent Children (AFDC) program, 105

Alabama Women's Commission (ALWC): proposed study to identify services available to Alabama women age sixty-five and older, 6–8; request for proposal (RFP) issued by, 6. *See also* Statewide needs assessment case study

Alternative hypothesis, 217–218

Ambiguous survey questions, 177, 178*fig*

Annotated Bibliography Entry Worksheet, 97*fig*

Annotated bibliography: description of, 66; journal article, 268; literature search for building, 66–67, 69

Annual reports, 249, 266–267

Anonymous human subjects, 43

Anonymous respondent comments, 150

ANOVA (analysis of variance), 223–224

APA Manual of Style, 32

Applied dissertations, 249, 270–271

Applied research: as creating knowledge about a problem and within served community, 57; distinguished from basic social science research, 2, 25–27; empirical analysis used in, 26; information literacy relationship to, 28–29; last thoughts on engaging in, 280–282; planning aspects of, 47–49*fig*; public administration, nonprofit studies, and other subfields of, 27–28; public service interest in, 1; purpose of, 25; understood as being a series of trade-offs, 16. *See also* Case studies; Decisions trees

Applied research design parameters/factors: bias or error, 100; degree of control, 99; ethical issues, 100; reliability, 100; research instruments, 100; sampling, 100; unit of observation, 99–100

Applied research design types: decision tree used to select, 127–129; decision tree used to select a, 127–129; experimental, 100–105; nonexperimental, 108–113; quasi-experimental, 105–108

Applied research designs: case illustrations of different approaches to, 113–116; general parameters of design, 99–100; sampling, 117–127, 129fig–130; types of, 100–113, 127–129. See also Research design

Applied research methods: case comparisons on variety of approaches and, 41–42t; integrating case studies into learning about, 2–3; introduction to the five case studies used to study, 3–15

Applied research process steps: 1: forming ideas and research questions, 21, 22fig, 23fig, 56–62; 2: developing theories and hypotheses, 21, 22fig, 23fig, 62–91fig; 3: constructing research design, 21, 22fig, 23fig; 4: implementing research design through data collection, 21, 22fig, 23fig; 5: data analysis, 21, 22fig, 23fig; 6: drawing conclusions and communicating research findings, 21, 22fig, 23fig

Applied researchers: participant observer role of, 153; passive observer role of, 152–153; qualitative researcher bias, 139; reciprocal relationship between community and, 56–57

Archival documents, 111
Argumentative survey questions, 179fig
Arthur, Brian, 203
Asset mapping, 256–258
Association of College and Research Libraries, 29, 30t–31t
Asymmetric measure, 221
Atlas.ti, 158
Availability sampling, 122–123

B

Back matter, 268
Backhoff-Escudero, Edurado, 270
Baker, Barbara, 87
Basic research: distinguishing applied research from, 2, 25–27; purpose of, 25–26; qualitative, 26; quantitative, 26–27; traditional approach to, 1
Before-and-after designs, 107t
Beliefs (applied disciplines), 38–40
Benchmarks: community organization program evaluation logic model and possible, 89fig; gauging process through logic model using, 84, 86
Beneficence principle, 43
Berman, Even M., 38
Berry, Frances Stokes, 126
Berry, William D., 126
Best case strategy, 123
Biases: agreement, 182; emotional, 179fig, 180; experimental design, 103–104; Hawthorne effect, 104, 153; qualitative reactivity, 139–140; qualitative researcher, 139; response set, 179fig, 180; selection, 103
Bibliographic listing. See Annotated bibliography
Biomodal, 212

Bivariate statistics: ANOVA (analysis of variance) for, 223–224; correlation coefficient for, 224–225; cross-tabulation for, 220–222t; crosstab table for soft skills class, 222t; description of, 207, 219; by level of measurement, 219t; t-tests, 222–223

Brown, Mitchell, 57, 87

Budget narrative, 259, 261, 263fig

C

Camasso, Michael J., 104

Capital-E experts, 252

Case studies: community garden initiative case study introduction, 4–6, 42t; criminal justice policy reform case study introduction, 13–15, 42t; election administration and technology case study introduction, 8–11, 42t; examples of scholarly sources used in, 67fig; national program evaluation of domestic violence program case study introduction, 11–13, 42t; statewide assessment of Alabama Women 65+ case study introduction, 6–8, 42t. See also Applied research; specific case study

Case studies (data collection strategy), 109t, 110–111; comparative case study research using, 159; construct validity of, 160; description and process of, 159; internal validity of, 160; method of agreement approach to, 160–161; method of difference approach to, 160; qualitative field research, 159–161; reliability of, 160

Causal argument conditions: identifiable causal mechanism, 73, 201; relationship cannot be spurious, 73, 201; temporal order, 73, 201; two concepts must co-vary, 73, 201

Causal mechanism, 73, 201

Census, 117

Central limit theorem (CLT), 119–120

Certainty: normal science, 40, paradigms linked to, 40; positivist school of thought on, 40

Ceteris paribus (all else equal), 226

Challenges. See Problems/challenges

Chicago Manual of Style, 69, 254–255

Citations: Chicago Manual of Style author-date system of, 69; example of paraphrasing using, 70; example of providing a direct quote using, 70; example of using an idea from source using, 70–71; examples of online database, 69–70

Closed-ended questions: qualitative research interview using, 146; survey research use of, 172

Cluster sampling, 121

Clusters, 121

Co-varying concepts, 73, 201

Code of Federal Regulations, 35

Codebooks: for election administration and technology project, 234fig–235fig; quantitative data, 208; for secondary data, 232–233; survey research, 173

Coding: behavioral, 174; intercoder reliability, 145; qualitative analysis, 143–144, 204–205; quantitative analysis, 208–209fig; survey research, 172–173, 174

Coefficient, 218

Cognitive interview, 144

Collinearity (or multicollinearity), 230–231

Communicable research, 26, 250

Communicating findings. *See* Presentations; Writing

Community: interviews with elite (or key informant) of the, 109*t*, 110; reciprocal relationship between researchers and, 56–57

Community garden initiative case study: comparing research question, theory, reasoning, and tools of, 42*t*; concepts and operationalization in, 76*fig*; introduction to the, 4–6; qualitative analysis used during, 236*t*; quantitative analysis used during, 237*t*; research design approaches of, 114*t*; research questions used in, 58; sampling approaches used in, 124*t*, 127; SWOT analysis display for the, 257*fig*; theory, literature, and hypotheses approach of, 74*t*; writing and presentations on the, 278*t*

Community organization program evaluation logic model, 88–90

Community-supported agriculture (CSA) model: beginning a civic initiative around broad concepts of, 4–6; for growing and distributing food via a network, 4

Comprehensive community change initiative (CCCI), 81–82, 86

Comprehensive Institutional Training Initiative (CITI; University of Miami), 44

Computer software data analysis, 158

Concepts: case comparison of operationalization and, 76*t*; causal arguments using, 73; causal mechanism tying together two, 73; co-varying, 73;

as element of theories and hypotheses, 73; operationalization of variables into, 24–25, 75–77; spurious, 73; temporal order of, 73. *See also* Variables

Conclusions section: funder reports, 265; journal article, 65, 268; needs assessment, 258; research process step of drawing recommendations and, 21, 22*fig*, 23*fig*. *See also* Outcomes

Confidence levels, 217

Confidentiality, 43

Construct (survey research), 186

Construct validity: qualitative research, 160; survey weighted index, 186

Constructive criticism, 251–252

Contamination (experimental): causes of, 103–104; example of, 104–105

Content analysis: description of, 109*t*, 111, 154–155; examining innovations in voter guides illustration of, 155, 156*t*–157*t*, 158; qualitative field research data collection using, 154–159; strengths and weaknesses of, 158–159

Content expert, 251

Context, 202

Context analysis, 202–203

Contrasting cases, 123

Control groups: contamination of, 103–104; description of, 101

Control variables, 201

Convenience case selection, 122–123

Cordero-Arroyo, Graciela, 270

Cornell-Peru project (1950s and 1960s), 154

Correlation coefficient, 224–225

Cosenza, Carol, 176

Cramer's *V,* 221

Credibility: as important component of quality research, 141; respondent validation to increase qualitative, 140; triangulation to increase qualitative, 140–141

Criminal justice policy reform case study: book published on the, 253–254; comparing research question, theory, reasoning, and tools of, 42*t*; concepts and operationalization in, 76*fig*; qualitative analysis used during, 236*t*; quantitative analysis used during, 237*t*; research design approaches of, 114*t*; research questions used in, 59–60; sampling approaches used in, 124*t*, 126–127; surveys used during, 192; theory, literature, and hypotheses approach of, 74*t*; on treating addiction and reducing criminal recidivism in, 13–15; writing and presentations on the, 278*t*

Critical cases, 123

Cross-tabulation: bivariate crosstab table for soft skills class, 222*t*; chi-square statistic calculation, 219*t*, 220; degrees of freedom, 220; description of, 220; nonparametric tests for, 220–222

D

Data: primary, 25; secondary, 25, 109*t*, 111–112, 112*fig*, 232–233, 271

Data analysis: case applications of qualitative and quantitative, 233–240; constructing the design for, 21, 22*fig*, 23*fig*; context and descriptive, 202–203; decision tree for approaching, 240–241*fig*; qualitative, 203–207; quantitative, 207–233; when it is time for, 201

Data collection: case illustrations of, 161–163; case studies, 109*t*, 110–111; constructing the design for, 21, 22*fig*, 23*fig*; content analysis, 109*t*, 111; decision tree used for, 163–165; direct observation, 109*t*, 110; elite or key informant interviews, 109*t*, 110; focus groups, 109*t*, 110; secondary data, 109*t*, 111–112*fig*; surveys, 109*t*, 111

David, Paul, 203

Deadlines, 250

Decision trees: for approaching qualitative and quantitative analyses, 240–241*fig*; choosing a sampling strategy, 129*fig*–130; choosing a sampling strategy using a, 129*fig*–130; data collection strategy selection using, 163–165; decisions about applied research and using a theory of change, 90–91*fig*; for making presentations, 277, 279*fig*–280; research process planning using a, 47–48*fig*; selecting a research design type using, 127–129; for selecting paper or web-based survey research, 193–194*fig*; for theory of change model, 90–91*fig*; for typical IRB review process, 48–49*fig*. *See also* Applied research

Deductive reasoning: comparing five case studies use of inductive or, 42*t*; theory building using inductive or, 71–73; theory-fact relationship in, 72*fig*

Degree of control, 99

Degrees of freedom, 220

Democratic functioning. *See* Voting

Demographics: description of, 111; survey questions on respondent, 188–189

Department of Motor Vehicles (DMV) experience scale, 182–183

Dependent variables: *ceteris paribus* (all else equal), 226; description of, 77; multivariate tests based on, 226*t*; regression with dummy, 231–233; regression with nominal, 232; regression with ordinal, 232

Descriptive (or univariate) statistics: description of, 119, 207, 210–211; frequency distribution example, 211*t*; graphic display of, 212*fig*; measures of central tendency, 211–214, 217*t*; measures of dispersion, 214–216*t*, 217*t*; statistical significance, 77, 216–219

Desk rejection, 269

Direct observation: description of, 109*t*, 110, 152; ethnography and thick description form of, 153–154; passive observer of, 152–153; qualitative field research data collection, 152–154

Directional hypothesis, 218

Disproportionate random sampling, 121

Dobyns, Henry F., 154

Dometrius, Nelson C., 276

Double-barreled questions, 177, 178*fig*

Double-blind peer-reviewed journals, 32

Doughty, Paul L., 154

Dummy variables: collinearity among independent variables fueled by, 230–231; description of, 227; regression with dependent, 231–232

E

Eatman, Timothy, 56

Election administration and technology case study: codebook example for, 234*fig*–235*fig*; comparing research question, theory, reasoning, and tools of, 42*t*; concepts and operationalization in, 76*fig*; Help America Vote Act (HAVA) [2002] impact on the, 8–9, 10; interest in causal relationships identified during, 238; introduction to, 8–11; qualitative analysis used during, 236*t*; qualitative data collection methods used during, 162–163; quantitative analysis used during, 237*t*; research design approaches of, 114*t*, 116; research questions used in, 58–59; sampling approaches used in, 124*t*, 126; theory, literature, and hypotheses approach of, 74*t*; writing and presentations on the, 278*t*. *See also* Voting

Election administration technology: DRE (direct-read electronic), 9; optical scan of paper ballot, 9; Voluntary Voting System Guidelines (VVSG) standards for, 9, 10, 238

"Elevator speech" explanation, 273

Elite (or key informant) interviews, 109*t*, 110, 146

Ellison, Julie, 56

Emerson, Sandra, 256

Emotional bias, 179*fig*, 180

Empirical analysis: comparing normative and, 26; description of, 26

Empirical theory: description of, 24, 71; funder report inclusion of, 265; journal article discussion on, 64, 268

Employment & Training Reporter, 63

Empowerment Zone/Enterprise Communities (EZ/EC) concept, 81

Encyclopedia of Public Administration and Public Policy (Berman), 38

Endogenous change, 103

Engaged healthy living activities index, 186–189

Estimated parameters: description of, 77; of the population, 119

Ethical issues: confidentiality and anonymity of participants, 43; as design factor, 100; incentive or compensation given to survey respondents, 173–174; informed consent, 43; national program evaluation case study and specific, 46–47; statewide needs assessment case study and specific, 45–46; three principles governing human subject research, 43. *See also* Institutional Review Board (IRB)

Ethnography, 153–154

Evaluation framework, 80. *See also* Theory of change

Executive summary: funder reports, 265; needs assessment and asset mapping, 257

Exhaustive response categories, 174

Expected value, 119

Experimental contamination: causes of, 103–104; example of, 104–105

Experimental design: bias in, 103–104; experimental contamination issue of, 103–105; internal validity issue of, 102, 104; measurement and intervention sequences for major forms of, 102*t*; public administration and nonprofit studies applications of, 104–105; purpose of, 100; randomness of, 103; treatment or intervention introduced in, 100; types of, 101–102*t*

Experimental design types: multiple-posttest design, 102*t*; multiple-pretest design, 101, 102*t*; randomized comparative change design, 101, 102*t*; randomized comparative posttest design, 101, 102*t*

Experimental group, 101

Explanatory variables, 201

Exploratory research, 24

External events (or history), 103

Extreme outliers, 212

F

F-test, 223–224, 228

Factorial designs, 107*t*

Faith-based and community organizations (FBCOs), 11–13

Falsibiability, 26

Feedback on writing, 251–252

Filter questions, 177–178

Findings section: funder reports, 265; journal article, 65, 268; needs assessment, 257–258. *See also* Outcomes

501(c)(3) nonprofit tax status, 62

Focus groups: description of, 151; ideal size of, 151; information gathered and outline for conducting, 152; nonexperimental data collection using, 109*t*, 110; piloting surveys using, 174

Form 990s, 249, 267

Fowler, Floyd J., Jr., 176

Funded research: description of, 60; national program evaluation study research questions for, 62; statewide needs assessment study research questions for, 61

Funder reports: description of the, 249, 264–265; sections included in the, 265–266

G

Gamma (γ), 221

Gantt chart: description of, 259; statewide needs assessment example of, 260*fig*

Generalizability: description of the issue of, 26; as element of theories and hypotheses, 73

Georgetown University, 64

Georgetown University Press, 64

Google Scholar, 38

Government Accountability Office (GAO), 35

Grand theory, 40–41

Grand tour question, 150

Grant applications: budget narrative included in, 259, 261, 263*fig*; description and requirements for, 258; Gantt chart used to display timeline in, 259, 260*fig*; letter of intent (LOI) in lieu of full grant proposal, 258; planning process example, 261*fig*–262; request for proposals (RFP) to start process of, 249, 258

Graphic displays (presentation), 272, 273

Gray, Tara, 250, 252

Grounded theory, 24, 203

H

Hale, Kathleen, 33, 36, 39, 57, 87

Handouts, 272, 273

Hankins, Ryan, 57

Hawthorne effect, 104, 153

Help America Vote Act (HAVA) [2002], 8–9, 10

History (or external events), 103

"Homeless women" information, 36–37*fig*

Huberman, Michael, 137

Human subject research: confidentiality and anonymity of participants in, 43; informed consent required in, 43; Institutional Review Board (IRB) rules

governing, 43–45; three principles governing, 43; typical research roles covered by IRB requirements in, 44*fig*

Hypotheses: alternative, 217–218; case comparison of approaches to, 74*t*; concepts of, 73; description of, 24, 62; developing research expectations and, 75, 77–79; directional, 218; generalizability element of, 26, 73; literature and building theory to develop, 23, 32–33, 37–38, 62–79; null, 77–79, 217; parsimonious nature of, 26, 73; research process of developing, 21, 22*fig*, 23*fig*. *See also* Research expectations

Hypothesis testing: Type I error, 78; Type II error, 78, 79

I

Independence assumption, 120

Independent variables: description of, 77; strong collinearity among, 230

Index: construct validity of, 186; creating a survey, 177; engaged healthy living activities example of a weighted, 186–188

Inductive reasoning: comparing five case studies use of deductive or, 42*t*; theory building using deductive or, 71–73; theory-fact relationship in, 72*fig*

Inferential statistics, 77

Information: finding high-quality, 37–38; quality and types of sources of, 29, 32–37, 63–65

Information literacy: applied research relationship to, 28–29; description of, 28–29; Information Literacy Competency Standards for Higher Education guidelines on, 29, 30*t*–31*t*

Information Literacy Competency Standards for Higher Education (ACRL), 29, 30*t*–31*t*

Information sources: primary, 25; secondary, 25, 109*t*, 111–112, 112*fig*, 232–233, 271; top news sources by media type, 34*t*; top ten information sources from Google search for "homeless women," 36–37*fig*

Informed consent, 43

Inputs: described as resources, 82; examples of, 82, 84

Institute for Community Peace, 203

Institutional Review Board (IRB): decision trees for typical process of, 48–49*fig*; description and research role of the, 43–45; institutional rules governed by, 43; level of disclosure requirement of, 150; providing compensation as perceived by, 173; three principles as guidelines for human subject research, 43; typical research roles covered by requirements of, 44*fig*. *See also* Ethical issues

Instruments: description of, 142; qualitative field research, 142–144

Inter-rater reliability, 205

Intercoder reliability, 145, 205

Internal validity: case study, 160; experimental design, 102, 104; quasi-experimental design, 108

Interval variables: description of, 210; measures of central tendency for, 217*t*; measures of dispersion for, 217*t*

Intervention, experimental design introduction of, 100

Intervention analysis, 107

Interview questions: closed-ended, 146; grand tour question starting interview, 150; how to write, 148–149; open-ended, 146–147

Interview types: semistructured, 147; structured, 146; unstructured, 146

Interviews: cognitive, 144; of key informants, 109*t*, 110, 146; major strengths and weaknesses of, 147–148; putting respondents at ease during, 149–151; qualitative field research data collection using, 146–151; reactivity bias of, 139–140; recording or taking notes during, 150–151; steps in developing effective, 148

Introduction section: funder reports, 265; journal articles, 264, 268; needs assessment and asset mapping, 257

Iterative research process, 22

Iterative writing process, 250

J

Journal Article Worksheet, 68*fig*

Journal articles: common format used for, 268; description of, 64–65; desk rejection of, 269; electronic-only journals and, 270; list of selected scholarly journals for applied research, 66*fig*; revision and resubmission of, 269–270; writing, 249, 268–270

JSTOR (Journal Storage), 38

Justice principle, 43

K

Kendall's tau (τ), 221

Keohane, Robert O., 40

Key informant (or elite) interviews, 109*t*, 110, 146

King, Gary, 40

Kuhn, Thomas, 40

L

Lambda (λ), 221

Landon, Alf, 118

Lasswell, Harold Dwight, 154

Leech, Beth L., 150

Letter of intent (LOI), 258

Levels of measurement: bivariate tests by, 219*t*; description of, 210; interval variables, 210; measures of central tendency and dispersion by, 217*t*; nominal variables, 210; ordinal variables, 210; ratio variables, 210

Levels of significance, 217

LexisNexis, 38

Likert scale, 185*fig*

Linear probability model (LPM), 231

Literature review: academic journal article inclusion of, 64–65; annotated bibliography built through, 66–67; case comparison of approaches to, 74*t*; conducting the, 65–69; description of, 23; funder report inclusion of, 265; hypothesis development by building theory and using a, 62–79; journal article, 64; sources of quality information for, 32–33, 37–38, 63–65; three forms of citations collected from, 69–71

Literature sources: academic journal articles, 64–65; popular press, 63, 64; quality information, 32–33, 37–38, 63–65; scholarly, 32–33, 64–65; top news sources by media type, 34*t*; top ten information sources from Google search for "homeless women," 36–37*fig*; trade and professional, 63–64, 64

Loeb, Susanna, 104

Logic Model Worksheet, 98*fig*

Logic models: benchmarks used as part of, 84, 86; description and basis of, 82; for increasing democratic functioning through voting, 85*fig*; for program evaluation for study of community organizations, 89*fig*; research applications and examples of, 82–84; study of community organizations using program evaluation, 88–90; writing the narrative that accompanies the, 87. *See also* Theory of change

Logistic regression, 231

Longitudinal study survey waves, 175

Lopzes, Maricela, 270

M

Manheim, Jarol B., 73

McNeal, Ramona S., 68*fig*

Means: description and examples of, 213–214; examining sample, 119; by level of measurement, 217*t*

Measures of central tendency: bimodal, 212; description of, 211; extreme outliers, 212; by level of measurement, 217*t*; mean, 213–214, 217*t*; median, 212–213, 217*t*; mode, 211–212, 217*t*

Measures of dispersion: description of, 214; by level of measurement, 217*t*; nominal data, 214–215; ordinal and scale data, 215; standard deviation from variance, 215–216*t*

Median, 212–213, 217*t*

Menkus, Royce, 256

Method of agreement approach, 160–161

Method of difference approach, 160

Methods section: funder reports, 265; journal article, 65, 268; needs assessment, 257

Middle-range theories, 41

MII Publications, 63

Miles, Matthew B., 137

Mill, John Stuart, 160

Misspecified model, 228

Mixed methods, 233

Mode, 211–213, 217*t*

Models: misspecified or underspecified, 228; multivariate test, 228–231

Multicollinearity (or collinearity), 230–231

Multiple-posttest design, 102*t*

Multiple-pretest design, 101, 102*t*

Multivariate analysis (or statistics): collinearity (or multicollinearity), 230–231; description of, 201, 225; misspecified or underspecified models, 228–231; ordinary least squares regression (OLS), 225–228, 230; regression, 231–232; relationship between soft skills course participant background and course attendance to posttest performance, 228–229*t*; tests based on dependent variable measurement, 226*t*

N

National Association of Drug Court Professionals, 15

National Media Award, 15

National program evaluation case study: comparing research question, theory, reasoning, and tools of, 42*t*; concepts and operationalization in, 76*fig*; interest in comparing grant-funded and nonfunded organizations during, 240; introduction to the Rural Pilot Program (RPP), 11–13; qualitative analysis used during, 236*t*; qualitative data collection

methods used during, 163; quantitative analysis used during, 237*t*; research design approaches of, 114*t*, 115–116; research questions in sponsored research of, 62; sampling approaches used in, 124*t*, 126; specific ethical issues of concern during, 46–47; surveys used during, 192–193; theory, literature, and hypotheses approach of, 74*t*; writing and presentations on the, 278*t*. *See also* Rural Pilot Program (RPP)

Needs assessments: asset map included in, 256; six components of, 257–258; SWOT analysis used in, 256, 257*fig*; writing, 249, 256–258

New Jersey FDP AFDC Section 115 Waiver welfare experiment, 105

New York Times, 63

Nominal variables: bivariate tests by level of measurement for, 219*t*; description of, 210; measures of central tendency for, 217*t*; measures of dispersion for, 214–215, 217*t*; regression with dependent, 232

Nonequivalent control group designs, 106–107*t*

Nonexperimental design: data collection used with, 109*t*–113; description of, 108; reflexivity issue of, 108, 112–113

Nonexperimental design data collection: case studies, 109*t*, 110–111; content analysis, 109*t*, 111; direct observation, 109*t*, 110; elite or key informant interviews, 109*t*, 110; focus groups, 109*t*, 110; secondary data, 109*t*, 111–112*fig*; surveys, 109*t*, 111

Nonparametric tests: Cramer's *V,* 221; description of, 220; gamma (γ), 221;

Kendall's tau (τ), 221; lambda (λ), 221; phi (φ), 220–221; Sommer's *d*, 221–222

Nonprofit organizations: 501(c)(3) nonprofit tax status, 62; Rural Pilot Program (RPP) partnership with FBCOs, 11–13

Nonprofit studies: ethical consideration specific to, 45–47; experimental design applications to, 104–105; as subfield of applied research, 27–28; values and beliefs in, 39–40

Nonrandom (or nonprobability) sampling: availability sampling, 122–123; description of, 121; quota sampling, 121–122; snowball sampling, 122

Nonresponse error, 189–190

Normal approximation rule, 119

Normal science, 40

Normative analysis: comparing empirical and, 26; description of, 26

Normative theory, 28

Null hypotheses: description of, 77, 217; how to develop a, 77–79

O

Odds ratios, 231

Office of Violence Against Women (OVW), 11–13

Open-ended questions: qualitative research interview use of, 146–147; survey research use of, 146–147

Operationalization: case comparison of concepts and, 76*t*; description of research process of, 24–25; reducing concepts to variables through, 75, 77

Ordinal variables: bivariate tests by level of measurement for, 219*t*; description of, 210; measures of central tendency for, 217*t*; measures of dispersion for, 215, 217*t*; regression with dependent, 232; relationship between soft skills course participant background and course attendance to posttest performance, 229*t*. *See also* Variables

Ordinary least squares regression (OLS), 225–228, 230

Outcomes: community garden case study time horizons and, 85*fig*; community organization program evaluation logic model and possible, 89*fig*; description as results of outputs or activities, 83; two time horizons for understanding, 83–84. *See also* Conclusions section; Findings section

Outcroppings, 154

Outputs (activities): community organization program evaluation logic model and possible, 89*fig*; description of, 83; example of, 84

Oxford University, 64

Oxford University Press, 64

P

p = values, 218, 222

Paradigm shifts, 40

Paradigms: certainty linked to, 40; description of, 40

Parameters: description of, 77; estimated, 77

Parsimony: description of the issue of, 26; as element of theories and hypotheses, 73

Participant observer, 153

Passive observer, 152–153

Path dependence: description of, 202; QWERTY touch-typing keyboard example of, 202–203

Pattern matching, 203–204

Peer reviews: of academia work, 32; feedback through, 251–252; journal articles, 269

Periodicity, 120

Phi (φ), 220–221

Piloting: interview process, 148; qualitative research instruments, 144; qualitative research protocols, 143*fig*, 144; survey research questions, 180–181; surveys, 174

Placebo effect, 104

Policy analysis, values and beliefs in, 39–40

Political theory, 28

Popular press sources, 63, 64

Populations: inadequate coverage of survey, 190–191; sample selected from a, 117; sampling interval used for small, 120

Positivist school of thought, 40

Poster presentations, 272–273

Posttesting: experimental design, 101; for major forms of experimental design, 102*t*

PowerPoint presentations: academic presentations and use of, 275, 276; tips on designing, 272, 274

Presentations: academic, 275–276; case illustrations of, 277, 278*t*; communicating research findings through, 21, 22*fig*, 23*fig*; decision trees for approaching, 277, 279*fig*–280; description and forms of, 271–272; "elevator speech" explanation of the project, 273; graphic displays used in, 272, 273; handouts used in, 272, 273; multiple learning styles of audience consideration in, 272; poster, 272–273;

PowerPoint, 272, 274; to stakeholders, 274–275; SWOT analysis format adapted for, 274; visual aids used during, 272. *See also* Writing

Presi, 276

Pretesting: experimental design, 101; for major forms of experimental design, 102*t*

Primary data, 25

Probability, 218

Probability sampling. *See* Random (or probability) sampling

Problems/challenges: applied research used to create knowledge about a, 57; description of, 82; example of, 84

Prompts (protocol), 147

Proportionate random sampling, 121

Protocols: description of, 142; develop, pilot, and revise, 143*fig*; prompts included in, 147; qualitative field research, 142–144, 147

Proxy, 75

Psychometrics, 176

Public administration studies: ethical consideration specific to, 45–47; experimental design applications to, 104–105; as subfield of applied research, 27–28; values, beliefs, and certainty in, 39–40

Public policy values and beliefs, 39–40

Public relations releases, 249, 267–268

Public service: applied research interest by, 1; definition of, 2

Purposive sample, 121

Push polling questions, 181

Q

Qualitative analysis: case applications of, 233–235, 236*t*, 238–240; coding used during, 143–144, 204–205; decision tree used for approaching, 240–241*fig*; description of, 203; grounded theory used in, 203; intercoder or inter-rater reliability of, 205; pattern matching process used in, 203–204; statewide needs assessment case study use of, 205–207; triangulation used in, 140–141, 205

Qualitative data collection: case comparison of case selection methods used for, 141, 142*t*; case illustrations of, 161–163; case studies, 159–161; content analysis, 154–159; decision tree to select strategies for, 163–165; direct observation, 152–154; focus groups, 151–152; interviews, 146–151; process of conducting field, 142–145; various methods of, 137–138

Qualitative research: data used for, 137; description of, 26; process of conducting field, 142–145; strategies to increase credibility of, 140–141; validity, reliability, and error in, 138–142

Quality information: academia or university-based work sources of, 32–33; description of, 32; literature sources for finding, 37–38, 63–65

Quantitative analysis: bivariate statistics used during, 207, 219*t*–225; case applications of qualitative and, 233–235, 237*t*, 238–240; coding used during, 208–209*fig*; decision tree used for approaching, 240–241*fig*; description of, 207; descriptive (or univariate) statistics used during, 119, 207, 210–219; levels of measurement, 209–210; multivariate statistics used during, 225–233

Quantitative research: description of, 26–27; explanatory variables and control variables examined in, 201; multivariate analysis for, 201

Quasi-experimental design: description of, 105–106; lower internal validity of, 108; major forms of, 106–108; SAMHSA study (1998) using, 106

Quasi-experimental design types: before-and-after designs, 107*t*; factorial designs, 107*t*; nonequivalent control group designs, 106–107*t*

Questions. *See* Survey questions

Quota sampling, 121–122

QWERTY touch-typing keyboard, 202–203

R

Radin, Beryl A., 35

Random (or probability) sampling: cluster sampling, 121; description of, 118–119; sampling intervals, 120; simple random sampling (SRS), 119–120; stratified sampling, 121

Randomized comparative change design, 101, 102*t*

Randomized comparative posttest design, 101, 102*t*

Randomly assigned subjects, 101

Range, 215–216

Ratio variables: description of, 210; measures of central tendency for, 217*t*; measures of dispersion for, 217*t*

Reactivity, 139–140

Readability: and appeal of written work, 252–254; of surveys, 175–176

Reasoning, 42*t*

Recursive enactment, 203

Reflexivity, 108, 112–113

Regression: with a dummy dependent variable, 231–232; with nominal dependent variable with two or more categories, 232; with ordinal dependent variable, 232

Reliability: case study, 160; as design factor, 100; inter-rater, 205; intercoder, 145, 205; psychometrics measure of survey, 176; qualitative research, 138–139

Replication of findings, 111

Request for proposals (RFP), 249, 258

Requests for proposals (RFPs): by Alabama Women's Commission (ALWC), 6; sponsored research questions included in, 60; statewide needs assessment study, 61

Research design: decision tree used to select type of, 127–129; inside the steps of the, 23*fig*; research process of constructing the, 21, 22*fig*. *See also* Applied research designs

Research design parameters/factors: bias or error, 100; degree of control, 99; ethical issues, 100; reliability, 100; research instruments, 100; sampling, 100; unit of observation, 99–100

Research expectations: case comparison of approach to, 74*t*; developing the hypotheses and, 75, 77–79. *See also* Hypotheses

Research instruments, as design factor, 100

Research process: applied research context of the, 25–27; decision trees used in planning the, 47–48*fig*; iterative nature of the, 22; Research Process Outline Worksheet, 54*fig*; six steps in the, 21–22*fig*, 23*fig*

Research Process Outline Worksheet, 54*fig*

Research process steps: 1: forming ideas and research questions, 21, 22*fig*, 23*fig*, 56–62; 2: developing theories and hypotheses, 21, 22*fig*, 23*fig*, 62–91*fig*; 3: constructing research design, 21, 22*fig*, 23*fig*; 4: implementing research design through data collection, 21, 22*fig*, 23*fig*; 5: data analysis, 21, 22*fig*, 23*fig*; 6: drawing conclusions and communicating research findings, 21, 22*fig*, 23*fig*

Research questions: applied to theories of change, 80–82; case illustrations of, 42*t*, 57–60; description of, 24; forming the, 21, 22*fig*, 23*fig*; how information and experience are used to create, 57; how to ask good, 56–60; national program evaluation study, 62; sponsored research and, 60–62; statewide needs assessment case study, 61

Researcher bias, 139

Researchers: participant observer role of, 153; passive observer role of, 152–153; reciprocal relationship between community and applied, 56–57

Respect for subjects principle, 43

Respondent validation, increasing qualitative research creditability with, 140

Respondents: anonymous comments by, 150; increasing qualitative research credibility by validating, 140; putting them at ease during interviews, 149–151; strata groupings of, 121, 188–189. *See also* Survey respondents

Response categories, 174

Response set bias, 179*fig*, 180

Riccucci, Norma, 39

Rockefeller drug laws (New York State, 1960s), 13–14

Roosevelt, Franklin, 118

Rural Pilot Program (RPP), 11–13, 42t. *See also* National program evaluation case study

S

Salmond, Rob, 276

Sample size, 123

Samples: inadequate coverage of population in the, 190–191; purposive, 121; selected from population, 117

Sampling: case illustrations of, 123–127; decision tree used to choose strategy for, 129fig–130; as design factor, 100; inadequate coverage of population by, 190–191; nonrandom or nonprobability, 121–123; process of, 117–118; random or probability, 118–121

Sampling frame: description and development of a, 117; *Encyclopedia of Associations* list as example of, 117; possible problems in selecting, 118

Sampling intervals, 120

Sampling unit, 117

Sampling with replacement, 120

Sampling without replacement, 120

Scale variables: bivariate tests by level of measurement for, 219t; Department of Motor Vehicles (DMV) experience, 182–183; general principles when using, 183, 185–186; illustration of ordered, 184fig; Likert scale, 185fig; measures of dispersion using, 215; relationship between soft skills course participant background and course attendance

to posttest performance, 229t; survey research, 182–183; weighted index created by using, 186–188. *See also* Variables

Scholarly publications: academic journal articles, 64–65, 66fig, 249, 268–270; Journal Article Worksheet, 68fig; list of selecting scholarly journals, 66fig; as source of quality information, 32–33, 64–65; university press books, 33, 64, 249

Secondary data: applied dissertation use of, 271; common sources of, 112fig; data collection using, 109t, 111–112; description of, 25, 232–233

Selection bias, 103

Self-editing, 251

Semistructured interviews, 147

Sigelman, Lee, 276

Simple random sampling (SRS), 119

Smith, David T., 276

Snowball sampling, 122

Social desirability of questions, 179fig, 180

Social Science Citation Index, 38

Social Science Research Network, 38

Soft skills class: bivariate crosstab table for, 222t; relationship between participant background and course attendance to posttest performance in, 229t

Sommer's *d,* 221–222

Sponsored research (or funded research): description of, 60; national program evaluation study research questions in, 62; requests for proposals (RFPs) questions used in, 60; research questions for, 60–61

SPSS, 158

Spurious concepts, 73, 201

Stakeholder documents: annual reports, 249, 266–267; Form 990s, 249, 267; public relations releases, 249, 267–268

Stakeholder presentations, 274–275

Standard deviation from variance: calculating, 215–216; calculation matrix for, 216*t*

Statewide needs assessment case study: comparing research question, theory, reasoning, and tools of, 42*t*; concepts and operationalization in, 76*fig*; Gantt chart used in, 260*fig*; introduction to the, 6–8; planning process for national replication of the, 261*fig*; qualitative analysis and data display during, 205–207; qualitative analysis used during, 236*t*; qualitative data collection methods used during, 161–162; quantitative analysis used during, 237*t*; requests for proposals (RFPs) issued during, 62; research design approaches of, 113, 114*t*; research questions used in sponsored research of, 61; sampling approaches used in, 123, 124*t*, 125–126; specific ethical issues during the, 45–46; surveys used during, 191–192; theory, literature, and hypotheses approach of, 74*t*; theory of change model used during, 238, 239*fig*; writing and presentations on the, 278*t*. *See also* Alabama Women's Commission (ALWC)

Statistical significance: description of, 77, 216–217; quantitative analysis using, 216–219

Strata groupings, 121, 188–189

Stratified sampling, 121

Structured interviews, 146

Style: *Chicago Manual of Style* guide on, 69, 254–255; illustration of table format and, 255*t*; used in reports and presentations, 254

Subjective information, 191

Summerfield, Giovanna, 87

Survey design: crafting quality questions, 176–181; readability and length issues of, 175–176; response categories, 181–188

Survey problems: caller ID and do-not-call lists, 190; inadequate coverage of the population, 190–191; nonresponses, 189–190; subjective information issue, 191

Survey questions: answers aggregated to form an index, 177; argumentativeness of, 179*fig*, 181; avoiding double-barreled, 177, 178*fig*; closed-ended, 172; crafting quality, 176–181; demographic, 188–189; emotional bias of, 179*fig*, 180; filter, 177–178; guidelines for wording of, 178*fig*–179*fig*; influence of word order and response set choices on responses to, 182, 183*fig*; minimizing ambiguity and confusing phrases in, 177, 178*fig*; open-ended, 172; piloting the, 180–181; psychometrics and validity of, 176; push polling, 181; response set bias of, 179*fig*, 180; social desirability of, 179*fig*, 180

Survey research: case illustrations of using, 191–193; construct of, 186; decision tree for selecting paper or web-based, 193–194*fig*; design used for constructing, 175–189; overview of, 171; problems and controversies in, 189–191; process of, 172–175

Survey respondents: behavioral coding of, 174; coding responses of, 172–173; demographics or strata of, 188–189; inadequate coverage of the population by, 190–191; incentive or compensation given to, 173–174. *See also* Respondents

Survey responses: agreement bias issue of, 182; categories of, 181–188; coding the, 172–173, 174; construct developed through, 186; influence of word order and response set choices on, 182, 183*fig*; nonresponse error, 189–190; predetermining response categories, 174; scaling, 182; verifying exhaustive response categories, 174; weighted index developed through, 186–188

Survey waves, 175

Surveys: closed-ended questions used in, 172; coding schemes assigned to responses of, 172–173; demographics included in, 111; multiple waves of a, 175; nonexperimental data collection using, 109*t*, 111; open-ended questions used in, 172; pilot testing, 174; psychometrics and validity of, 176

SWOT analysis: adapted for presentation audience, 274; needs assessment, 256, 257*fig*

Systematic observation, 26

T

t-tests, 222–223

Telephone survey problems, 190

Temporal order of concepts, 73, 201

Test statistics, 120

Testable, 56

Theories: comparison of five case studies use of, 42*t*; concepts of, 73; empirical,

24, 64, 71, 265, 268; generalizability element of, 26, 73; grand, 40–41; grounded, 24; hypothesis development through literature review and building, 62–79; middle-range, 41; normative, 28; parsimonious nature of, 26, 73; political, 28; research process of developing, 21, 22*fig*, 23*fig*

Theory building: case comparison of approaches to, 74*t*; causal arguments used in, 73; empirical theory role in, 24, 71; generalizability used for, 26, 73; inductive and deductive theories used for, 42*t*, 71–73; literature used for, 23–24, 32–33, 37–71

Theory of change: applied to research questions, 80–82; community garden study time horizons, outcomes, and model of, 85*fig*; comprehensive community change initiative (CCCI) collective approach to, 81–82, 86; decision tree for making applied research decisions using, 90–91*fig*; description of, 79–81; for increasing democratic functioning through voting, 85*fig*; needs assessment or asset map precursor for developing, 256; statewide needs assessment case model development of, 238, 239*fig*; steps for development of, 86–88, 86–90, 90. *See also* Evaluation framework; Logic models

Thick description, 153–154

Time horizons: community garden study theory of change model, outcomes, and, 85*fig*; two types for understanding outcomes, 83–84

Time series analysis, 107

Tolbert, Caroline J., 68*fig*

Trade and professional sources, 63–64, 64

Treatment groups: contamination of control group by, 103–104; experimental design use of, 100

Triangulation, 140–141, 205

Tufte, Edward, 276

Type I error, 78

Type II error, 78, 79

Typical cases, 123

U

Underspecified model, 228

Unit of observation, 99–100

Univariate statistics. *See* Descriptive (or univariate) statistics

University of Miami, 44

University press books, 33, 64, 249

"Unraveling the Effects of the Internet on Political Participation?" (Tolbert and McNeal), 68*fig*

Unstructured interviews, 146

U.S. Census Bureau, 111, 112*fig*, 232, 271

U.S. Code, 35

U.S. Department of Housing and Urban Development, 81

U.S. Department of Justice, 11, 47

V

Validity: construct, 160, 186; as design factor, 100; internal, 102, 104, 108; qualitative research, 138; survey, 176

Values (applied disciplines), 38–40

Van Ness, Kathy, 256

Variables: control, 201; dependent, 77, 226*t*, 231–233; description of, 77; dummy, 227, 230–232; explanatory, 201; independent, 77, 230; interval, 210, 217*t*; nominal, 210, 214–215, 217*t*, 219*t*,

232; operationalization of concepts into, 24–25, 75–77; ratio, 210, 217*t*. *See also* Concepts; Ordinal variables; Scale variables

Verba, Sidney, 40

Vicos community project (1950s and 1960s), 154

Voluntary Voting System Guidelines (VVSG), 9, 10, 238

Voting: DRE (direct-read electronic) of ballots, 9; logic model/theory of change to increase democratic functioning through, 85*fig*; optical scan of paper ballot, 9; Voluntary Voting System Guidelines (VVSG) standards for, 9, 10, 238. *See also* Election administration and technology case study

W

Washington Post, 63

Waves (survey), 175

Weighted index: description of, 186; example of engaged healthy living activities, 186–189

Westlaw, 38

Wolcott, Harry F., 137

Wolfinger, Raymond E., 251

Worksheets: Annotated Bibliography Entry Worksheet, 97*fig*; Journal Article Worksheet, 68*fig*; Logic Model Worksheet, 98*fig*; Research Process Outline Worksheet, 54*fig*

Writing: annual reports, 249, 266–267; applied dissertations, 249, 270–271; asset mapping, 256–258; case illustrations of, 277, 278*t*; *Chicago Manual of Style* used for, 69, 254–255; communicating research findings through, 21, 22*fig*, 23*fig*; Form 990s, 249, 267; funder reports, 249, 264–266; grant applications, 258–259, 261–264; journal articles, 64–65, 66*fig*, 249, 268–270; needs assessments, 249, 256–258; public relations releases, 249, 267–268; request for proposals (RFP), 249, 258; stakeholder documents, 266–268; university press books, 33, 64, 249. *See also* Presentations

Writing tips: communicability principles of research, 26, 250; on deadlines, 250; on feedback and constructive criticism, 251–252; iterative nature of the writing process, 250; a note about style, 254–255*t*; for productive writing process, 250–251; on readability and appeal, 252–254

Y

Yin, Robert K., 159, 160

Z

z-scores, 218, 222